Also by Fred Goodman

The Secret City: Woodlawn Cemetery and the Buried History of New York

The Mansion on the Hill: Dylan, Young, Geffen, Springsteen, and the Head-on Collision of Rock and Commerce

FORTUNE'S FOOL

EDGAR BRONFMAN JR., WARNER MUSIC, AND AN INDUSTRY IN CRISIS

FRED GOODMAN

Simon & Schuster
New York   London   Toronto   Sydney

Simon & Schuster
1230 Avenue of the Americas
New York, NY 10020

Copyright © 2010 by Fred Goodman

First Simon & Schuster hardcover edition July 2010

SIMON & SCHUSTER and colophon are
registered trademarks of Simon & Schuster, Inc.

For information about special discounts for bulk purchases,
please contact Simon & Schuster Special Sales at
1-866-506-1949 or business@simonandschuster.com.

The Simon & Schuster Speakers Bureau can bring authors to your
live event. For more information or to book an event contact the
Simon & Schuster Speakers Bureau at 1-866-248-3049 or visit our
website at www.simonspeakers.com.

Designed by Jill Putorti

Manufactured in the United States of America

10   9   8   7   6   5   4   3   2

Library of Congress Cataloging-in-Publication Data is available.

ISBN 978-0-7432-6998-8
ISBN 978-1-4391-6050-3 (ebook)

To Our Lady of Perpetual Revisions, Ruth Fecych. My patron saint.

Contents

The great American drama is the clash of adolescence with middle age.

−Frank McCourt, *Teacher Man*

I'm not sure if *music* got a future. We have all these electronic ways to download and steal music and get music, but there's no money in makin' music. That money's startin' to dry up. So what's gonna happen in twenty years, twenty-five years, when the new artists of the day are all, "There ain't no money in music, so I'ma go use my creative talents to do something else"? World never hears of great talent, because it's all dried up. Now what are you gonna put on your iPod? Now what are you gonna download, when there's nobody making music?

−Ice Cube, interviewed by Nathan Rabin for
The Onion's A.V. Club, January 16, 2008

PROLOGUE

The Opening Bell

Wednesday, May 11, 2005

Edgar Bronfman Jr. is famous for two things; one annoying and the other unforgivable. The annoying thing is that though he was born rich as Croesus, he has opted to work hard every day. The unforgivable thing is that he managed to lose $3 billion while doing so.

Today is the first day of public trading in the stock of the Warner Music Group (WMG), the troubled recording and music publishing company that Bronfman purchased a little over a year ago from Time Warner with a group of private equity investors. As the new company's chairman and CEO, Edgar is here to ring the exchange's opening bell. He is also here to get back some of his money and all of his pride by becoming the man who saved the embattled music business.

The record industry has become the canary in the internet coal mine. It is the first commercial medium to feel the gale force of cyberspace, and the entire business, including the Warner Music Group, has been blown off its foundation. The industry faces the most basic questions about its future—not just how it will price, distribute, and control its product in the digital era, but whether it even *has* a future in a world remade by file trading and rife with free digital copies of virtually any recording. Indeed, no one can say with certainty that artists and performers will continue to need or even want record companies. Because of the internet, all bets are off. Warner is literally in a fight for its life.

Despite a well-known passion for the entertainment business, Edgar is a most unlikely candidate for savior. The heir to the Seagram liquor fortune, he skipped college to pursue a career as a theater and film producer, and when he followed his father and grandfather as the chairman of the family-controlled and publicly traded company, he acted on those interests and recast the liquor giant as an entertainment company. In 1995, he purchased MCA, and then two record companies, Interscope and PolyGram. The controversial strategy split the Bronfman family into warring factions and polarized Wall Street, where investors who had liked Seagram for its regular dividends decried the moves, and those who predicted the internet would bring new value to intellectual property, like films and recordings, embraced them. The debate became moot when Edgar orchestrated one deal too many by merging with France's would-be media giant Vivendi, a decision that quickly reduced the family empire—and its shareholder value—to rubble.

The Vivendi disaster was as high-profile a humiliation as any businessman not sent to prison is likely to endure. The normally circumspect *New York Times* crowned Bronfman "Wall Street's favorite whipping boy."

Edgar claims the failed venture barely scuffed the Bronfman fortune. "The story that's told is that I squandered the family money," he says. "I made all the money I squandered." That could very well be: estimates by *Fortune* and *Canadian Business* still place the family's fortune somewhere north of $5 billion. But Seagram was a powerful vehicle for the Bronfmans' wealth and influence and part and parcel of their identity—and it vaporized in his hands. Without the freedom and extraordinary clout that comes with controlling your own empire, Bronfman's just another guy with money, and in the Warner deal he is a minority partner. Edgar has come down in the world, and everybody he deals with knows it. He is like Dylan's Napoleon in rags—stripped of not just his army but also his mystique. The Warner Music Group is how he will get back up. When he succeeds, it will be sweet revenge and a rehabilitation as public as his downfall. Except this isn't a slam dunk.

Bronfman is wagering that a reinvention and turnaround isn't up for grabs but an eventuality. In his view, the downloading and the explosion in freely traded music that shrank worldwide CD sales from $38 billion in 1999 to $33.6 billion in the five years before he purchased the Warner Music Group can be turned into a money fountain by creating new internet products that are superior to free music files. When asked if record companies can get the genie back in the bottle, Bronfman holds up a bottle of water. "Why do people buy this when they can get water for free? The same is going to be true of music. There will be advantages, points to pay for such as being virus-free, reasonably priced, and a better product." He says that time will prove he picked up Warner's music publishing and recorded music holdings for a song. "I wrote my check because I believe these libraries will be fundamentally revalued, just as video did for TV and film," he has been telling potential investors. "Cell phones, iPods—I think it all cuts very favorably for a company like ours."

That's hardly the way things have played out so far. The internet storm caught the record business off guard, and in no way has it exhibited the fortitude, imagination, or strategic planning needed to adapt to the new and evolving environment. Its best managers have the skills to find, record, and promote music—and that's all. Edgar will have to change that.

Bronfman doesn't consider himself a record executive so much as a special breed of money man. Whatever mistakes he made at Seagram, Edgar has learned to read between the lines of a balance sheet as well as his equity partners, and he knows enough about the quirks of the music business to be expected to make good hires and thoughtful investments. He's a manager and investor with an understanding and passion for both the art and commerce of music who is prepared to lead the search for a new way of doing business by being the bridge between the financial world and the record executives—the heart between the head and the hands. For WMG to survive, he has to assemble and direct a team of executives who can be more than traditional record men.

To lead the record operation, he has chosen Lyor Cohen, the former president of Def Jam Records. Cohen is a controversial choice considering the difficult challenges Warner Music faces. He became rich and successful by mastering the old and increasingly irrelevant industry system that rewards executives for chart success and market share, but he is neither wildly creative nor an iconoclast in the mold of Def Jam's two other well-known executives, Rick Rubin and Russell Simmons. He isn't tech-savvy enough to program his own smartphone, let alone craft an internet delivery system for music. What he is, is intimidating and rapacious, and he has created exceptionally focused and effective labels. But Bronfman is betting that Lyor's hunger for power, recognition, and more money, and his willingness to do anything to win, makes him the man for the job.

The Warner Music Group's recent past is as dismal as Bronfman's. The company he and his partners have brought to market is not the same one that launched the careers and hits of Buffalo Springfield, the Doors, Cream, Led Zeppelin, Joni Mitchell, the Eagles, Fleetwood Mac, Prince, and Madonna. Time Warner ceased caring about the record business ten years ago and embarked on a strategy that practically halved the company's market share from 25 percent to 13 percent, and in the United States it dropped from first place to fourth. It was a stark contrast to the glory days of the 1960s when the Warner Music Group—comprised of the Atlantic, Elektra, and Warner Bros. labels—became the gold standard of the music business and powered the rise of Steve Ross's wide-ranging media empire, Warner Communications, Inc. Time Warner chairman Gerald Levin inherited that marketing might and extraordinary catalog of popular American recordings from Ross but didn't have the slightest interest in them. As far as Levin was concerned, cable television was the only business that could raise the company's share price. When conservative politicians criticized popular music, the company became fearful for its cable licenses and knuckled under, selling its hottest record label. By the time Bronfman and his partners came along in the fall of

2003, Time Warner was buckling under the crushing debt incurred by Levin's horrendous merger with AOL, and the record company had devolved into a caricature of itself. Unloading the music division, long the right thing to do given the company's lack of interest or commitment, became the only option left.

The financing was neat and clever. Bronfman and his partners put up half of the $2.6-billion purchase price and borrowed the rest. After today's IPO, they will have used a combination of bonds, extensive layoffs, roster cuts, and the stock offering to recoup all of their own money. They will also still own 75 percent of the company and have unfettered control of its board. All in all, an excellent return on a year's work.

Bronfman is unlikely to get much credit, since his partners are three of the country's best regarded private equity funds: Thomas H. Lee Partners, Bain Capital, and Providence Equity Partners. The respective heads of Bain and Providence, John Connaughton and Jonathan Nelson, have seats on the Warner Music Group board but their involvement is largely passive. The big-money player and boardroom force at the Warner Music Group is Lee Partners, and Tom Lee and his managing director, Scott Sperling, were key in making and structuring the deal along with Bronfman. At the end of today they'll still own 38 percent of the company. Bronfman, by comparison, controls just 12 percent.

Lee, sixty-one, has generally shared Wall Street's aversion to the record industry, so his involvement with Bronfman is something of a surprise. His A-list fund also owns American Media, publisher of the supermarket tabloids the *Star* and the *National Enquirer,* but he isn't viewed as an entertainment industry player. The deal that solidified his reputation and fortune was his purchase of the beverage company Snapple for $135 million in 1997, which he sold two years later to Quaker Oats for $1.7 billion. A few months before acquiring Warner Music Group, a Bronfman-led group that included Lee Partners failed to buy Universal Studios and their record company back from Vivendi.

Sperling is the Lee partner with an interest in the music business, going back to his days booking concerts as a Purdue undergraduate.

After taking an MBA at Harvard, Sperling became a manager of the Aeneas Group, the fund that handled a quarter of Harvard's then $5-billion endowment. There, he learned what a crap shoot entertainment can be. Aeneas's $8-million investment in TriStar Pictures became $30 million when Sony bought the company; its $5-million bet on Avenue Entertainment, the company that produced Robert Altman's hit film *The Player* but still went bankrupt, was a total loss.

If Bronfman is to remain CEO he's going to have to keep Lee and Sperling happy—and they're not giving him a very long leash. Sperling responded to press questions about Bronfman's role by publicly putting him on notice. "The deal with Edgar is he does a good job or someone else comes in to do a good job," Sperling said.

That will require more than just getting the financing right with Warner Music, and more than getting the company back on its feet. If he wants to prove that his steadfast belief in the continuing value of entertainment had him on the right road when he crashed with Vivendi, Bronfman will have to be right about the value of music copyrights in an age when perfect replicas of recordings can be made and traded virtually for free.

It is difficult to divine how his prior failure has affected Edgar. Just two weeks shy of his fiftieth birthday, he is as languid and patrician as a French king. A lifetime of extraordinary wealth has made him skilled at keeping others at arm's length, and he exudes the lack of doubt characteristic of people who are used to running things. Still, he can be disarmingly unpretentious in conversation, a mensch. Yet something is there in his voice and in the sharp darting of his eyes when the subject of his reputation is raised. Beneath the ingrained good manners and the practiced calm, Edgar Bronfman Jr. is seething. He's here to prove he's no one's whipping boy.

The longer Bronfman and his team are running Warner Music, the more obvious the limits of their power to affect the future become. For starters, Warner Music doesn't have the expertise to develop or dictate online technology. Edgar can only react, using his rights as a copyright owner to pick who the company will fight or support from among an endless parade of new music applications and models. "The days of the record industry dictating formats to the consumer are gone, and they're not coming back," Bronfman admits.

Even if they do find systems and services they like, it's not clear that Edgar can get the whole industry to move with him—and Warner Music doesn't have the market share to force its will on anyone. Bracketed by antitrust laws on one side and competitive distrust on the other, the major record companies have rarely been able to develop a unified strategy for even the smallest issue, so coming to a consensus on something as momentous as the internet may be impossible. That's particularly bad news. While the majority of consumers say they are willing to pay for music, the fact is they don't have to, and the industry, steadily contracting for the last five years, now appears to be on the brink of free-fall as the all-important younger music fans rapidly lose the habit of owning recordings; they see music as both ubiquitous, and free. Time is not on his side, and Bronfman may find he has little choice but to try to force-feed his competitors a cocktail of common sense and fear.

Bronfman's first order of business at Warner Music was to trim the staff by 10 percent and the roster by 30 percent, but there's nothing in the current music market to suggest that it has hit bottom. The steady erosion in CD sales recently bankrupted Tower Records, the high-profile, full-catalog superstores that carried virtually everything the record labels manufactured; the country's largest record chain, the 1,300-store Musicland, appears to be right behind them.

The weakening industry faces one more major challenge: because contracts have always apportioned the lion's share of profits to the labels, artists could be less inclined to sign with them as their marketing prowess—and financial clout—declines. Each day it becomes increasingly obvious that artists who were once the backbone of the company, like Eric Clapton—who became a guitar god during a forty-year career on the Atlantic and Warner Bros. labels and generated hundreds of millions of dollars for them—probably wouldn't sign if he were starting now. "I think it's finished, I think it's had its day," remarked Clapton of the record business not long after the Warner IPO. "I don't know where it's going, and I don't care."

Edgar is well aware of the problems. He's glad to have former Led Zeppelin guitarist Jimmy Page on hand to perform as part of the opening bell ceremony, even if the sixty-two-year-old rocker wasn't the first choice. The company had hoped Linkin Park, a popular young hard-rock group, would play, but the week before the IPO the group released a statement condemning the company as cynical and correctly pointing out that virtually all of the offering's potential $750 million will be used to pay back investors, with only $7 million earmarked for operations and none for artists. Calling the company "weakened," they announced that they intended to leave Warner Bros. Records.

Bronfman responded by saying that Linkin Park still owes Warner Bros. several albums and wasn't going anywhere. "The joy of this business is that you have long-term assets," he told potential investors. "But those assets do tend to talk back to you. Linkin Park is a big act with a long-term contract and this is just a negotiating situation." Bronfman has made clear to the band that Warner might be willing to improve their contract—depending, of course, on what additional products and rights Linkin Park is willing to give in return—but management, and not the artists or their handlers, will decide how the company spends money. Behind closed doors Linkin Park's public gambit is viewed as poorly conceived and amateurish. "They immediately fired all their bullets," Lyor Cohen remarked dismissively. "What are they going to do now? *Throw the gun at us?*"

These are the issues awaiting Bronfman. But today proves that he and his partners were smart enough to acquire control of a company worth north of $2.6 billion by laying out half of that amount for just a year. The twenty-four hours leading up to this morning have been brutal: a breakfast meeting in Baltimore, a phoner with potential investors from the car on the way to a Philadelphia lunch, and a final road show stop in Radnor, Pennsylvania. Then it was a 3:30 helicopter back to New York to meet with lead underwriter Goldman Sachs to fix the stock price.

Word on the street yesterday was that the book was weak—that there weren't a lot of takers at Goldman's projected offering range of $22 to $24 a share. It was a perception guaranteed to drive the striking price down. While disappointing, it wasn't unexpected, and when Bronfman got on the helicopter in Radnor, it looked like the deal was coming together at $18—a significant reduction, but something he'd considered in advance and deemed livable. But by 4:00 even that was suspect.

It had been another down day in a lackluster market, and the New York Stock Exchange closed off 109 points. Worse, DreamWorks Animation, a well-received entertainment industry IPO when it debuted just a few months earlier, had chosen that day to announce it would not make its projected numbers for the quarter—a cold shower sure to send a shiver through an entertainment offering like WMG. Most ominous, Bronfman could sense that the usual grumbling about private equity offerings had begun to turn nasty in the face of an uncertain market. More and more of the portfolio managers he spoke with on the road show were feeling abused, and it was becoming harder to sell an equity stock flip. Suddenly the question before Goldman Sachs and the rest of the underwriters wasn't just how low Bronfman and his partners were willing to price the IPO. It was, had they mistimed it? Should they pull the IPO and hope for an improved market?

In the end, no one balked. Lee and the rest of the partners agreed to trim the offering back to 27.2 million by foregoing plans to sell 5.4 million shares of their own holdings, a move that would have put $93 million in their pockets. It was a disappointment but hardly a defeat, and they told Goldman Sachs to lock the deal at $17 per share. Looked at in another light, cutting the stock offering by holding their own shares felt like a no-brainer. Though WMG was almost certain to trade down on its first day, they were all betting that the stock was eventually going up. Having completely recouped their investment in WMG, Edgar and his partners were in no hurry to sell more stock at $17.

At 9:25, Jimmy Page, looking puffy-eyed but as well coiffed and suspiciously smooth-skinned as a Palm Beach widow on the make, is tuning his guitar when Edgar and his wife, Clarissa, along with

Tommy Lee, Lyor Cohen, and several other senior WMG executives, join him in the gallery overhanging the trading floor. At 9:29, Page cranks up the volume on a stack of amplifiers, stands on a chair, and launches into "Whole Lotta Love," windmilling his arms and grinning down at the floor traders hooting and cheering him on. Edgar bobs his head stiffly and, at precisely 9:30, rings the opening bell. Thirty seconds later Page tosses his pick over the rail to the traders as if they are the girls in the front row at Madison Square Garden. As Bronfman had expected, WMG marks its first day as a public company by trading down and closing at $16.17. The next day the *Toronto Globe and Mail,* the leading newspaper in the country where the Bronfmans first made their fortune, declares the WMG deal just one more example of Edgar Bronfman Jr.'s imbecility.

It's the usual verdict. Bronfman is a dilettante, too dumb and ungrateful to just clench his teeth and hang on to that silver spoon. But he is neither naïve nor ungrateful. Bronfman has never scorned his family or cursed his incredible good fortune. On the contrary, Edgar is delighted to have been born rich. He just doesn't accept his birth as the sum total of his life. In a poor man, that's admirable; in a billionaire, it's risking the winning hand. Yet Bronfman can't help himself, and it's not because he is a fool with a fortune but because he's fortune's fool, put on the spot by history. The business he needs to measure himself in isn't the same carefree dream factory he fell in love with as a young man, but a battered industry taking the brunt of a new century's cataclysmic shift in technology and commerce. Whether he really has the tools to reinvent it and point the way for other media is a question for the future. How the fates of Bronfman and the Warner Music Group came to be intertwined, and why Edgar needs to risk so much, can only be found in the past.

1

Family Business, or the Tale of Two Edgars

Edgar Bronfman Jr. has always been an enigma to the music business. When he bought MCA in 1995–which he would use to build Universal Music into the world's largest record company–people in the record industry noted that he didn't conform to stereotype. He was neither a "killer," the cutthroat executive who'd chewed his way through everyone ahead of him on the corporate ladder, nor a "real record man," the romanticized and no less Machiavellian music maven with a feel for the street and the will and raw ego to transform a lifelong obsession with music into a commercial empire cut in his own image. "I'm not sure what he brings to the table," one second-generation record executive said dismissively at the time. "He's not book smart and he's not street smart."

In 1955, the year Edgar was born, his family's liquor empire, Seagram, supplied one of every three drinks sold in the United States. His father, Edgar Sr., is the only person to have made the *Forbes* list of America's five hundred wealthiest individuals every year since its inception, and his mother, Ann, is a Loeb, of the historic Wall Street investment bank Kuhn, Loeb & Company. Home for young Edgar was a duplex penthouse at 740 Park Avenue, the celebrated building where Jacqueline Onassis grew up and Time Warner founder Steve Ross owned a thirty-two-room penthouse. On the weekends, Edgar swam and played tennis at the family's Georgian-style mansion in Purchase, New York, and played with the other wealthy Jewish children at the Century Club. Once asked what it was like to grow up a Bronfman, Edgar laughed. "It's terrific. I thoroughly recommend it."

Being a Bronfman hadn't always been such a great deal. In 1888, Edgar's great-grandfather, Yechiel, a Bessarabian miller and tobacco farmer, fled a pogrom with his family to become part of what proved an unsuccessful Jewish agrarian community in Wapella, Saskatchewan. Yechiel grubbed for work in the frontier towns dotting the western lines of the Canadian Pacific Railway. There, along with his oldest sons, Abe and Harry, he sold scrap wood in the summer and frozen whitefish in the winter.

According to family legend, the Bronfmans discovered the liquor business through the circuitous route of trading horses. It was a tradition to seal those deals with a drink—and usually the only place to do that was the bar in the small hotel that marked each railroad town. The Bronfman boys saw that dispensing drinks was a better deal than buying them and cobbled together the money for a small hotel in Emerson, Manitoba. It proved a good idea: by World War One they owned hotels in Yorkton, Saskatchewan, as well as in Port Arthur and Winnipeg, the latter managed by a younger brother, Sam, who was just twenty-two. The last son born in Russia, Sam engineered the Bronfmans' almost inconceivable change of fortune, moving them in one generation from the shtetl to the castle. Faced with lifelong accusations that their hotels had been little more than brothels, the rapacious and unapologetic Sam would declare, "If they were, then they were the best in the West!" When Canadian prohibition hit in 1916, the Bronfmans gave the first indication that they were a business family to be reckoned with.

Their economic salvation lay buried in a loophole of Canadian law. When the country went dry, each province determined the specifics of prohibition within its borders, while the federal government retained control over sales between provinces—which remained legal. Unable to sell alcohol in their hotels, the Bronfmans moved into the mail-order liquor business and opened warehouses around the country for the sole purpose of using the federal provision to ship whisky from province to province. And when World War One rationing later banned alcohol sales for any but medicinal purposes, the Bronfmans obtained drug wholesaling licenses and sold their wares to drugstores. In the end, the brief-lived Canadian prohibition proved a boon to the Bronfmans, a tune-up for what was to come in the United States.

By the time of the Volstead Act in 1920, the Bronfmans had warehouses—"boozoriums"—in small border towns from British Columbia to Ontario, where Americans could purchase all the liquor they wanted legally. It was a rough-and-tumble business, and a Bronfman brother-in-law managing several of the warehouses was shotgunned to death by bootleggers in 1922.

Harry, who ran the business, had a ready supply of Canadian and Scotch whisky but saw a chance for the family to do even better by making its own. The Bronfmans' first forays into distilling were reputedly nothing more than rotgut: four parts water, one part pure grain alcohol, a few gallons of someone else's good whisky for flavor, a touch of caramel for color, and a dash of sulfuric acid for a little kick and the illusion of age. The famous aged Scotch whiskies Glenlivet (which the Bronfmans would eventually own) and Johnnie Walker inspired the family's fake brands—finger-numbing two-day wonders "Johnny Walker" and "Glen Levitt." They were a howling success. And though hardly alone in the perfectly legal business of selling alcohol in Canada to Americans, they were far and away the most aggressive. They would one day agree to a settlement with Canadian and American tax authorities amounting to a de facto admission to having provided 50 percent of all whisky smuggled in from Canada.

In 1924, the Bronfmans purchased the shuttered Greenbrier Distillery near Louisville, Kentucky, tore it down, and shipped the equipment to Montreal, where they built a new distillery in Ville LaSalle on the St. Lawrence River. Two years later they started Distillers Corporation Ltd. as a partnership with the Distillers Company Ltd. of Great Britain—then the world's largest distiller—and became the exclusive Canadian agents for many of the world's best Scotches. In 1928, they purchased Ontario's Joseph E. Seagram & Sons, a small distiller with a good reputation. In one of their most prescient moves, the Bronfmans held back their best and better-aged liquor and sold parched Americans such now-forgotten beverages as Chickencock (sold in a can), stockpiling their superior distillations against the day Prohibition would be repealed and consumers could afford to be more selective. More than any other, this move made the Bronfman fortune. When Prohibition ended in 1933, Seagram was sitting on 3 million gallons of aged and select whisky. Overwhelming their competitors, they bought US distillers, brands, and distributors, and by 1938 claimed to be the leading company in the US spirits market.

Throughout much of Prohibition, Sam and Harry had each held 30 percent of the company. But Harry found himself indicted on various bootlegging and related bribery charges. He eventually beat them, but the publicity—particularly regarding his flair for convincing key witnesses of the financial merits of moving beyond the reach of the courts—made him a less-than-ideal candidate to head the rapidly expanding and increasingly respectable company now known as the Distillers Corporation–Seagram's, Ltd. As Sam made the company more and more his own, he would present his brothers and sisters with a succession of revised share plans, until he personally held 37.5 percent out of the family's 51 percent stake in the company. At that point, he and Allan, the youngest brother and Seagram's attorney, were the only ones retaining significant shares and input—and Sam always made sure Allan knew the score. "The business is mine," Sam told him. "You must understand that the words 'we' and 'us' no longer apply."

Taking over, Sam—or Mr. Sam, as he was now called by his employees and associates—concentrated on expanding the business in the United States and treating himself like a pasha. He acquired a chauffeured Rolls-Royce and moved the family to Westmount, the English-speaking suburb that most of Montreal's affluent Jews called home. There, Sam and Allan occupied adjacent mansions at the top of Mount Royal. Sam usually spent his weeks in New York, traveling back and forth to Montreal by private sleeper car on Friday and Sunday nights. His apartment at the St. Regis Hotel—which he kept for thirty years—was the largest in the hotel and boasted an oak-paneled living room, a library, three bedrooms, a full kitchen, a maid's room, and two butler's pantries.

Nursing an irrational fear that Prohibition could return, Sam strived to make drinking as respectable as possible. Seagram urged consumers to drink moderately and following World War Two, made several prestigious European purchases, including both Perrier-Jouët and Mumm's champagne, cognac maker Augier Frères, and the highly successful wine shipper Barton & Guestier. But Sam's greatest feel was for marketing and selling whisky, and he was justly proud of his creation and launch of the company's two premium whisky blends, Crown Royal and Chivas Regal. He acquired the Aberdeen-based Chivas Brothers for £80,000, intent on making the small, well-regarded distiller into the greatest name in blended Scotch whisky. Crown Royal, packaged in its signature purple jewelry bag, was a triumph of marketing and likely Sam's greatest moment as a liquor executive. It commanded top dollar and for more than twenty years had no real competitors.

Despite the newfound wealth, Mr. Sam spent much of his adult life and large chunks of his fortune in a fruitless attempt to deny his past and wash away the stain of bootlegging. Driven by a near maniacal need for acceptance, he falsely claimed to have been born in Canada, affected an English accent, and became a devout Anglophile. He gave millions of dollars to both the Liberal and Conservative parties in a vain quest for one of Canada's ceremonial senate seats. When he attempted to join such exclusive Montreal institutions as the Mount Royal Club, he was rebuffed with a potent cocktail of anti-Semitism and elitist disdain for the way the arriviste Bronfmans had made their formidable fortune. Unwelcome in society, he grew dictatorial in the world that he could control, erecting a cult of personality in which he was all things Seagram: master blender, marketing genius, infallible corporate titan. In order to avoid inheritance taxes, Sam and

Allan had jointly placed their 3.3 million shares of Seagram stock into trust for their children through Seco Investments, a holding company with two parts: Cemp—for the 2.2 million shares for Sam's children Charles, Edgar, Minda, and Phyllis—and Edper, which held the 1.1 million shares of Allan's sons, Edward and Peter. However, Sam made sure that his majority share in Seco gave him the right to vote all of its stock and subsequently used his absolute control over his brother's shares to bar Edward and Peter from coming to work at Seagram. Finally, in 1960, Sam announced that he wanted to buy 600,000 of Edper's 1.1 million shares—at a discount, of course. His nephews agreed, partly out of a perceived threat that Sam would strip their father of his Seagram vice presidency if they refused. Over the next few years they earned a measure of revenge by unloading all of their Seagram shares and launching an investment and real estate empire of their own.

Tyrannical and abusive, Sam would berate employees, his favorite all-purpose sobriquet "cocksucker" applied continuously and without prejudice to salesmen, lawyers, board members, and secretaries— and even at the dinner table until his wife, Saidye, shamed him into silence. "Cocksucker," she mused. "Isn't that a charming word? *Cocksucker*. I'm going to learn to use that." His greatest vitriol was aimed at his younger brother, Allan, whose acquiescence to being abused only seemed to provoke him further. Sam once threw an ashtray at Allan's head during a meeting. When Mr. Sam's longtime attorney and advisor, Lazarus Phillips, was offered Sam's coveted seat as Canada's token Jewish senator by the Liberals, Sam went berserk. After three decades as the Bronfmans' go-between, deal maker, and consigliere, Phillips found himself cut dead by Sam, who now described the man who was arguably Canada's most sophisticated barrister and deal maker of the day as "a two-bit lawyer—I made him a millionaire."

In front of his children he was never seen in less than a jacket and tie, even on the hottest summer Saturday. "Next to my father," his eldest son, Edgar Sr., would later say, "Queen Victoria looked like a swinger." Growing up in the Westmount mansion was torture for Edgar. Slaves to their father's WASP pretensions, kept at arm's distance by their mother, the four Bronfman children were placed under the care and tutelage of European governesses and nannies until they were old enough to go to boarding school. Contact with their parents was limited to two weekend meals for which they were required to dress, and Saturday evenings were set aside for "Life Lessons," Mr. Sam's lectures on how to work hard and carry oneself in the world.

Edgar loved his father, but he neither liked nor trusted him. "One thing I never saw Father do was give a compliment," he said. He never forgot watching his father curse out Allan in the middle of an annual shareholders' meeting or throw a glass of ice water at him during a lunch. Regarding Sam's treatment of Lazarus Phillips, Edgar recalled, "The language Father used to describe a man whom he had often called his best friend was beyond foul," leading him to the conclusion that "this man could turn on anyone—meaning *me*. Consciously or subconsciously, I lived with this all my life. The idea that I was only conditionally loved was reinforced by what I observed of Father's conduct toward others."

Miserable, Edgar was less than warm and considerate toward others. In a story his mother liked to tell, one of Sam's business associates, Julius Kessler, discovered that Edgar was impressed with his pocket watch and promised to give it to Edgar as a bar mitzvah present. The boy shook his head: "You're an old man and you might be dead by the time my bar mitzvah comes around," he said. "You better give it to me now."

"My father was an empire builder," Edgar once said. "And, true to the customs of his times, the emperor needed a male heir. As the first son, I was destined to be that heir. In truth, Sam Bronfman wanted a clone." Sadly, what Edgar didn't want, his oldest sister, Minda, craved. Tough-minded and temperamental, she was the child most capable of standing up to their father, for she was most like him, and probably best suited to be his successor. But such a role was unimaginable for a girl—least of all any daughter of Mr. Sam. With no future in Montreal, she moved to Paris and became a baroness. Over the years, both before and after her father's death, Minda made repeated attempts to become more active in Seagram business. Each effort was rebuffed.

Once he left home, Edgar grew ever more rebellious. At Waspy

Williams College, where his main interests were drinking and chasing coeds, he briefly became engaged to an Irish girl in a bald attempt to anger his parents. A string of drunk driving accidents culminating in a motorcycle crash brought him back to Montreal. There, he saw Ben Raginsky, a psychotherapist Sam and Saidye had previously hired to explain the facts of life to Minda and Phyllis. Seemingly ready to accept that there might ultimately be more positives than negatives in being a Bronfman, Edgar completed his education at McGill and in the summer of 1951 went to work at Seagram.

While he accepted Seagram as his life, he still longed to be somewhere other than Montreal and spent as much time as possible in New York. It was there, filling in for his brother, Charles, on a date, he met Ann Loeb, daughter of the investment banker John Loeb, and the two soon decided to marry. Sam, who had repeatedly counseled his sons not to waste any time dating poor girls, was delighted with such a responsible match. The bride's family was just as pleased: at the wedding reception, John Loeb quipped, "Now I know what it feels like to be the poor relation."

Spending the summer of '53 in New York, Edgar studied at the elbow of his father-in-law's colleague Sam Steadman. A partner at Loeb, Rhoades & Co., Steadman pursued the then-unorthodox strategy of evaluating companies on their potential rather than their current asset value. Edgar returned to Montreal in the fall for a year in his father's office before taking command of the US company. It was a role that some Seagram executives—and his own mother—believed him unsuited for.

Edgar himself was deeply ambivalent about his career at Seagram. On one hand, he harbored a grudge over having to become his father's successor, yet he was eager to prove himself capable of running the company should his father ever let him. Still, Edgar bristled at any challengers, real or perceived. Whatever shame he felt over his father's despicable treatment of his uncle and cousins, the notion that they should even *think* there was a place for them at Seagram could set him off. Like a jealous prince, he ruminated on who among his father's aides and executives would get to stay—and who would taste the axe.

The transformation of Seagram from its opportunistic, wild-and-wooly beginnings into a respectable international corporation drove Sam in his later career. He crafted an image for the company that bore little relation to its roots. The new company motto implied a storied past: "Integrity, Craftsmanship, Tradition." By the mid-fifties, the future of the company was in New York, not Montreal. When Seagram planned its new corporate headquarters on Park Avenue, Mr. Sam envisioned something in the moat-and-drawbridge school, but his younger daughter, Phyllis Bronfman Lambert, persuaded him to make what she characterized as a more "significant" statement. Given free rein, she hired the already legendary architects Ludwig Mies van der Rohe and Philip Johnson. Today, the Seagram building at Park Avenue and Fifty-second Street is considered one of the greatest buildings of the twentieth century. It was a triumph for Seagram and the Bronfmans—and further proof of just how much family talent Mr. Sam had overlooked when he anointed Edgar over his daughters.

When Edgar assumed the presidency of the US distiller in November 1957, he was nowhere near as involved in the day-to-day running of the company as his father had been. "I don't much like details and I'm not really suited to being a hands-on operating executive," he admitted. "I'm better at laying out long-term strategy."

Sating the old man's ego was nearly impossible, but Edgar was audacious enough to succeed occasionally. When Ann was expecting the couple's first child, Edgar told his father that he wanted to name his first son for him. It was a startling suggestion: Sam was far from a religious man, but the gesture flaunted Jewish tradition. "My husband was well aware that in Orthodox Jewish tradition a child is not supposed to be named after a living person," Saidye said. "He sat perfectly silent and he didn't say a word. Later, when we went upstairs to bed, he confessed that he was very pleased but was so taken aback by what Edgar had proposed that he simply didn't know what to say. He mulled it over and next morning, with a twinkle in his eyes, gave the children his consent." Sam didn't remain abashed for long: when Minda named her second child Charles Samuel, he tried unsuccessfully to have the boy's name changed legally to Samuel Charles.

The family trust, Cemp, also gave Edgar Sr. an opportunity to show his savvy, particularly when he steered the family into an early investment in Polaroid and expanded the Bronfmans' oil holdings. In the early '50s, Sam bought a stake in western Canada's Royalite. "If it's good enough for the Rockefellers, it's good enough for us," he liked to say. In the following decade, Edgar convinced him to invest in the Oklahoma-based Forrest Oil and to create an exploration firm, Frankfort Oil. And in 1963, Seagram purchased Texas Pacific Coal and Oil for $65 million.

When it came to maximizing their profits, the Bronfmans demonstrated a near mania for minimizing taxes. Sam was adept at exploiting the fact that Seagram had both US and Canadian operations, claiming to be based in one country or the other depending on the tax advantage. When Charles secured an extraordinary advance tax ruling in 1991 to transfer a family trust worth $2.2 billion out of Canada without paying taxes—saving the family $750 million—it became a government scandal.

Restless at Seagram, Edgar yearned to be in the film industry, which he called "uniquely satisfying." In the mid-1960s, Cemp cashed out its position in Polaroid for $20 million, and Edgar reinvested the money in Paramount Pictures, giving Cemp nearly a third of the studio's stock. It was a remarkable stake at a bargain price. But Mr. Sam was rarely willing to venture beyond what he already knew and thought the Paramount purchase insanity. "I don't want you in the goddamned movie business," he thundered at Leo Kolber, the financial advisor who oversaw Cemp. "We've got whisky. We've got real estate. We've got oil. What the hell else do you want?" At Sam's insistence, the stock was unloaded in 1966 to Charles Bluhdorn, who used it as the cornerstone for his far-flung conglomerate, Gulf+Western, the predecessor to Paramount Communications.

Undeterred, Edgar made a second bid to get into the film business through Cemp two years later, agreeing to buy a 15 percent stake in Metro-Goldwyn-Mayer at a premium. Once again, Sam was less than impressed. "Tell me, Edgar," he said. "Are we buying all this stock in MGM just so you can get laid?" Edgar was unfazed. "No, Pop. It doesn't cost $40 million to get laid."

Though smitten with the entertainment business, Edgar had also gone into the MGM deal with a bigger target. He knew that Time Inc. had quietly been acquiring MGM stock and he hoped to buy a controlling interest in the studio and merge the two companies—a prescient move that would have predated Time's 1989 merger with Warner Communications by twenty-one years. By the following year he'd accumulated enough stock to become MGM's chairman, but he was forced out three months later when Las Vegas developer Kirk Kerkorian amassed a 25 percent block. When Edgar made the mistake of attending comedian Don Rickles's show at a Hollywood nightclub, the put-down king quipped, "Hey, there's Edgar Bronfman! He was chairman of MGM for five whole minutes!" Cemp eventually sold out its position for a $10-million loss, but Edgar held on to a block of personal shares and claimed a profit when Kerkorian built the MGM Grand Hotel.

Denied a studio, Edgar formed Sagittarius Productions in 1967 to make movies for domestic television and foreign theatrical release and wound up compiling a better-than-respectable track record: a biography of union organizer Joe Hill won the Jury Prize at Cannes in 1971, and an animated version of E. B. White's children's classic, *Charlotte's Web,* has enjoyed a long and profitable life on television and home video. On Broadway, the company produced *1776* and *The Me Nobody Knows.*

In 1971, with Edgar finally and firmly at the helm of Seagram, Sam died of prostate cancer. Edgar's younger brother, Charles, by then cochairman, saw their father's passing as a rare opportunity to exorcise the greed and intrafamilial rivalries that had characterized Sam's consolidation of power. He seemed genuinely mortified by Sam's shabby treatment of his brothers and sisters and, either out of morality or self-interest, didn't want family history repeating itself. In contravention of Jewish tradition, which expressly forbids revisiting a grave until a week after the burial, Charles convinced Edgar to return the day after their father's funeral and swear an oath that the business would never split the family. Edgar's reaction to his father's passing was a bit less introspective if no less dramatic. As in his professional life, Edgar had been forced to make certain personal choices in order to remain in his father's good graces. As soon as Sam was in the ground, he began a second adolescence.

"I had been unhappy for some time," he said of his marriage, which had produced five children, of which Edgar Jr. was the second. "While Father was alive, however, I couldn't bring myself to consider divorce, knowing how strongly he would disapprove." Indeed, Edgar had always styled himself something of a swinger and with Sam's death all bets were off. He and Ann split, and Edgar embarked on a bizarre and rapid series of romantic adventures. He married four times over the next two decades—including twice to the same English barmaid and once to the very unladylike Lady Carolyn Townshend, who, despite having been his employee and mistress, reportedly told friends on the eve of their wedding that she was only marrying Edgar for his money and would never have sex with him after they'd taken their vows, a promise she apparently kept. The humiliating story lit up society columns from New York to London. But even worse was the revelation that Bronfman had happily granted Townshend's request for a phenomenally generous premarriage agreement and reportedly handed over his Westchester estate, $115,000 worth of jewelry, and $1 million in cash. He was forced to seek an annulment to recover the gifts and a semblance of pride.

A potentially far more tragic event was resolved when Sam II, Edgar's eldest son, was kidnapped in August 1975. The family paid the ransom, and he was returned unharmed. The events took a more bizarre twist when Sam's captors were apprehended and proved to be acquaintances. At their trial, the two men claimed not only that Sam was in on the kidnapping, but also that he'd had an ongoing sexual relationship with one of them. Though Edgar and the family vehemently denied the story, it apparently found some traction with the jury: the defendants were convicted of extortion, but not of kidnapping.

While Edgar was experiencing the mother of all midlife crises, Seagram's stock price was slipping, and it fell largely to Charles to keep things going. But he was still based in Montreal where a good deal of his time went to managing his new baseball team, the Montreal Expos. Minda, in France and still smarting at being passed over by Sam, flew to Montreal and proposed to Leo Kolber that they use the Cemp shares in Seagram to oust Edgar as chairman. Though Kolber was no fan of Edgar, he feared the impact a palace coup could have on Seagram, particularly its stock, and demurred.

Edgar's continuing hunger to prove the old man wrong would ultimately diversify and reinvigorate Seagram. By the early '80s, Seagram's stake in Texas Pacific was worth $566 million. Yet the capital-intensive nature of the business and the fact that oil now accounted for a sizeable percentage of the liquor company's earnings appeared to make Edgar nervous: he said he feared that the Texas Pacific Coal and Oil tail was wagging the Seagram dog. In 1980, after the Iranian revolution created an oil shock and sent crude to $30 a barrel, Edgar saw an opportunity to sell out Seagram's oil stake, arguing that any company with American oil reserves was likely to fetch a premium. He was right. The following year they unloaded Texas Pacific to Sun Oil for $2.3 billion, clearing over $2 billion in profits.

Seagram now had the best kind of problem: what to do with all that cash. Though he had argued that Texas Pacific was taking Seagram away from its core business, Edgar had no interest in plowing those profits back into the operation. His prior Hollywood adventures testified to his ambivalence to liquor, and he hired banker Felix Rohatyn of Lazard Frères to scout new opportunities. After mounting an unwelcome and unsuccessful takeover bid for the mining firm St. Joseph Lead, Edgar's next target was Conoco. Investment banker Mark Millard, who had shepherded the Bronfmans in and out of their investment in Texas Pacific, noticed that a small Canadian firm, Dome Exploration, had made a tender offer for a portion of Conoco, intending to swap the stock back for the company's Canadian oil and gas holdings. When Dome's offer was wildly oversubscribed, Millard deduced that Conoco's stock—already selling relatively cheap—was ripe for acquisition. Edgar and Charles met with Conoco's CEO, Ralph Bailey, and offered to acquire 25 percent with a five-year standstill agreement. But Bailey had been making plans of his own, talking quietly with DuPont about an outright purchase of

Conoco. He listened politely to the Bronfmans but said he wasn't interested. Nevertheless, two days later, Seagram made a tender offer for Conoco.

DuPont and Mobil also made offers, and Conoco accepted DuPont's offer of $97 a share. Then, in an inspired move, Seagram found a way not just to get to the table, but also to wind up with a sizeable stake in DuPont—a far better prize than Conoco.

DuPont's offer was to be paid in cash and stock, but Seagram suspected that the arbitrageurs holding most of Conoco's stock would be willing to take a bit less for all cash, and offered $92. The name of the game was to acquire at least 20 percent, which would enable Seagram to consolidate the earnings into their own financial statements. In July 1981, they wound up with just over 20 percent of Conoco—and promptly accepted DuPont's swap offer.

It was a triumphal moment for both Seagram and Edgar. Seagram's stake in DuPont would eventually grow to 25 percent, largely due to an aggressive DuPont buyback plan that shrank the pool of available stock. Edgar had engineered a world-class deal that redefined the Bronfmans as more than booze barons and promised to make the already formidable family fortune secure beyond his father's dreams. And it allowed Edgar Sr. to finally lay his most insistent ghost to rest. As Leo Kolber put it, DuPont was the kind of prize that "would have had your father dancing in the streets."

The upheavals of Edgar Bronfman Sr.'s midlife crisis were the markers of Edgar Bronfman Jr.'s adolescence: he turned sixteen in 1971, the year his parents divorced, and twenty the summer of his brother's abduction. Like his own father, who felt closer to the chauffeur than to his parents, Edgar Jr. was left largely on his own through much of his adolescence, and he had a reputation as a spoiled kid. Arriving for an interview at a New Hampshire boarding school, he was asked by the headmaster if the man accompanying him was his father. "No," he replied, "he's my pilot."

"My clearest memory is of him cheating on the tennis court," says a former classmate at Manhattan's Collegiate School. "You know, insisting shots that were out were in. I remember thinking, 'He's so fucking entitled—he thinks *everything* has to go his own way.' "

Within the splintered family, he tried to be a healer and remained devoutly loyal to his mother. His relationship with his father—though sometimes strained—never completely ruptured.

Indeed, it was his father to whom Edgar Jr. would owe his lifelong fascination with the entertainment business, and it was to Sagittarius Productions, his father's entertainment company—and not school— that he gravitated. "From the time I was ten, I always knew—but *always*—that I would never go to college," he said. "School bored me to death." Indeed, by the time he was a senior at Collegiate, he was spending more time running the school's switchboard than attending class. In his headstrong second son, Edgar Sr. saw a kid who knew how to "avoid what he didn't want and get what he did. We sent him away to camp," said Edgar Sr., "and he made it clear that wasn't for him. Nor was he going away to prep school. Nor college." Said his brother Sam: "Edgar was always older than his years. He wanted to be grown up."

And why not? On his twenty-fifth birthday, Edgar Jr. would gain full access to a trust worth millions of dollars. It certainly couldn't be argued that missing school and becoming a determinedly crude man had done Mr. Sam's career much harm, and Edgar Sr. was, by his own admission, an executive who wasn't interested in sweating the details. Similarly, Edgar Jr. would later claim that his grandfather had anointed him as the future leader of Seagram. "He was the one who first decided I was going to run the company, when I was fifteen," Edgar said. It was part arrogance and part reality: the reality was that being a Bronfman meant living and breathing the business. The arrogance was in believing that you couldn't fail.

While still in high school, Edgar picked up a script that had been sent to his father for financing, an Alan Parker project entitled *Melody*. Taken with the story, Edgar convinced his father to invest in the film— and got himself hired as an assistant to its producer, David Puttnam, who would produce *Chariots of Fire* and *The Killing Fields* and briefly run Columbia Pictures. He spent the next two summers in London living with Puttnam's family and his father's friends Apple Records president Ron Kass and his wife, actress Joan Collins. Unpretentious and earnest, Edgar made a good impression on his English hosts. "I wish the sons of our very rich families were like him," Puttnam said, recalling that Bronfman pitched in around the house with chores and was "idolized by our kids." Puttnam's family hung Edgar Jr. with a nickname, Efer, a joking reference to an ad for eggs ("E for B—eggs for breakfast"). The name stuck.

Back in New York, Edgar showed a script he'd written to the Broadway producer Bruce Stark. Whether it was Efer's precocity or his father's bankroll, Stark liked the youngster well enough to agree to develop films and plays with him. Though nothing came of the partnership, it was an indication of the way the Bronfman name could open doors. He had a similar relationship with producer James Walsh, working first as a gofer on a rock opera, *Soon,* in which his father held a stake, and then, when he was twenty-two, investing in and producing another play with Walsh, the poorly received *Ladies at the Alamo.* After teaming with Stark, Edgar Jr. produced Terrence McNally's 1978 play, *Broadway, Broadway,* with his father's financial backing. But when it received poor reviews during tryouts in Philadelphia, Efer was summoned to a meeting in the back of his father's limousine outside the theater and, an hour later, he closed the play. If it was easy to knock Edgar Jr. as a rich brat playing producer, it was just as easy to forget that he was working to establish himself in a highly competitive business that he felt passionately about rather than playing tennis until his trust fund came due.

After working on a television show featuring Dionne Warwick, Edgar began dating one of her friends, an African American actress named Sherri Brewer. The relationship didn't please either family. When Edgar Sr. urged him to end it, Efer asked if his objections meant he could never become the head of Seagram. His father said they didn't, and he hosted a small reception for the couple after they eloped to New Orleans in 1979.

Edgar Jr. moved to Hollywood, where the Bronfman name bought him meetings with Robert Redford, director Sydney Pollack, and Paramount Studios head Barry Diller, who would become a friend, sometime mentor, and eventually a business associate. Diller, the ambitious son of a successful Hollywood real estate developer, had skipped college and started in the William Morris mailroom, where he'd famously taught himself the rudiments of the entertainment business by reading the agency's contract files. As someone who made his own luck, he recognized Edgar's seriousness. "As a teenager I always acted older than I was," Diller said. "You see that in someone else and you gravitate to it."

At Universal, Bronfman produced *The Border*, the 1982 film that teamed actors Jack Nicholson and Harvey Keitel with the noted British director Tony Richardson. It was a mild dud. When music publishers Frank Military and Jay Morgenstern introduced Efer to songwriter Bruce Roberts, he took up writing song lyrics. "They put us together and we disliked each other instantly," says Roberts. "He wrote a lyric that was extremely difficult to set and I thought, 'Screw him, I'll do it.'" Instead, the two quickly became friends, and their partnership survives still—"If he's in Los Angeles, he'll come out to the house and we'll grind for an hour"—and has produced songs like "Whisper in the Dark" for Dionne Warwick and "In Your Arms" for Ashford and Simpson. Back then Edgar's songwriting income was negligible. "I didn't have much money at that age," he said, claiming he lived on his per diem from Universal.

Following the premier of *The Border*, Edgar Jr. took his father to dinner at La Côte Basque in New York and confessed that he was fed up with being a producer. "From his standpoint, it wasn't a 'business,'" Edgar Sr. said. Sensing the moment was right, he invited his son to drop by the office the next day, at which point he asked him to come to work at Seagram.

The offer was hardly a surprise, but Edgar Jr. had nursed a dream of making his reputation as something more than the heir to Seagram. He never denied who he was—he'd used his father's connections and worried that his marriage might preclude a chance to run the company—yet he craved validation of his own abilities. He hadn't achieved it as a film or theater producer, and that was deflating. But in his father's offer was the promise of a larger validation. He was paving the way for Edgar Jr. to become guardian of the family's immense fortune. Wasn't that a bigger and better stage for proving himself worthy of the Bronfman mantle of empire builders? He told his father he'd do it.

It would prove the first step in the dissolution of both Seagram and the Bronfman family.

2

The World's Most
Expensive Education

In 1982, Efer's first job as Seagram's anointed heir was special assistant to company president Phil Beekman. The twenty-seven-year-old already knew his father's and uncle's guiding principle: everything at Seagram, no matter how singular or closely tied to the Bronfman family legend, was for sale at the right price. Exhibit A was the landmark Seagram Building. In 1978, when the company had exhausted the building's twenty years' worth of tax advantages, Edgar Sr. and Charles unloaded it on a retirement fund for $75 million. For all the building's fame as an architectural masterpiece, the sale was barely noted, which suited the family just fine. As Edgar Sr. liked to put it, Seagram was "a publicly held family business," an oxymoron suggesting that the other shareholders should understand exactly whose interests would be served first.

Not surprisingly, Edgar Jr. was more precocious and a good deal less in awe of Beekman than the typical Seagram junior executive. Beekman discovered that his new assistant was less likely to carry out his decisions than to question them. After only three months, Edgar

Sr. bailed out Beekman by asking Efer if he'd like to move to London to head the company's smaller but promising European operation. "I'd kill for it," he said. An amused and no doubt relieved Beekman suggested that that probably wouldn't be necessary.

In London, the hot potato of guiding Efer was passed to Edward Francis McDonnell, the president of Seagram International. "I was very reluctant to take him," McDonnell admitted, fearing that having a Bronfman at his shoulder would complicate his job. His fears proved ungrounded. McDonnell found him hardworking and serious. "After a few months I came to the conclusion that he was the youngest fifty-year-old I'd ever met," he said. "He was part of the team. What he didn't know, he asked about."

Edgar helped expand the operation by championing the purchase of two British liquor retail chains and a German winery, and he became an advocate of emerging overseas markets like China and Southeast Asia. Within the year, he was lobbying to come back to New York and run the company's flagship, the House of Seagram, the domestic liquor division. He got the job in 1984 and immediately hit the road to see the operation firsthand. What he saw didn't cheer him.

The post-Prohibition liquor business had once looked limitless to Mr. Sam, but its best days were now behind it: hard liquor sales were down, wine sales flat. Edgar Jr. laid off 15 percent of the division's employees and eliminated distributorships. In search of new products, he sank millions into an advertising campaign for Seagram wine coolers featuring the actor Bruce Willis that catapulted the company from fifth to first place in that niche market. But the success proved short-lived and within a decade the category had all but disappeared.

Among his executives, Efer was respected for his transparency and hard work, but he was producing decidedly mixed results: he'd trimmed costs and tried new products but failed to invigorate Seagram's liquor business. In truth, his track record was inconsequential, since the only person whose opinion really mattered was Edgar Sr. As chairman and CEO, his public position was that "nobody comes to work here thinking they're in line to be chief executive," but the reality was quite different. Edgar Sr. had only achieved complete executive autonomy with his father's death in 1971, but he was already looking for the exit when he pulled Efer on board a decade later. The stewardship of Seagram had to be pried from Mr. Sam, but Edgar Sr. seemed in a hurry to hand the company off to his own son. Indeed, when Efer joined Seagram, Edgar Sr. informed his oldest son, Sam, that he intended to pass him over and give Seagram to Edgar Jr. "You're good," explained his father, "but an unfortunate fact of your life is that you'll always be compared with your brother. And as my successor, he's better."

The blunt rejection stung. But it was civil compared to Edgar Sr.'s blindsiding of his brother, Charles, who learned the company was being turned over to Efer when he read about it in *Fortune* magazine. Charles was furious: he had his own son, Stephen. As vice chairman, he had to sign off on the pick, but Edgar Sr. had short-circuited any debate by announcing it as a done deal. Nevertheless, he'd staked his whole life on being the family peacemaker and couldn't bring himself to do more than complain privately to his brother. It was likely the kind of timid response Edgar Sr. had expected if he considered his brother's reaction at all.

Charles's good friend Leo Kolber, the family advisor and Seagram board member, was far less circumspect. "Edgar was mesmerized by his son," he said. "There's no other way to describe it. Edgar Jr. is a very nice man, very diffident, a good listener, and not a show-off in any sense of the word. He is anything but stupid. But he had no business running Seagram, and if he hadn't been named Bronfman, he wouldn't have been."

Following the brief Sturm und Drang, Efer's ascension took on an almost leisurely pace. He joined the Seagram board in 1988 and was named president and COO of Seagram the following year—a title he held until being named CEO in 1994. As chairman, Edgar Sr. did his best to mend fences with Sam and Charles, admitting that his use of the press to preclude any serious discussion of succession was "a huge mistake."

"What I should have done, of course, was discuss the issue with my brother, Charles, then with Efer and Sam," he said, before adding a litany of excuses including conflicted feelings, an aversion to confrontation, and poor planning. "If there's anything to be said in my defense, it is that I didn't extend the drama over succession, as Father did. I blundered badly, but never did I try to manipulate my sons to increase my own sense of importance."

Whatever excuses he proffered regarding his mismanagement of the succession, Edgar Sr. showed an earnest desire to let his own son lead the company without undue constriction or fealty to the past. That was admirable, but it was not hard to see the repudiation of his own father and the humiliations and frustrations he'd suffered in his shadow, particularly in his deals for Paramount and MGM, in the quick carte blanche he gave Efer to remake the company to his liking. He fancied himself a tough master, but Edgar Sr. seemed incapable of believing he himself or his son could make a real miscue. And with 38 percent of Seagram's stock under Bronfman control, all other shareholders could either accept dynastic rule or sell.

Leo Kolber thought Edgar Sr. "mesmerized" by his son, but he was actually responding to his own perceived reflection. Edgar saw in Efer all the attributes he believed he himself possessed: confidence, style, command, good looks, "a lady-killer." Yet his son had an earnest and even quixotic streak that, if not completely alien to Edgar Sr., did not define his personality.

That earnestness had two sides. On one, Efer was a sentimentalist. Divorced in '91, he wooed his second wife, Clarissa, by sending her two dozen roses and orchids every day for years. As a songwriter, his tastes and standards were those of a hack, his lyrics unapologetic adolescent syrup. But as a businessman, he was serious, unpretentious, open to counsel, and hardworking, eager both to accept the responsibility and determined to be proven worthy of the office, even if he had received it as a birthright. "It bothers me when people do a bad job and there are no consequences," Edgar said. He made it a point to visit every Seagram operation worldwide and spent half his first year as COO on the road—certainly not something the employees would have expected from his father—and visited Seagram operations in twenty-six countries in 1992 alone. Back in New York, he mounted a photograph of his grandfather behind his desk, along with the old empire builder's most famous and relevant charge: *"Shirtsleeves to shirtsleeves, fortunes have come and gone. I'm worried about the third generation."* As Edgar, with his father's approval, set about to remake Seagram in his own image, the words hung there like the sword of Damocles.

The problems that Seagram faced in the 1990s were new. Sam Bronfman had the great good fortune to be in the whisky business in Canada when the US Congress shut down his American competitors. Edgar Jr. was forced to make his own luck, and he tried to tailor Seagram to a maturing marketplace. In 1987, he purchased Martell, the two-hundred-year-old cognac firm, for $1.2 billion as part of a dual strategy to take Seagram upscale and make inroads in the Far East, where the brand was particularly well regarded. A few years later he sold nearly two dozen of the company's "bar brands" such as Calvert whisky, Wolfschmidt vodka, Ronrico rums, and Leroux cordials, and became the distributor for Sweden's increasingly popular top-shelf vodka, Absolut. The emphasis on higher-margin brands worked: in 1996, Seagram posted record profits for North America even though sales were down by 2 percent.

Yet Wall Street couldn't be enticed to belly up to the bar. Alcohol was viewed as a stale or even dying business. By '91, Seagram stock was trading at $30 a share and slipping. Upscale or not, Sam Bronfman's grandson's company was a dowdy investment, with many shareholders acquiring the stock as a backdoor to owning DuPont shares. Edgar Jr.'s most ambitious attempt to broaden Seagram had been the purchase of Tropicana in 1988 for $1.2 billion. It plunged the company into what proved to be an intensely competitive business: its biggest rival, Minute Maid, was owned by Coca-Cola—a company with a good deal more supermarket clout than Seagram. The cost of competition was steep: although Tropicana had a nearly 40 percent share of the US orange juice market and accounted for 20 percent of Seagram's revenue, its earning never topped 5 percent. Worse, Edgar took a brief flyer with Soho Beverages, a New York soda company, but had no idea what to do with it. Seagram bought it in '89, Bronfman tinkered with its packaging and flavors, watched its sales plummet, and dumped it in '92.

Even before he became CEO, Edgar Jr. was dissatisfied with the company's investment in DuPont. With a market value of around $9.4 billion, Seagram's 156 million shares in DuPont provided the company with a lot of cash and security, but Bronfman felt as if he were collecting an annuity rather than growing Seagram. "I'd already sat on the board of DuPont for a number of years, and I did not think having a noncontrolling share of another company was the best way to go," he said. "The asset was worth a lot and not really delivering for shareholders." Convinced that Seagram needed a transforming acquisition to get its stock out of the doldrums, Edgar wanted to finance it by selling DuPont. Before he could suggest that to his board, he'd have to identify a more promising deal.

Unlikely to find it in beverages, Edgar looked at several other industries, including fragrance and luxury goods, briefly steering Seagram into a stake in French couturier Herve Leger. But he kept returning to his—and his father's—favorite business: entertainment. "We became convinced that the communications-media-entertainment area was one in which a lot of money would get made," said Stephen Banner, then Seagram's CFO.

Edgar envisioned worldwide demand for entertainment exploding with the coming wave of new technology and media opportunities. Outside of Seagram, he'd been dabbling in media investments. His brother-in-law, Alejandro "Alex" Zubillaga, a Venezuelan entrepreneur with a background in the oil services business, acquired a national cable license in the early '90s and, with Bronfman's backing, formed a joint venture with Comcast to create a Venezuelan cable company. When the Venezuelan banking system collapsed in '94, Comcast pulled out and the plan was abandoned, but Bronfman and Zubillaga put $10 million into eQuest Partners, a venture capital firm investing in Latin American media startups, managed by Zubillaga. The Bronfman name helped attract $150 million from Merrill Lynch, JP Morgan, and others.

Regardless of whether it was software, cable, or wireless, Edgar believed that each new medium would only be as attractive as the programming it offered. Whoever owned the content—movies, music, television programming, literature, and news—would make money every time a new technology took hold. The record industry provided the clearest example.

The vinyl LP, invented by Peter Goldmark and introduced by Columbia Records in 1948, had enjoyed a nearly forty-year life and fueled the record industry's postwar growth. Then, beginning in the 1960s, the increasingly rapid development of home entertainment technology began to shrink the life of each subsequent configuration and increase the record industry's profits. Eight-track tapes barely lasted a decade before being replaced by the cassette. The Sony Walkman reinvigorated the music business in the late '70s and early '80s when it made prerecorded music completely portable. But the real revolution came in 1982 with the introduction of the compact disc.

Invented and jointly patented by Sony and Philips Electronics, the CD boasted pristine digital sound and created new markets for both the hardware companies and the record industry. Based on its quick acceptance, Philips and Sony envisioned a world where succeeding generations of software and hardware would be introduced every ten to fifteen years.

The CD proved a bonanza for the labels, effectively doubling their wholesale prices by replacing vinyl albums with their suggested retail price of $8.98 with $15.98 CDs. Simultaneously, the companies invoked clauses in recording contracts allowing them to pay reduced artist royalties on new technologies. And although the higher prices were initially justified by the fact that it was a good deal more expensive to manufacture CDs than LPs, those production costs soon dropped dramatically—but wholesale and consumer prices never followed. Even better for record companies, the new configuration reinvigorated back catalogs as buyers replaced favorite albums with CDs. Electronic hardware companies were also delighted to sell the new players. The company that really reaped the bonanza was Philips, which manufactured players and coowned one of the world's largest record companies, PolyGram. In 1988, Sony, which coowned the patent on CD technology along with Philips, followed their example and purchased CBS Records for $2 billion. Two years later, Sony's rival, the Japanese industrial conglomerate Matsushita, bought MCA for $6 billion.

The music business's new rosy forecast was not lost on the financial community, which had traditionally viewed the entertainment industry as something less than a business. (Mr. Sam's disdain for Paramount and MGM was far from atypical.) The leading labels like Warner Bros., RCA, and Columbia had been subsumed in larger conglomerates, so there weren't any pure record stocks to trade, and the labels' numbers were rarely reported in depth. As a result, virtually no one on Wall Street had the vaguest notion of how to assess the value of a record company catalog. Al Teller was senior vice president and general manager of Columbia Records during much of that label's explosive growth in the '80s. "We were part of CBS, which of course was a public company, but Wall Street felt the record operations' earnings were erratic and didn't understand it," he said. Bob Dylan had made dozens of albums for Columbia—what were they worth? What would they be worth in ten years? Twenty years? Fifty? Wall Street's answer was to roll its eyes and presume probably not much. But the quick success of the CD—especially the immediate doubling of retail prices and its rejuvenation of a label's back catalog—changed Wall Street's mind. If you still couldn't find someone who knew exactly what Dylan's catalog was worth, one thing was now obvious: if you accepted the premise that the CD boom would be replicated several times in the coming years with successive technologies, then the recorded work of Dylan or any other artist who could demonstrate lasting appeal was very valuable indeed. That was certainly the view of Edgar Bronfman Jr., and to advise Seagram on possible acquisitions, he turned to two high-profile entertainment industry deal makers who had acted as advisors to Akio Tanii, the president of Matsushita, in the acquisition of MCA: Herb Allen and Michael Ovitz.

As CEO of the private investment banking firm Allen & Company and a former chairman of Columbia Pictures, Allen was widely viewed as the entertainment industry's savviest and most preeminent deal makers, having advised Rupert Murdoch, Barry Diller, and cable magnate John Malone. His annual weeklong retreats in Sun Valley, Idaho, are legend—rarefied but well-publicized powwows for such media and investment barons as Warren Buffett and Bill Gates.

Ovitz, a former talent agent at William Morris, was cofounder and chairman of Creative Artists Agency (CAA), where he represented Steven Spielberg, Tom Cruise, Dustin Hoffman, Michael Douglas, and Barry Levinson. And when he made a movie star of his former martial arts instructor, Steven Seagal, it appeared he could do anything. By the mid-'80s, Ovitz had reportedly grown tired of being a hand holder to the stars and began to use his influence in Hollywood to fashion a new role as a corporate deal maker.

Ovitz introduced himself to Bronfman during that period, although the reason for the overture was far more personal. Ovitz's father, David, had spent his working life as a salesman for a Seagram distributorship and was being forced to retire. The agent implored Edgar to help him. "If my dad can't work, he'll die," he said. Bronfman arranged for the elder Ovitz to keep his job, his office, and a company car. Ovitz was grateful, but it soon became clear to Bronfman that he was also trying to cultivate him as a client. "He's a great salesman," says Edgar, "and he tried to figure out how to sell me. He asked me if I wanted to meet Marty Scorsese. I said, 'No.'"

In the spring of 1993, Edgar and his advisors began focusing on Time Warner, which appealed to Bronfman because it marketed American culture worldwide across the entire media spectrum. Created in January 1990 when Time Inc. acquired Warner Communications, Inc. (WCI) for $14.9 billion, it was a global empire of first-class brands: HBO and a part interest in Turner Broadcasting System; Warner Brothers Pictures; Time Warner Cable; the Time Inc. group of magazines including *Time, Sports Illustrated, Fortune, People,* and *Entertainment Weekly;* and the Warner Music Group, the largest domestic record company. But the company lacked a dominant shareholder, and its management was unsettled. Steve Ross, the formidable founder of WCI and the driving force behind the merger with Time, had been in rapidly failing health and had died in December 1992 before the companies could be fully integrated. It remained to be seen whether Time Warner's new and largely untested CEO, Gerald Levin, could accomplish what Ross had not.

Owning Time Warner held a personal allure for Bronfman. He had been a huge fan of Ross and frequently cited him as someone he sought to emulate. "I think he, more than anybody, knew how to manage an entertainment company," Bronfman says. "He had an incredible ability to be smart and tough with numbers and also to know where value is created and make people feel appreciated." Getting Ross's company—or at least a substantial chunk of it—was much more appealing to Edgar than owning a stake in DuPont, and he certainly believed it had a greater upside. Since Time Warner was loaded with debt and an outright acquisition was far too expensive, Edgar's long-term strategy was to replace Seagram's 25 percent stake in DuPont with a 25 percent to 30 percent stake in Time Warner. At the February '93 Seagram board meeting, Edgar and his father took the first step and convinced the members to approve the purchase of 4.9 percent of Time Warner—just under the 5 percent threshold requiring public disclosure.

The following month, Edgar began lobbying the board to sell Seagram's position in DuPont. The proposal exacerbated the simmering family rift between Edgar and his father on one side and Charles on the other and their very different visions of Seagram.

For Charles, who'd been told all his life that his goal should be to not muck things up, the name of the game was preserving the family wealth. "I'm a very different person than my father," he said. "I wasn't an entrepreneur, for God's sake. I was the inheritor." He considered Seagram's stake in DuPont an unassailable security—the financial equivalent of the Rock of Gibraltar—and to divest of it just because his nephew thought something else more promising and exciting was insane. "I don't like the entertainment business," he declared. "Someone once told me that the business of business is to make money. Once you've made the money, you can do any damn thing you want. That always stuck with me."

But the Edgars didn't view themselves as just shepherds of the family portfolio. They were the successors to the empire builder, and they measured themselves against him. Edgar Sr. saw no reason why Efer should run Seagram as if it were a stock fund instead of a corporation. "Unless you're growing a company, you're losing ground because the rest of the world is always moving forward," he said. "My son was Seagram's CEO. He understood the [entertainment] business and wanted to grow Seagram through a vehicle we controlled rather than through a passive investment. Charles had no such incentive, and was more interested in finding a safe investment—keeping what we had with DuPont—that would protect the family fortune."

Kolber, who sided with Charles, was aghast. When Edgar Jr. told him selling DuPont was the right thing to do and denigrated the chemical giant as "just a commodity play," Kolber groaned. "He actually seemed to believe what he was saying," Kolber later said. "Some commodities. Nylon. Dacron. Teflon. Textron. As it turned out, the stupidity of it was breathtaking."

The two Edgars remained adamant, arguing the chemical giant had seen its best days. "DuPont is a great name," Edgar Sr. said, "but the basis of its success is research and development; they manage to make the same commodity cheaper than anybody else. For that reason, it won't go on forever. You can't keep technological innovation secret—it's just a question of time." Edgar Jr. wondered aloud at a board meeting if the 1984 disaster at Union Carbide's Bhopal pesticide plant—when a deadly gas leak killed at least 13,000 people and severely sickened over 100,000—couldn't just as easily happen at a DuPont facility. "DuPont is a great company," he told the board, "but you're one accident away from conflagration." If that sounded more like self-justification than hard analysis, Edgar Jr. could point to the similar conclusions reached by the consultants at the Boston Group, whom he'd hired to analyze Seagram.

It would take two years for the board to come to an agreement on DuPont. In the interim, Seagram continued to acquire Time Warner stock. In May, when they hit the 5 percent mark, Edgar Jr. telephoned Levin to say he planned to buy more. "This is a benign investment," Edgar said, comparing it to Seagram's role in DuPont.

Levin was dubious. Seagram had steered clear of squabbles with

DuPont, but it still designated 25 percent of the company's board of directors—something Levin did not want to see at Time Warner, where he'd just reduced the size of the board and brought it under his control. Even if the Bronfmans were earnest about being just investors, it was impossible to forget how Laurence Tisch had engineered a successful takeover of CBS in 1986 with just 25 percent of the stock.

At Levin's urging, Time Warner's board adopted a poison pill provision. If Seagram acquired in excess of 15 percent of the stock, they would have to pay a huge bonus or make an all-cash offer for the entire company, a near impossibility. It proved an effective brake: Seagram sank approximately $2 billion into Time Warner but stopped at the 15 percent line. Repeated requests for a Seagram presence on the board fell on deaf ears. "Jerry never believed me when I said we wanted to stop at twenty-five or thirty percent," Bronfman says.

And on Wall Street the Time Warner buy hurt Seagram's stock. "I was getting pounded by the market, and eventually it seemed like not a great idea," admits Edgar. Apparently, Seagram's investors liked the idea of a passive investment in DuPont much more than they liked owning Time Warner stock. "The market took it all off our market cap. It was as if we'd taken the money and burned it."

Nevertheless, neither the failed run at Time Warner nor Wall Street's negative reaction dampened Edgar Jr.'s desire to sell DuPont and use that money to move Seagram away from liquor and into entertainment. When rumors of Bronfman's intentions started to circulate in the financial community, the reaction was overwhelmingly negative. Two credit rating agencies, Moody's Investors Service and Standard & Poor's, commented that selling DuPont could have a negative effect on the credit rating of Seagram's debt, while Brian Lomas, an analyst with Canada's ScotiaMcLeod Inc., went much further. "We don't think the rumored changes make much sense," Lomas wrote. "If the sale of Seagram's DuPont investment occurs, we would become urgent sellers." But in the end, the Bronfmans controlled the company and could pretty much do what they wanted—and what at least two of them wanted was to shed DuPont. "Beyond these issues, both Efer and I felt that DuPont was a boring investment," Edgar Sr.

would later write in his business memoir, *Good Spirits*. "DuPont is still a great company, just not an exciting one."

If Charles didn't like the entertainment business, Edgar managed to find one reason to sell DuPont that his uncle approved—a wrinkle in the tax code that could net Seagram $1.5 billion. DuPont chairman Edgar Woolard Jr. was very eager to regain the Seagram block, and in early 1995 he helped the Bronfmans exploit an extraordinary tax loophole that would benefit both companies. In return for purchasing Seagram's 156 million shares at a discount—DuPont paid $56.25 per share when the stock was trading above $60—the chemical company sold Seagram the right to buy 156 million shares at inflated prices, a slick but legal sleight of hand that qualified the deal as a stock redemption instead of a sale. Seagram booked the sale as an $8.8-billion dividend—taxed at $615 million—rather than the $6-billion capital gain that it actually was, which would have been taxed at $2.1 billion.

"I told the board, 'Only one person gets to use this tax advantage—then Congress gets rid of it,'" says Edgar. "Which they did." The swap outraged members of the House Ways and Means Committee, but it took Congress a month to alter the law and by then Seagram had its money and DuPont had its stock plus an additional $1 billion accumulated via the sale's unique structure.

Weekly Corporate Growth Report assessed the sale as a big win for DuPont but a dud for Seagram. "Even with this tax break, Seagram's return on its fourteen-year DuPont investment hardly exceeds what the company could have earned purchasing a Standard & Poor's 500 Index fund. Without the tax break, Seagram's return would have trailed behind the S&P." That conclusion wasn't much different from Edgar's. But in the coming months, as DuPont's stock price rose steadily—fueled in large measure by the fact that Seagram's shares had been withdrawn from the marketplace—Edgar Jr. continued to be criticized for rocking the boat and costing Seagram hypothetical billions. "Perhaps it would have been better for Seagram and the Bronfman family fortune if Edgar Jr. had been a feckless playboy with no ambition and if his father had chosen to retire in the 1980s and collect the family's share in the DuPont dividends for the rest of his life," concluded Graham D. Taylor, a professor of history at Canada's Trent University.

If the criticism bothered Bronfman, he didn't show it. But then, he had plenty to occupy him.

While Seagram worked on its DuPont divestiture, a lawyer from Matsushita came to see Seagram CFO Steve Banner. Recalled Bronfman: "He said, 'We see your purchase of Time Warner stock—would you be interested in MCA?'"

Matsushita's purchase of MCA had been a strategic response to archrival Sony's acquisition of two American entertainment companies, CBS Records and Columbia Pictures. But if ever a company seemed ill-suited for doing business in Hollywood it was Matsushita, a far-ranging Japanese industrial giant with a formal, hidebound business philosophy that reportedly included a five-hundred-year plan. The American executives leading MCA were the Hollywood agent-turned-studio-head Lew Wasserman and his protégé Sid Sheinberg, and neither showed any taste for taking orders from Japan. At one point, when Matsushita executives refused to meet with Wasserman and Sheinberg to discuss MCA's possible purchase of CBS and then flatly turned down a more modest request for $1 billion to buy Virgin Records—a move that would have complemented the US-based MCA Records with an international operation—the studio's irate management gave Matsushita executives an ultimatum: they could succeed in Hollywood only if they granted Wasserman and Sheinberg complete autonomy.

It was not the kind of behavior Matsushita was used to from its employees—especially managers who had just received several hundred million dollars in compensation from the purchase of their company—and Matsushita appeared at a complete loss as to how to tame a foreign holding whose business they barely understood. When a multimillion-dollar recall of refrigerators created a crisis in Matsushita's core business, Tanii was replaced as president by Yoichi Morishita. He desperately wanted Matsushita to get back to its knitting.

Bronfman was certainly interested. MCA did not have Time Warner's strength and diversity of assets—there were no magazine or major cable operations—and while it had a large film and television library, its motion picture division, Universal Studios, underperformed. The company's Universal theme parks were a distant second to Disney, and its record operation, MCA, disparagingly known as the Music Cemetery of America, had no presence outside the US. Still, it was the kind of US-based entertainment conglomerate that Edgar craved. Having failed to gain a meaningful stake in Time Warner, he was willing to settle for the smaller MCA and build it up.

As Bronfman tells it, the timing was simply fortuitous. "Everyone naturally assumes that we sold DuPont to buy MCA, but they were unrelated," he maintains. "When I wanted to sell, the board asked, 'What do we do with the money?' I felt it doesn't matter—if the right thing is to sell the asset, then sell it." But it was no coincidence that Matsushita knew Bronfman had the interest and was about to get the money: his advisors, Ovitz and Allen, as well as Seagram's law firm, Simpson Thatcher & Bartlett, had all advised Matsushita on the acquisition of MCA.

Matsushita was very clear on one point: they did not want an auction. Any agreement with Seagram would have to be concluded quickly and quietly. On the morning of March 6, 1995, Edgar boarded the Seagram Gulfstream IV jet at Teterboro Airport in New Jersey for Osaka, Japan, and a secret meeting with Morishita. Bronfman's chief concern was Matsushita's rumored asking price of $10 billion, and he spent much of the flight reading Morishita's speeches in an effort to find the proper tone for the negotiations. Whether by design or luck, his decision to make the trip alone proved a good one. Although Morishita spoke no English and Bronfman no Japanese, Edgar's earnest desire to work out an agreement one to one stood him in stark contrast to MCA's American executives. Well aware of other possible suitors including TCI, News Corporation, and Bertelsmann, Bronfman was eager to avoid a bidding war. Within two days a framework for a possible sale was devised. Matsushita would open MCA's books to Seagram and give the company an exclusive window of eighteen days in which to make a bid. In return,

Bronfman agreed to keep the negotiations a secret, especially from Wasserman and Sheinberg.

On April 9, just three days after Seagram completed the sale of its DuPont shares and a month after Bronfman's meetings with Morishita, Matsushita sold 80 percent of its stake in MCA to Seagram for $5.7 billion. Retaining a 20 percent stake was a way for Matsushita to save face and downplay a mistake. Its Hollywood foray had proven at best a wash and at worst a costly waste of time and attention. For its part, Seagram gradually shed its 15 percent position in Time Warner, allowing Bronfman to claim the failed run had still earned Seagram shareholders $1 billion.

It was hard to argue that Bronfman hadn't gotten a good deal for MCA. But Wall Street, which had thumbed its nose at Seagram's maturing liquor business, the Time Warner flyer, and the DuPont divestiture, didn't like the MCA purchase, either. News of the acquisition dropped Seagram's stock from $44.38 to $37, taking nearly 20 percent off the $16.5-billion company's value. That translated into a $1.1-billion paper loss for the Bronfmans. Charles Bronfman could only watch the price of DuPont rise steadily and gnash his teeth.

During the negotiations, Edgar had succeeded at keeping Sheinberg and Wasserman in the dark, which virtually guaranteed their exit from MCA once the deal was done. It's hard to imagine any circumstance in which giving MCA executives the opportunity to look for other buyers or make their own bid would have been to Seagram's advantage, but Edgar sought to mollify them by offering Wasserman a seat on the Seagram board of directors and underwriting an independent production deal for Sheinberg. Neither man was Bronfman's choice to run the studio. The man he wanted was Ovitz, whose connections could quickly bring in choice projects and cast Seagram as a bold new player in Hollywood.

Running a studio was Ovitz's dream job, but he also wanted a dream contract that guaranteed jobs for two of his top CAA associates, Ron Meyer and Bill Haber. And as eager as he was to move beyond CAA, Ovitz insisted on a compensation package that took into account what he might have made if he'd stayed there. Additionally, he'd been holding on-again, off-again conversations with Disney chairman and CEO Michael Eisner about joining that company. Indeed, when Ovitz told Eisner that Bronfman wanted him to run Universal, the Disney chief tried to dissuade him, characterizing the Bronfmans as fickle and ruthless and predicting they'd be hard to work for. "Why would you want to go to Universal when you could come to Disney as my partner?" Eisner asked him.

Bronfman offered Ovitz a package variously valued at between $150 million and $250 million. Nevertheless, Ovitz seemed unable to take yes for an answer, and negotiations dragged out as he piled on demands for stock options, planes, limousines, offices, and anything else he could think of. Bronfman, who could find someone qualified to run Universal for a fraction of what he was offering Ovitz, got queasy.

"There's a great saying: you learn something about somebody when you start to negotiate with them," Bronfman says. "I knew within a week that I'd made a terrible mistake because everything was focused on control. It was like a bright line: I knew it was over. Mike asked for some outrageous package for the three of them. When I asked what the split on the Universal equity was, ninety percent was going to Ovitz."

It was also too much for Charles Bronfman and Leo Kolber. They'd gone along reluctantly with the DuPont divestiture and MCA purchase, but they howled at the idea of writing a $250-million executive contract. Kolber found it so unconscionable that he considered its approval a breach of the board's fiduciary duty. "I'm telling you right now I'm voting against this," he told Charles when briefed on Ovitz's proposed package. "This is criminal, you can be put in jail for this."

"Everyone was uncomfortable from day one, my uncle more than anyone," Bronfman said. Nor had he forgotten that one of his earliest mentors, producer David Puttnam, had paid a heavy price for running afoul of Ovitz. "David Puttnam came to Hollywood and started poking CAA in the eye and they shut Columbia down," Bronfman says. "I had to get out of the deal with him having the victory. I needed to let Mike beat up on me publicly. And he did, but too much." Ovitz later claimed that he had declined the position at MCA because Edgar's father and uncle were actually calling the shots at Seagram, and Edgar couldn't deliver. Says Bronfman: "There's lasting enmity."

With no obvious alternative to head the studio, Bronfman took the advice of David Geffen—whose own antipathy toward Ovitz dwarfed Bronfman's—and offered the job to Ovitz's top lieutenant at CAA, Ron Meyer. Though widely perceived as little more than a talent agent, Meyer would prove a solid—and far less costly—choice to help lead Universal Studio's turnaround. "I like Ron," says Bronfman. "He was still a seller when he came to Universal, but he had relationships and credibility. If CAA was a ship, Mike was the tug and Ron was the rope: people are loyal to Ron."

Geffen along with Barry Diller were two of the sharpest, most feared, and most opinionated operators in the business. They met Bronfman in 1973 when he was just eighteen and beginning his career as a producer, and came to constitute something of a kitchen cabinet for him. It was a connection from which Geffen and Diller would reap substantial benefits. Almost immediately after Edgar bought MCA, Geffen and Bronfman personally negotiated a deal for Universal to distribute films made by DreamWorks, the company Geffen had cofounded with Steven Spielberg and Jeffrey Katzenberg, and a few months later Edgar made an unorthodox and controversial deal that placed MCA's television operations under the control of Diller's USA Networks. In each case it was clear that Bronfman was paying a lot of money in order to be in business with proven hit makers, and he couched each deal as an act of trust, virtually allowing the men to name their own prices, which Geffen did. In Diller's case, associates say, he thought the deal Bronfman was offering was so good that he insisted Edgar not mention it to Geffen, fearing he would advise against it. The business press and the rest of Hollywood seized on both transactions as proof that Bronfman had come to town to get hosed. "He's like a *piñata*," one anonymous executive gleefully told the *New Yorker*. "Hit him and money comes out."

Bronfman needed a success story. With an untested head in place at the lagging film studio, he turned to the music division. MCA Records, though a perennial wallflower, was one of the few divisions that might be rapidly improved. "I didn't see any way we could be number one in film," he says of his earliest assessment of MCA. "We can't compete on cable. So it's music."

Bronfman had inherited a seasoned and respected record division head in Al Teller, who'd risen through the ranks at CBS Records before coming to MCA. But having weathered Matsushita's ownership, Teller didn't seem keen to work for the Bronfmans, whom he privately belittled. "Al didn't always come across as if he believed it was Edgar's company," says another MCA executive. Bronfman was soon looking for a replacement, an executive with the drive and vision to bring the record company from last place to first.

Bruce Roberts, Edgar's songwriting partner, suggested to him that the man he wanted was Doug Morris, the powerful chairman and CEO of Warner Music US. Morris's experience, wealth of artist and business contacts, and ready-made senior staff could put a quick charge in a sluggish record operation like MCA.

Though Edgar didn't know Morris, Roberts's suggestion made perfect sense to him. After all, when he first decided to move Seagram into entertainment it was the far-ranging Time Warner, and not the much smaller MCA, that was his preferred target. Why shouldn't he find the best executive to head MCA Records at Warner Music?

Trying to hire Morris was, in fact, a smart call and Doug's mastery of the business was real. Balding and paunchy, the affable Morris seemed more like a favorite if somewhat mysterious uncle than the kingmaker and grand master of corporate intrigue that he was. The fifty-eight-year-old had risen through the ranks at Atlantic and in the last ten years had breathed new life into the rock and R&B label cofounded in the 1940s by the great music man Ahmet Ertegun. Atlantic's success during the '60s and '70s—along with that of its sister label, the California-based Warner Bros. Records, run by another legend, Mo Ostin—put the early financial muscle into Steve Ross's media conglomerate, Warner Communications, Inc. (WCI), and helped turn it into everything that MCA was not. But by the late '80s the tightfisted and old-school Atlantic had become stale. Named Atlantic's chairman in 1990, Morris empowered a cadre of label presidents, and their success and loyalty made him more than a music industry force: he became the defining executive of his era. Morris's rise coincided with a period of massive transformation in the music industry, and he was a master of two worlds. As Ahmet's protégé in the traditional record business, he knew how to deliver hits, but he had also become a consummate corporate gamesman. The last man standing in a bitterly fought executive range war, Doug was on the verge of taking complete control of Time Warner's worldwide record operation. Over the coming months, Bronfman would bet much of Seagram's future as a media company on the record business, and he needed someone he could lean on to make key decisions and teach him the business. Morris hadn't simply survived music's transformation from a niche industry to a key component of a worldwide media industry—he had thrived like no one else.

Yet if Edgar had taken a look beyond the sunny story of Morris's own success, he might have seen the storm clouds gathering over both Warner Music—a company he would one day own—and the record industry.

Whatever could be said of Morris, his rise coincided with a period of greed and self-interest that was exceptional even for the record business. The easy windfall from CD profits made some executives who knew nothing about the business look savvy—and it spurred many who did to reach for ever more wealth and executive power. The result was a generation of label managers who thought almost exclusively about the immediate results that could boost their own bonuses and make them more powerful than their rivals, and not at all about where the business—and particularly the technology supplying its robust growth—was going. Add in a parent company like Time Warner, whose own executives increasingly viewed the record business as a burden rather than a boon, and the results should have been foretold. In a few years the internet would challenge every aspect and basic assumption of the industry's business model. And those executives who once looked so savvy wouldn't have a prayer.

3

The Rainmakers

Doug Morris was an aspiring songwriter with hitches in the army and Columbia University when he scored his first real record business job in the mid-'60s as a song plugger, convincing A&R people to record songs published by producer Bert Berns, who coowned the small record company Bang. His next stop was Laurie Records, where he worked on several hits including "Little Bit o' Soul," by the bubblegum group Music Explosion, and "Sweet Talkin' Guy" for the girl group the Chiffons. Before long Morris was feeling confident enough to go into business for himself. "I realized that if you have good product you can do okay," he says of his 1970 decision to cofound Big Tree Records.

Like Laurie, Big Tree was a modest but wide-ranging pop label aiming squarely for Top 40 radio, still at the height of its popularity. Unlike FM's emerging album-oriented rock radio, Top 40 was an extraordinarily democratic format: a station would play virtually any record regardless of style—soul, rock, R&B, middle-of-the-road, even country—if it was a big enough hit. Big Tree tried to live up to its name by spreading out and offering a bit of everything and anything: after starting with a dud cover of Joni Mitchell's "Big Yellow Taxi," the company made its mark with a string of gooey and immensely popular soft-rock hits by Lobo and England Dan and John Ford Coley. The label also scored unique hits, including the dance track "You Sexy Thing" by Hot Chocolate and the Michigan rock band Brownsville Station's anthem for aspiring juvenile delinquents, "Smokin' in the Boys' Room." Before long the acts were coming Morris's way. One was the English group Magic Lanterns, and in 1974 he purchased their single "One Night Stand." Morris quickly put it out and sat back, ready to watch it climb the charts. Instead, he says, he got an unexpected phone call.

"Doug Morris? This is Ahmet Ertegun at Atlantic Records. Why are you putting out my Magic Lanterns record?"

Atlantic had released "One Night Stand" several years earlier and still owned its rights. Fearing the worst, Morris ran to Atlantic to head off a lawsuit. Ertegun liked the younger man's drive and instead of suing Big Tree, he struck a deal for Atlantic to distribute the label. In short order, the two were mentor and protégé.

Morris's blunder and ultimate triumph is just the kind of story record men love to tell about themselves. A hustler runs into trouble and, by dint of luck or cunning, comes out smelling like roses. In 2006, Ertegun, a still-sharp eighty-three, couldn't recall how he met Doug Morris and the mention of the Magic Lanterns drew a blank. But he did remember that it was love at first sight. Had he been a baseball scout, Ertegun would have judged Morris a five-tool player.

"Doug is a terrific record guy—an old-time record guy," Ertegun said. "He'd been a songwriter, even a performer, I think, and he had all the aspects of the business within him plus a feel for the times. On top of all that, he was a great promotion man, and we had that in common."

In joining Atlantic, Morris was moving up to the big leagues. Ertegun was a record industry legend.

The worldly son of a Turkish ambassador, Ertegun was a music maven who borrowed $10,000 from the family dentist in 1947 to start Atlantic as a black music or "race" label. In 1953, music journalist Jerry Wexler joined as a partner and before the end of the decade Atlantic was the home of Ray Charles, Ruth Brown, Joe Turner, the Coasters, and the Drifters. A leader in the field of rhythm & blues—a term, not coincidentally, coined by Wexler—the label's cachet made it a magnet for the next generation of white rock musicians. Ertegun, a jet-setting sophisticate and sybarite who was hipper than his competitors, proved irresistible to rockers and their managers, and he landed the best and bestselling of the British bands including Cream, Led Zeppelin, and ultimately the Rolling Stones. Nonetheless, Ertegun and Wexler were essentially small business owners who enjoyed a well-earned reputation as tightfisted negotiators with a talent for getting what they wanted—and leaving a smile on your face. "Those were two of the cagiest cats on the planet," says an admiring Jac Holzman, the founder of Elektra Records.

In 1967, Wexler had convinced Ertegun to sell Atlantic to Seven Arts Productions for $17.5 million. A New York company that syndicated movies and cartoons to television, Seven Arts had purchased the famed but down-on-its-heels Warner Brothers Studios from Jack Warner for $32 million a few months earlier. That company included two small but growing record labels, Warner Bros. and Reprise Records, and with the addition of Atlantic, the new company, Warner–Seven Arts, was positioned to become a power in the record industry just as the underground rock movement of the late '60s brought explosive growth. But in 1969 Warner–Seven Arts was sold to Kinney National, an unlikely conglomerate of funeral parlors, parking lots, and cleaning services. The $400-million pricetag—about 13 times what Seven Arts had paid for Warner Brothers just three years earlier—left Ertegun and Wexler with a massive case of seller's remorse. Clearly, they'd sold too cheap, and they did not envision going to work for someone from the mortuary business. But Kinney mastermind Steve Ross was nothing if not charming, and generous to a degree almost beyond imagination. He granted the record executives extraordinary autonomy and paid them more lavishly than they'd ever been paid in their lives.

In 1970, Ross purchased Elektra Records for $10 million from Jac Holzman, and created the Warner Music Group—a three-headed giant whose combined roster boasted Led Zeppelin, Aretha Franklin, Crosby, Stills, Nash and Young, and the Rolling Stones on Atlantic; James Taylor, Jimi Hendrix, Joni Mitchell, and the Grateful Dead on Warner Bros./Reprise, and the Doors on Elektra.

Ross allowed Ertegun, as well as Warner Bros. Records chief Mo Ostin, to run their operations as each saw fit. As long as they performed, it was an unending honeymoon, celebrated with progressively generous bonuses and stock options. "I remember the days of Steve Ross," says a wistful Sheldon Vogel, who was the controller and vice president of finance for Atlantic at the time of the sale to Kinney. " 'You do your thing, you make some money for me, and I don't know what you're doing.' " But for all his laissez-faire management style and the corporate goodies he doled out, Ross was savvy. Vogel remembers getting a new contract several years later—and being surprised to discover that Doug Morris, by then the president of Atlantic, had simultaneously received a shorter one. "Doug asked Steve Ross why I got five years and he got three," Vogel says. "And Ross said, 'Unless he gets Alzheimer's, Shelly isn't going to forget how to do his job. You could lose your feel.' Ross didn't give long contracts to people on the creative side."

By 1977, eight years after the formation of WCI, operating income and revenues for the record division had grown sixfold and the music group supplanted CBS as the US market leader, a position that would continue for more than twenty years. With the music operation providing financial stability, Warner had flowered into one of America's great media companies. In 1976 it had acquired the video game company Atari for $28 million and anything—cable, books, comics, theme parks—seemed possible on the cash flow produced by the music division and, later, the reinvigorated studio.

In 1978, Ertegun bought out Morris's stake in Big Tree and named him president of a new Atlantic division, Atco and Associated Record labels.

It was a great opportunity for Morris. One of Ertegun's other protégés, David Geffen, had become a millionaire while still in his twenties by taking Ertegun's advice and using Atlantic's distribution and financing to start Asylum Records, the label that became home to Jackson Browne, Linda Ronstadt, and the Eagles. But unlike the entrepreneurial Geffen, Morris was not in it to become an owner; he'd already done that. He hadn't missed how well Ertegun or Ostin were doing under Ross and adopted Ross's management style by assembling and enabling a team of creative executives. "I build an environment," Morris says when asked to describe his key function as head of a record operation. "That's what Steve Ross did." Says Ron Shapiro, who under Morris became president of Atlantic: "Doug identified executive talent and nurtured it. He was always more interested in the executives than the artists."

Doug was nonetheless determined to prove he had better rock chops than Big Tree acts like Lobo would suggest. His first Atco signing was Pete Townshend, the guitarist and songwriter for the Who. His second big signing was a joint venture for a new associated label, Modern Records.

Atco's partners in Modern were two young record executives, Paul Fishkin, the former president of Bearsville Records, a small label started by Bob Dylan's manager Albert Grossman, and Danny Goldberg, who had been the US vice president for Led Zeppelin's Atlantic-distributed label, Swan Song. Perhaps Modern should have been named Modest, because it had just one artist: Fishkin's girl-friend, Stevie Nicks. A member of the immensely successful band Fleetwood Mac, Nicks was far from a sure thing as a solo act. For her first album, *Bella Donna,* Modern paired her with a twenty-seven-year-old record producer from Brooklyn named Jimmy Iovine.

Iovine had produced Tom Petty and the Heartbreakers' *Damn the Torpedoes,* the group's 1979 commercial breakthrough. When he had to find a single for Nicks, Iovine knew where to look. Petty had a song, "Stop Draggin' My Heart Around," that he couldn't fit on *Damn the Torpedoes* and Iovine suggested to him that it would be a hit as a duet with Nicks. He was right: the single rose to number 3 and by September of '81, *Bella Donna* was at number 1 on the *Billboard* Top 200.

The son of a longshoreman, the fast-talking, streetwise Iovine had been a gofer only a few years before at one of New York's top recording studios, the Record Plant. He quickly hustled his way into remixing Meat Loaf's *Bat Out of Hell* and working on John Lennon's *Double Fantasy,* and Bruce Springsteen's *Born to Run.*

"He was kind of the janitor," recalled *Bat Out of Hell* producer Jim Steinman. "He swept up, but he also assisted. But Jimmy's an amazing person, and he absorbed like a sponge. From the first day I knew him, he always had one goal. He always would say, 'You know, Steinman, I just want to make a hundred million dollars.'"

There was something fun and seductive about the frank Brooklyn hustler who seemed less like a record executive than the neighborhood hotshot who was always buttering someone up for a crack at his sister. Artists found they couldn't get enough of Iovine's shtick, even if they knew what he might do to their sister—and them—if given half the chance. Five years removed from sweeping the floors at the Record Plant, he was one of the industry's most successful producers, working on albums for U2, Patti Smith, Simple Minds, Dire Straits, and Graham Parker.

By the mid-'80s, however, Iovine grew impatient with the grind of recording and hand holding. Moving to Los Angeles, he dabbled in artist management and redesigned A&M's studio. Yet Doug Morris still believed Jimmy was a born hit maker and wasn't going to let him get away.

When Ertegun added the presidency of Atlantic to Morris's portfolio in 1980, Doug had made it his mission to modernize and expand the label. The company's incredible catalog notwithstanding, Atlantic had a reputation as an old-fashioned sweatshop where the boss kept his eye fixed on the bottom line, in stark contrast to Mo Ostin's artist-oriented haven at Warner Bros.

"Ahmet certainly had an austerity philosophy when it came to things on the inside," says Danny Goldberg. "All the frills—packaging and the cutesy advertising they did at Warner Bros.—that was peripheral, and they didn't do it. What mattered was the record and getting it on the radio; the philosophy was 'get great artists, get it in stores, and get it on the radio.' Warner Bros. had a much bigger overhead than Atlantic. They just had all these departments—people to go out on the road, bigger staffs. At Atlantic, we felt we were the scruffy ones who didn't win the Grammy Awards but always had better profit margins."

The person largely responsible for keeping Atlantic's expenses in check was Sheldon Vogel, the company's powerful chief financial officer. Vogel had served as a convenient excuse for resisting artists' financial requests since joining the company in 1963. "I remember when Aretha Franklin's contract came up—she wanted $1 million per album," Vogel said. Far from an unreasonable request from an established artist today, it was way beyond what Atlantic was willing to pay her in the 1970s, despite her being second only to Ray Charles in historic importance to the label. "She was very precious to Atlantic. She was also a singles artist. I presented it to Ahmet, and he told her, 'Sheldon's not letting me do this deal.'" Vogel still smiles at the notion that any employee ever told Ahmet Ertegun or Jerry Wexler which deals to sign or for how much. Franklin left the label.

Throughout the '50s, '60s, and '70s, Atlantic had enjoyed successful partnerships with independent labels like Stax, Capricorn, and Rolling Stones Records. But by the time Morris got there, Atlantic's financial model wasn't good enough to attract the better startups. Seymour Stein, the cofounder of Sire Records, had unsuccessfully tried to cut a deal with Warner Bros. in 1973. "Mo turned us down," he recalled. "Then, when I had Talking Heads signed and two Ramones records out, Jerry Wexler came to me and said, 'You should be with us.'" Leery of Atlantic's penny pinching, Stein politely passed. "I said, 'No offense, Jerry, but I don't want to be with Atlantic.'" Wexler respected Stein and didn't want WCI to lose him or Sire, and he helped broker a deal for the label to go to Warner Bros. Eventually, Sire brought Warner Bros. Madonna, Seal, k. d. lang, the Pretenders, Depeche Mode, and Barenaked Ladies.

In 1988, Morris and Ertegun offered Iovine the financing for his own Atlantic-distributed record company, arguing that it was the chance to make the kind of money he'd always wanted. Recalled Ertegun, "I advised Jimmy, 'Don't just work for anyone—you gotta *own*.'"

Iovine liked the idea, but at the same time the film producer Ted Field, heir to the Marshall Field department store fortune, was searching for executives for a new record company, Interscope. Along with investing $50 million, Field planned to partner with a major label that would handle distribution and give Interscope a substantial war chest by taking an additional equity position. One of the first executives he hired was Tom Whalley, the head of A&R at Capitol Records, who'd just been fired in a senior executive purge, and John McLain, the veteran A&R executive who'd signed Janet Jackson to A&M, also joined the startup. Then Paul McGuinness, the highly respected manager of U2, told Field that he should meet Jimmy. "Paul said, 'It's too bad Jimmy's already made his deal with Doug,'" Field recalled. But impressed by Field's bankroll, Iovine changed his plans and joined Interscope as a partner.

Whether by design or luck, the involvement of Iovine—whom Morris desperately wanted to keep at Atlantic—made him eager to become Interscope's distributor and financial partner. Says Field: "It took Doug a moment to adjust. Doug kidded me about sweeping his boy off his feet."

Investing in Interscope—Atlantic started with a 25 percent stake in the label and eventually raised it to 50 percent—required a green light from corporate. A few years earlier, the deal would have gone directly to chairman Steve Ross for approval. Consumed with negotiating WCI's merger with Time, Ross had delegated day-to-day supervision of the Warner Music Group to Robert Morgado, whom he'd appointed chairman and CEO of the division.

Morgado was not a typical WCI senior executive—which is to say he was not a seasoned entertainment executive, a gifted accountant, or part of Ross's crew of cronies. He was the former chief of staff for New York governor Hugh Carey, for whom Ross had been a major fund-raiser. Ross hired him in '82 as a favor to Carey and created a position for him in WCI's office of the president. But Morgado proved his value to the company the following year when Atari, which had risen like a rocket, fell to earth.

By 1980, Atari's profits had increased tenfold to $70 million; the following year it posted profits of close to $300 million. In 1982, Atari accounted for 75 percent of WCI's revenues. But in 1983 the video game industry crashed and nearly overnight Atari posted a crippling loss of $500 million—the majority of it in a single quarter—and WCI's stock tumbled from $60 to $20. It was a mess of epic proportions, and Ross needed the company's other operations to help close the enormous shortfall.

Doug Morris, then the president of Atlantic, was in his office at 75 Rockefeller Center when his boss, Ahmet Ertegun, nattily attired in a tan suit, popped his head in to inform him of the post-Atari retrenchment.

"He said Steve Ross wanted to see us the next day to hear our tactics," Morris recalls. "I said, 'Do you want to talk now?' He said, 'Nah.'"

When Morris showed up at Ross's office the next morning at 9:00 he was surprised to discover Ertegun wasn't there. Twenty minutes into the meeting, Ahmet slipped in, wearing sunglasses and the same tan suit—albeit looking a bit lived in. "When it comes time for him to talk about our plans, all Ahmet says is, 'Doug and I are going to have more hits.' It was like watching Peter Sellers in *Being There*! And, you know, we did have more hits. We had a tremendous year."

Along with stepped-up profits, Ross was in desperate need of someone to engineer across-the-board savings at corporate. He gave the job to Morgado, who proved adept at it. "Morgado was a hatchet man," says Vogel, who estimates the company's eventual losses from Atari at $2 billion. "His job was to fire enough people for us to stay in business." Around Warner, Morgado became known as "the smilin' Hawaiian." Said one executive: "When he smiled, you knew the knife was coming."

As a reward for slashing the corporate staff from 900 to 150, Ross groomed Morgado to replace David Horowitz, the retiring president of Warner Music, in 1985. The laid-back Horowitz had left the label chairmen to their jobs and never inserted himself into the one-on-one relationships they had with Ross. Morgado, however, was prepared to exercise a much stronger mandate than Horowitz—or anyone short of Ross—had before.

"To understand Morgado, you have to realize that he's Portuguese-Hawaiian-American," says Jac Holzman. "They were the overseer class in Hawaii, brought in by contract with the Portuguese government in the 1890s when Hawaii was a republic. It was about creating a professional middle class between the hands who worked the fields and the landowners. They were the ones with the shiny boots that cracked the whip in the field."

The respective heads of Atlantic, Warner Bros., and Elektra Records—Ertegun, Ostin, and Bob Krasnow—saw no reason for things to change, especially when profits were beginning their CD boom. What they failed to recognize was that while the record industry was healthy, WCI was not. Atari had put a scare into Ross, and he wanted to keep his executives on a shorter leash. "Ross encouraged Mo and Ahmet," says Danny Goldberg. "Over the years the record operation had thrown off a lot of cash and he had a soft spot for it. But he used Morgado to control costs."

It was not a welcome change. "I saw Ross once a month and we socialized about once every three months," said Krasnow. "And no one was closer to Steve Ross in the music division than Mo Ostin. They vacationed together, took boat trips, went to the Hamptons. Their wives were very good friends." Krasnow and Ostin bristled at the notion that they should take marching orders from a bureaucrat.

The success of Warner Bros. Records was due in no small part to Ostin taking a long view of the creative process that, at first glance, didn't look cost-effective. Unique and adventurous artists like the Grateful Dead, Neil Young, Randy Newman, and Joni Mitchell grew at their own rate and proved the greatest source of the label's long-term financial and artistic strength. "My feeling was always follow the artist, follow the music," Ostin said. "It will lead you to the money." Eventually, established stars who took their careers and reputations seriously—including George Harrison, Miles Davis, Paul Simon, Elvis Costello, Tom Petty, Quincy Jones, and John Fogerty—flocked there, frequently for less money than they could have gotten at another label. The Red Hot Chili Peppers, who would score six platinum albums for Warner Bros., initially accepted, but then jettisoned, a more lucrative deal with Sony Music because they wanted to be with Ostin. "We signed with Warner Bros. because of Mo," said Flea, the group's bassist. For twenty-five years, Ostin had run Warner Bros. with a free hand—and built it into perhaps the most admired record company in the world. His disdain for Morgado was understandable—and evident.

Ostin failed to appreciate that the 1990 Time-Warner merger fundamentally changed the character of the company and the distribution of power. It was no longer the old WCI. Management had to prove to shareholders that the deal—whose mechanism had devolved into a costly $14.9-billion purchase of WCI stock when Paramount made an unwelcome bid for Time—had been worthwhile. Time Warner needed to show quarterly growth and as quickly as possible. Just as consequential, it had to do it without Ross, whose battle with cancer was sidelining him. By 1992 the former HBO executive Gerald Levin was Time Warner's chairman and CEO. Morgado was clearly running the music division, and the label executives wanted no part of him.

Part of the friction was a matter of style. Morgado, who kept an old-fashioned, glass-domed stock ticker in his office but no stereo equipment, was asocial and brusque to the point of rudeness. To the freewheeling label presidents—especially Krasnow, who liked to have a good time and made no secret of his recreational drug use—the straitlaced Morgado was from another planet. Krasnow got his first real taste of how different things were going to be when he bumped into Morgado at the company's annual sales meeting in 1991.

"Henry Droz, who ran the distribution company, used to have his meetings in August at the Diplomat Hotel in Miami—it was like ninety-nine degrees," Krasnow recalls. "We used to call it 'the Dumplomat' and make up T-shirts with cockroaches on them. We were walking to the hotel elevator and Morgado says, 'I want you to close your office in London.'"

Krasnow was stunned. He'd signed several of Elektra's hottest artists, including the Cure, Simply Red, and Howard Jones, through that office. "He said, 'Rob Dickins [the chairman of Warner Bros. Records UK] can take care of London.' I said, 'Hey, we've signed all these great acts.' Morgado says, 'This is not a debate.'"

Krasnow—who, since taking over in 1982 had raised Elektra's share of the music division's sales from 7 percent to 28 percent—wouldn't comply. He cut the office's overhead but kept it open.

"Morgado came off as an innocent," says Tom Silverman, whose hip-hop label Tommy Boy Records was then part of Warner Bros. Records. "He wasn't good or bad, he just saw the world in a different way from Steve Ross, Mo, or Ahmet. And," he adds with a laugh, "certainly a different way from Bob Krasnow." Says Goldberg: "Morgado was perceived by the record guys as a freak. But he was a typical corporate manager. In reality, it was Steve Ross who was the anomaly."

Even Morgado's advocates had to admit he could be hard to take.

"What I saw was the brilliance," says a former Time Warner executive who frequently worked with Morgado. "It's *Rashomon:* people around Nixon found him brilliant, and I found Robert Morgado able to see solutions I couldn't see. He always saw things in the most abstract ways; he'd describe systems and distribution organs and processes. But he had a tragic flaw: he was unable to develop personal relationships with anyone. He never appreciated that humans had to do this; you felt he thought people were fungible in a large company. Whatever it was in him—shame, fear—there was a stiffness that people found offputting and that fed the image."

When Morgado attempted to reduce risk and improve profits by solidifying release schedules and sales projections, it was viewed by the record executives as further proof that he was out of his depth. Morgado clearly had no idea what a record company might have to go through to get a finished album or maintain a relationship with a star. Says Goldberg: "He was convinced that there were patterns to be managed. He tried to take the risk out of the business, and that doesn't work."

Warner Records executive Howie Klein, an Ostin loyalist who was then general manager of Sire, received an angry call from Morgado—with whom he'd previously never spoken—demanding to know why an album by the band Ministry hadn't been completed. "He doesn't even say hello—he just starts yelling," Klein recalls. "'Where's the Ministry album?' I said the lead singer hadn't turned it in yet. 'What? It's on the sheet!' So I explained that the guy was in rehab. Morgado says, 'What do you mean?' I said, 'Drugs.' 'What? Is that what you're dealing with?' I said, 'Hey, we're not selling shoes here.'

"There was corporate pressure to put down these absurd numbers," says Klein. "It so fucked up the record business. Look, Alanis Morissette kept Time Warner's entire global record operation open for two years. That album [*Jagged Little Pill*] was budgeted at twenty-five thousand copies. It sold twenty-three million. Calling for numbers on records that haven't been made is moronic!"

Krasnow openly defied Morgado, while Ostin ignored him. "There was no dynamic—they never spoke," says Silverman. Though cordial in meetings, Ostin refused to report to Morgado, and it was impossible to miss the insult.

Two different corporate cultures were now firmly dug in at Warner Music Group, each fighting for control of the business. When WCI was on the rise under Ross, all the power went to the record men, the rainmakers who could identify, develop, and sell talent. Now Morgado and his cadre of managers were arguing that finding talent was no longer enough. "There's a tendency within the music business to dis anyone who is a business person," says Paul Vidich, Morgado's former executive vice president of business development. "It's an easy and cheap shot to take. But if you look, the division had its greatest growth under Morgado. He expanded internationally and significantly grew the company. But the music people definitely had a resistance to the notion that there was a guy in the center who brought value to the enterprise. There are a multitude of businesses, and you've got to be in tune with so many things. The head of a label's principal job is to have a relationship with a group of important artists. This other stuff is not their area—yet they'll say the music business is *only* signing artists and having hits. The world is now more complex. Bob recognized that."

Warner Music was a company at war with itself, and the risks were obvious—especially the likely losses of both executives and market share to competitors. Yet both sides plunged forward. Looking to bring Ostin down a peg, Morgado built up Doug Morris by encouraging his expansion plans. When Doug and Ahmet wanted to invest in Interscope, Morgado was happy to approve the money. "Morgado wanted to mold Doug into a force against the West Coast operation," says a former aide who worked closely with him. "His attitude was

'Good—go form Interscope.' He wanted to give Doug a base and counterbalance the Mo problem."

Ertegun named Morris and Vogel cochairmen of Atlantic in 1990, but the fiscally conservative Vogel objected to Morris's plans and soon found himself on the losing end of a badly mismatched power struggle. To reinvigorate the company's commitment to black music, Morris revived East West Records for Sylvia Rhone, a protégée plucked from the promotion department at Elektra. And he made a concerted effort to expand Atlantic's roster beyond the stale supply of cookie-cutter heavy metal bands and R&B acts. Danny Goldberg, who had sold out his position in Modern at the height of Stevie Nicks's success and then managed Bonnie Raitt and Nirvana, was brought back by Morris in January 1991, first as Atlantic's West Coast general manager and then as its president. Stuart Hersch, an entertainment lawyer who'd run the television syndication company King World, was hired to create a new video company, A-Vision, which initially focused on Atlantic's music videos but soon moved into exercise, children's tapes, and soft-core porn.

Morris defined his job as attracting and nurturing executives with an ear for talent. "A record company can be run by a creative person with other skills," Morris says. "Sure, I have business guys. But how would a guy like that know what to cut? You need professional music managers—and you have to understand who the rainmakers are. End of discussion."

Vogel argued against the deals Morris was making, calling them costly and accusing him of building his own career at company expense. "Doug wants to be number one," Vogel says. "His philosophy is volume. I wanted to make money for the company, not create prestige. I don't care about gross—I wanted to beat Warner Bros. on the bottom line. Doug's philosophy was bringing in joint ventures, signing big acts. In all joint ventures, you're giving up ownership. Wouldn't we be better off doing it ourselves?"

But Morris was succeeding in his bid to modernize Atlantic and raise its profile. East West scored a string of big hits with the vocal quartet En Vogue, and Atlantic Records went multiplatinum with the pop-rock band Hootie and the Blowfish. The label struck pay dirt when a secretary, Jenny Price, encouraged them to sign a teenage singer-songwriter from Southern California named Jewel. Goldberg made distribution deals with Matador and Mammoth Records. Neither of those nervy labels gave Atlantic a big hit, but they provided something just as important for Morris and his new team: cachet.

The real star of Atlantic's rebirth was Interscope. Between Atlantic and Field, the company had unusually deep pockets for a startup. And unlike the old Atlantic, it wasn't afraid to spend money. Interscope's first hit, 1991's "Rico Suave" by the hunky singer Gerardo, was pure teenybopper beefcake, but the label signed the industrial bands Nine Inch Nails and Primus and scored an international hit with 4 Non Blondes's *Bigger, Better, Faster, More!*.

"Ted was very willing to spend whatever money it took to not only get the artist in the door but to build their career," said Whalley.

In 1992, Interscope struck the deal that would transform it into the most successful record company of the decade when John McLain negotiated a deal to release albums by a new Los Angeles rap label, Death Row. Its first album, *The Chronic* by Dr. Dre, quickly sold 3 million copies. Dre, a former member of the controversial rap group N.W.A (for "Niggas With Attitude"), was one of the new label's cofounders and already one of rap's premier producers. On the drawing board was the debut album of Dre's protégé, a lanky, sloe-eyed Long Beach rapper named Calvin Broadus who went by the moniker Snoop Doggy Dogg. But Death Row's other cofounder was virtually unknown in the business. Marion "Suge" Knight was a 6'4", 330-pound ex–football player whose chief claim to fame was the report that he'd "negotiated" Dre's release from his prior recording contract with Ruthless Records by visiting the label's owner, N.W.A founder Eric "Eazy-E" Wright, with a crew of associates toting baseball bats.

Knight's business style should have set off alarm bells at Interscope, but it didn't. Iovine, who oversaw Interscope's dealings with Death Row, liked and got along with Knight—"He was a really sweet guy back then," Iovine says—and was convinced that Dre and Death Row could make records that would "cross over" to white buyers. And that was exactly what happened. The effect on Interscope and the entire Atlantic group was galvanizing, and Ertegun gave the credit to Iovine and Morris. "The connection with Jimmy Iovine is really what made us successful here," he said in assessing Morris's years at the helm of Atlantic. "Both Doug and I have been very appreciative of Jimmy's talents from the beginning—and Doug is his great champion."

Despite the successes, Vogel continued to denigrate Morris's deals, and Ertegun counseled him not to take on the company's rainmaker. "I told Shelly, 'Look, push comes to shove, Doug is a person who arranges to have hit records made, and you're a financial guy,'" said Ertegun. "Guess who's going to win?"

Morris cautioned him, too. "He said he was a street fighter and he knew what to do and that he would beat me because I didn't," Vogel said. When Morris arranged for Vogel's assistant, Mel Lewinter, to be named Atlantic's CFO and for Sheldon to be kicked upstairs to Morgado's office, he was outmaneuvered. "I can't fault Doug—he even warned me."

With Vogel dispatched and Ertegun taking a new title as chairman emeritus, Morris became the Atlantic Records Group chairman and CEO, and all of the attributes that would soon make Morris so attractive to Bronfman were in place. As a record executive, he was the complete package: he not only knew whom to sign and how to make and promote hits, but had a core of handpicked, loyal label heads—Iovine, Goldberg, Rhone, Hersch—reporting to him. "Doug wasn't as well known as Clive Davis or Mo Ostin," says Goldberg, "but we thought he was great—our little secret. He was extremely motivated and focused."

Atlantic was clearly on the rise. In the midst of Ostin's ongoing feud with Morgado, Warner Bros. Records was becoming even more demoralized by a new problem, a controversial song by the rapper Ice-T, "Cop Killer." The tempest around the song was comparatively brief, but its ramifications for Time Warner would prove far-ranging, ultimately leading the company to surrender first its involvement in rap music and then its position as the top U.S. record company out of fear that the music could jeopardize its other businesses.

• • •

Tracy Marrow grew up in the tough south central Los Angeles neighborhood Crenshaw. "I used to write rhymes before I knew there were raps," he said. "I used to write gang slogans and things on the wall: 'Crips don't die, they multiply' and shit like that. And I had these stories I used to tell in rhymes, and everybody thought they were real cool." There would soon be a name for his graphic and violent style—gangsta rap. Marrow took a new name, Ice-T, in tribute to the writer Iceberg Slim.

Unknown among white readers, Iceberg Slim—the pen name of Robert Beck—was the author of a series of books purporting to be the memoirs of Beck's life as a hustler. The most popular, 1969's *Pimp: The Story of My Life,* reportedly sold 2.5 million copies. Sensational, gripping, and repulsively misogynistic, *Pimp* both enshrined and decried the life of a ghetto gangsta. Slim spun a web of macho fantasies not unlike those in blaxploitation movies like *Superfly,* a story of a drug dealer whose only rule is to brook no bullshit and possess the cunning to survive in a rough world. But unlike those films, Beck was also telling a story of a man with deep self-loathing who realizes he has been stripped of all dignity by poverty and racism and reduced to the basest, crudest creature imaginable. In no uncertain terms, *Pimp* was a story of black rage.

Signed to Sire in 1987, Ice-T released albums that were filled with graphic tales of a violent outlaw life. The explicitness hadn't been an issue for his label. "Mo and those guys were always supportive," says Ice-T's manager, Jorge Hinojosa. "They never gave us shit." Ice-T's work hadn't bothered anyone at corporate, either: they even asked him to be a last-minute replacement when Richard Nixon backed out of a scheduled chat with Time Warner's senior executives.

In 1992, Ice-T released an album entitled *Body Count.* He initially wanted to call the album *Cop Killer,* the title of the last song on the album, but he dropped the idea when the label suggested retailers wouldn't carry it. The song's lyrics came up for discussion when the album was previewed in the Warner Bros. Records weekly meeting. Russ Thyret, the head of creative services and the son of a campus security guard, suggested that "Cop Killer," told in the profanity-laced voice of an enraged man who'd been brutalized by the police, could be offensive. It fell to Howie Klein, as general manager of Sire, to broach the subject to the artist and his manager.

"It doesn't condone killing cops," Hinojosa flatly told Klein. "Look, if they don't want to put it out, they can just give us the record back and kiss my ass. Ice-T has made you nothing but money. Ice is the shit—he's the ideal artist on so many levels. So take it or leave it."

They took it. "It was a typical Warner Bros. thing: 'Anybody can do anything,'" says Bob Merlis, then the label's senior vice president of publicity. "We never thought the record was about killing cops—it was Ice-T's rock record."

The song was performed live without incident when Ice-T went out with the Lollapalooza tour, but the album was not a hit. Then, about six months after *Body Count*'s release, the company began to receive mail, mostly from Texas, complaining about the song. "We got the news on Wednesday," says Hinojosa, "and by Thursday it's pretty intense. Friday it's a national story. I figured the weekend would cool it. But somebody was actively stoking it."

"It was a clearly orchestrated effort," says Merlis. "And it made its way to corporate."

The furor began when the Combined Law Enforcement Associations of Texas urged Time Warner to pull "Cop Killer" and pushed other police organizations and their pension funds to divest of Time Warner stock. After President George H. W. Bush termed Ice-T's work "sick" and Vice President Dan Quayle said the recording should be taken off shelves, Levin responded with a guest editorial in the *Wall Street Journal* on June 24. He defended Ice-T and the company on First Amendment grounds. Entitled "Why We Won't Withdraw 'Cop Killer,'" it was penned by speechwriter Peter Quinn. It argued, in part,

> Time Warner is determined to be a global force for encouraging the confrontation of ideas. We know that profits are the source of our strength and independence, of our ability to produce and distribute the work of our artists and writers, but we won't retreat in the face of threats or boy-

cotts or political grandstanding. In the short run, cutting and running would be the surest and safest way to put this controversy behind us and get on with our business. But in the long run it would be a destructive precedent. It would be a signal to all the artists and journalists inside and outside Time Warner that if they wish to be heard, then they must tailor their minds and souls to fit the reigning orthodoxies.

The editorial was greeted with relief at Warner Bros. Records, but the good feeling didn't last long.

On July 16, Time Warner held its annual stockholders meeting at the Beverly Wilshire Hotel in Los Angeles with Levin filling in for the dying Steve Ross. It quickly became apparent that "Cop Killer" would be the only topic of consequence.

Actor and National Rifle Association president Charlton Heston condemned the company from the floor and belittled Levin for having compared "Cop Killer" to "Frankie and Johnny" in his editorial. He then recited some of the lyrics to the squirming board members, including opera star Beverly Sills and Henry Luce III, the son of *Time* magazine editor and founder Henry Luce.

" 'I'm 'bout to dust some cops off. Die, die, die pig, die,' " intoned Heston. "Catchy little number, isn't it?" For an encore, he quoted from the equally graphic *Body Count* song "KKK Bitch."

After Heston, several police officers who had been shot and maimed in the line of duty demanded the record's recall. Dewey Stokes, president of the 238,000-member Fraternal Order of Police, termed the song "a justification for murder" while Tom Scotto of the National Association of Police Organizations attacked Levin as "a sick mind running a sick company." An attorney for Oliver North's Freedom Alliance suggested Time Warner's assets could be seized through a RICO action; he was booed.

In case no one thought the company could possibly look worse, Ice-T was at that moment driving past the hotel in his Rolls-Royce. He exchanged words with the protesters, who were wearing signs reading "Time Warner Puts Profits Over Police Lives," and gave them the finger. Naturally, the moment was caught on film.

The board meeting confirmed Hinojosa's fear that the company's First Amendment argument didn't address the real issue: that the complaints were an emotionally loaded misrepresentation of the song, sometimes by police and sometimes by political factions with a larger agenda. "The song doesn't say 'Go kill a cop,'" he says. "Listen to the lyrics and make your own decision." More pointedly, he wondered what difference there was between Ice-T's record and the critically acclaimed Warner Brothers film *Unforgiven,* in which a vengeful, nearly satanic Clint Eastwood slaughters a crooked marshal and his deputies. "Gene Hackman plays a dirty cop—only [Eastwood] is white and he's wearing a cowboy suit," Hinojosa says. "Of course we believe in the First Amendment. We're just not going to become your Willie Horton."

Two weeks later, after the Burbank offices of Warner Bros. Records had to be emptied twice for bomb threats—some executives believed they'd been phoned in by policemen—Ice-T held a press conference.

"It's not a Warner Bros. fight, it's my fight," the rapper said. "Warner Bros. is taking the sweat for me, and the cops feel this record was done for money. So I'm going to pull the song off the record just to prove to them that it ain't about that." Ice-T continued to give away copies of "Cop Killer" at his concerts, but on the album the song was replaced by a new track, "Freedom of Speech."

Still, as the only publicly traded American corporation to own a major record company, Time Warner continued to be a target of protesters' ire. Nearly two months after the withdrawal of "Cop Killer," Chrysler cited the song when it canceled a large ad campaign slated for Time Warner's magazines. C. Delores Tucker, a veteran civil rights activist, and William Bennett, the former Bush administration drug czar turned right-wing moralist, mounted a media campaign against rap in general.

The company made a quick about-face. In Morgado's office, attorneys began screening lyrics and artwork. Projects no one had thought twice about were suddenly off the release sheet—especially if they were by rappers.

"I had to get rid of a Paris album called *Killing Bush,*" recalls Tom

Silverman. "It had a cover of a masked man lurking behind a shrub in front of the White House as the first President Bush came out." Atlantic shelved a rap album it had invested $1 million in.

Not surprisingly, the project corporate was most nervous about was Ice-T's next album, which was delivered in December of '92, the same month Steve Ross died. Taking its inspiration from a series of Los Angeles break-ins in which families had been held hostage, the album was dubbed *Home Invasion,* and it fell to public relations consultants Jaime Willett and Josh Baran to give its lyrics an intense review. After reporting that it was a typical Ice-T record—which is to say the language was graphic and the subject matter violent—they found themselves in a meeting with Levin.

Levin reiterated what he'd said about free speech in the *Wall Street Journal,* but threw in the new caveat that he had an entire company to think of and not just any one particular division. Baran and Willett left the meeting a little perplexed regarding the game plan. They turned to one of Levin's aides. "So we put out the record, right?" Baran asked. The answer stunned them. Time Warner was fearful its cable franchise in Texas might be revoked if there were any more problems—so they were instructed to get Ice-T off the label.

The record executives—already having been unpleasantly surprised by Morgado's approach to the music business—were now dismayed to discover that Levin viewed the business as an irritant rather than an opportunity. The record division, the financial engine for Steve Ross's WCI, was, at Levin's Time Warner, viewed as a side business. And politics and the culture war were transforming it into a liability. "Levin made an analysis and decided that the key to driving stock up was the cable business," says Danny Goldberg. "The others made money, but the perception on Wall Street was that cable was valuable. And there's no denying that his Wall Street analysis was right: he damaged the record operation, but he was right in seeing it as irrelevant to the stock price. That was a terrific shock to the record executives. Under Ross, the rule was that if you always make your numbers, you can do whatever you want. And suddenly you're part of a corporation where the numbers don't matter—they only have a sense that the record industry is creating controversy."

Not wanting to own up to what they were doing—Time Warner believed in the First Amendment, after all—an assistant to Morgado suggested to executives at Warner Bros. Records that they manipulate Ice-T into asking for his release. When the company made it clear that they were going through the album line by line and wanted Ice-T to make some changes, he reacted as they had predicted. "Ice said, 'I'm not changing shit,'" says Hinojosa. "I wrote to Mo and these guys saying we want off the label."

Angry as they were, Ice-T and Hinojosa were also crestfallen. When Hinojosa met with the senior Warner Bros. Records staff to discuss the letter, he found it difficult to contain his emotions. "Do you know how much I enjoyed working with you?" he asked. "I don't want this—this is fucked. We love the people in this building." Sire's Howie Klein, a staunch ACLU member who considered Ice-T and Hinojosa friends, broke down in tears.

Two days later, Ostin and Klein took Hinojosa to lunch and told him the record company would honor his request and release Ice-T from his contract. The master recordings and an HBO pilot were included as further compensation; it was a generous deal. But Hinojosa was crushed. "A part of me would have liked Mo to say, 'Jorge, we'll let you out, but we want you to stay. We're willing to endure the slings.' Part of me was hoping to get that speech."

Ice-T quickly landed on the much smaller but rap-savvy Priority Records where he never duplicated the success he'd had with Warner Bros. As a new generation of hard-core rappers—including Ice Cube, Tupac Shakur, Snoop Doggy Dogg, and Notorious B.I.G.—came in his wake, Ice-T turned to acting. By 2000, he would be best known for his role on the television drama *Law & Order: Special Victims Unit*. He played a cop.

Severing ties with Ice-T was depressing Warner Bros. But the mood at Atlantic couldn't have been more buoyant. In 1991, Morris bought Beat Records, a year-old techno and dance label begun by Craig Kallman, a young club DJ and avid record collector. "He said, 'I'll teach you what it's like to play in the big leagues,'" recalls Kallman.

"I just watched Doug in action. If he met a talented exec, he'd want them—and then figure out a place for them. It was 'You can never have too many stars.'" A&R man Jason Flom, whom Morris hired as a favor to Flom's father, Joseph, senior partner in the New York law firm Skadden, Arps, brought the label several successful acts, including Twisted Sister, Skid Row, Tori Amos, and Stone Temple Pilots. Morris rewarded him with his own Atlantic-financed label, Lava Records. Morris later exercised Atlantic's option to buy out Flom and Jason became a multimillionaire. Not surprisingly, Morris's executives loved him. "He created incredible loyalty," said Atlantic president Ron Shapiro.

Morris's success also benefited Morgado, who was eager to exploit it in his ongoing problems with senior executives at Elektra and Warner Bros., who continued to resist and ignore his directives. "Morgado wanted to stuff Atlantic down Mo's throat," says the former head of another Time Warner division.

Looking to trumpet its new direction—and Morris's success—Atlantic mounted a press campaign. Its biggest piece was a fawning *Los Angeles Times* article that used Atlantic's data and sales reports from SoundScan to show that the company had overtaken Warner Bros. in market share. It was clearly intended as a throw-down in the label's hometown newspaper.

Staffers at Warner Bros. were outraged. "The relationship with Atlantic became sort of adversarial," says former Warner Bros. publicity head Bob Merlis. "They trumpeted themselves as the most successful, and we felt they were fudging."

The suspicion that Atlantic's numbers weren't all that good was at least partly correct. "I think we provoked people," a former Atlantic publicist says of the *L.A. Times* article. "It was the beginning of SoundScan, and we utilized it to illustrate our growth. But we were accused of throwing in the kitchen sink to get our figure that Atlantic grossed close to $1 billion globally." The executive chuckled. "I *know* we threw in the kitchen sink for that." Still, there was no denying that Danny Goldberg had strengthened the label. And by 1994 Interscope, thanks to Death Row and multiplatinum hits from Snoop Dogg and Tupac Shakur, was a cash machine.

Atlantic was soaring. At Warner Bros., Ostin's contract expired and Morgado offered him a new one in early 1994 in which Mo would remain chairman of the West Coast label but relinquish the title of CEO to his protégé, Lenny Waronker. Unhappy with being eased out of his day-to-day role, Ostin didn't sign it.

Morgado played his next card in June at a senior staff meeting in Montreux, Switzerland, when he announced Morris's appointment to the newly created post of CEO of Warner Music US. Couching it as the domestic parallel to the job held by Ramon Lopez, the chairman of WEA International, Morgado essentially made Morris the boss over the other label chairmen—an arrangement he had to know Krasnow and Ostin wouldn't accept. Says an executive at the meeting: "Morgado promoted Doug and created this realm of nothing in order to empower Doug and get rid of Krasnow and embarrass Mo. Of course, as soon as he did this, Kras didn't want to report to Doug. And Mo, contractually, couldn't be made to. It was a mistake. Morgado was creating a Frankenstein."

Following the meeting, Krasnow was vacationing in Milan when he got word that Morgado wanted to see him in his office the Tuesday after the Fourth of July. Ertegun tipped him that Morgado was going to ask him to resign, which proved to be true. Krasnow's replacement at Elektra was Morris's protégée, Sylvia Rhone, a clear sign Morgado was giving Morris the reins to run the US record division and choose his own team. Ertegun also told Krasnow that Morgado would soon ask Ostin to resign as well. "I called Mo and he didn't believe me," said Krasnow. "But sure enough, that Friday, he asked Mo." If Ostin was asked to resign in July '94, he won't say. But the following month he tendered his resignation. By year's end his thirty-six-year relationship with Warner would be over. In October, Lenny Waronker informed Morris and Morgado that he had decided not to succeed his mentor Ostin. (He and Ostin would soon join David Geffen's new DreamWorks Records.) They should have been cheered by the news: now they could select their own head of Warner Bros. Records. But Morgado would soon wonder if he had given Morris too much power.

For the 1994 "Power Issue" of *Entertainment Weekly,* an annual listing of the most influential people in the business, Morris's publicists successfully lobbied for him to share a Top 20 slot with Morgado. But when Morgado got an early notice of the rankings, he had an assistant call the magazine to say that including Morris would be a slight to Ramon Lopez, the head of WEA International, adding that Morgado and Morris were not equals. Morris and his photo were removed.

Everything Morgado's aide had told the magazine was true; Morgado and Morris were not equals. But that didn't prevent Doug from feeling humiliated and angry. "We loved the man and felt indignant about any assaults or insults," says Shapiro. "He's respectful of both people above and below, and if you're there for him, he's there for you. But if he feels he's been unjustifiably fucked, then he goes to a place of genuine hurt. I think he felt that Morgado had set him up."

Now wary of each other, Morgado and Morris had to consult on Ostin's replacement. Not surprisingly, neither had any interest in selecting a candidate who had been groomed by Ostin in Burbank. Among the names bandied about were Jimmy Iovine, Danny Goldberg, and Rob Dickins, the head of Warner Bros. UK. Morris wanted Goldberg, a subordinate with whom he was particularly close.

"Suddenly Morgado sees the Frankenstein," says a former Time Warner executive. "Doug will have his stalwarts running the three labels."

Looking to put the brakes on Morris, Morgado asked Gerald Levin to mediate a meeting over the Warner selection. Levin, a master at keeping his hands clean, stayed five minutes, just long enough to instruct the two executives to work it out. As soon as he left, the meeting descended into a pitched battle, and Morgado called Levin and said he wanted to give the job to Rob Dickins as soon as possible.

"I got an urgent message at one a.m. from Morgado," recalls Dickins. " 'We want you to run Warner Records. Get out here now—we're going to hold a noon press conference to announce your appointment.' "

On October 27, Dickins flew to New York on the Concorde and immediately phoned Morgado, who sounded surprisingly distracted. "Something's come up," he said. "We'll call you."

It was more like a palace revolt. Having heard the prior evening that Dickins was to be appointed head of Warner Bros. Records, Morris had rallied his supporters. At 1:00 a.m. New York time, Mel Lewinter, the Morris loyalist who had replaced Sheldon Vogel as Atlantic's CFO, called Fred Wistow, an attorney in Morgado's office. "We're not coming in tomorrow," Lewinter said. "I think you should call Morgado right now and tell him." Wistow did, and Morgado and Gerald Levin then tried to figure out a response to the record group insurrection.

No easy answer was forthcoming. By the time Dickins arrived in New York, Morris and his key executives—Danny Goldberg, Mel Lewinter, Sylvia Rhone, Atlantic chairman Val Azzoli, Jason Flom, and company attorney Ina Meibach—were closeted in the Central Park South apartment of Stuart Hersch, the president of A-Vision. Ahmet Ertegun acted as a go-between and, in a series of telephone conversations with Morgado and Levin, the senior executives made it clear that they were not coming back to work unless Morris was given a free hand to run the US music operation.

Unaware of the battle raging around his appointment, Dickins checked into the Carlyle Hotel, laid out a fresh suit to wear to his press conference, and waited for the phone to ring. After several hours he tried unsuccessfully to reach Morgado. When the phone finally did ring, it was David Geffen. "Something's up," Geffen told him.

Dickins, obviously upset, said he suspected Morgado was backing out. Geffen did his best to soothe him. "David was really lovely and probably saved me from a nervous breakdown," says Dickins. "He was just starting DreamWorks, which was the hottest thing around, and he said, 'I don't want you getting upset—come work with us. Go home, rest, and then call me.' His offer certainly got me through that period." Geffen clearly saw what Time Warner management did not, that Morgado was destroying the record division by discarding or alienating his most experienced and respected record executives.

Faced with the prospect of firing his senior executives or caving on Dickins, Morgado, pressured by Levin, capitulated. Danny Goldberg was put in charge of Warner Bros. Records and Morris got the additional title of chairman of Warner Music US and contract provisions that would make it difficult to fire him. Says a Time Warner attorney who drafted the agreement, "By the time Doug got to the lobby, the *Wall Street Journal* was calling asking about Danny being the new head of Warner Bros."

One person Morgado hadn't bothered to contact was Rob Dickins. "The day was full of people calling as they heard things," says Dickins. "By half past five I was getting calls: 'We've just heard Danny Goldberg is taking over Warner Bros. Records.' I tried to get Morgado on the phone every half-hour. He finally takes my call and says, 'Rob, I've had a terrible day.' *He's* had a terrible day!" The two men never spoke again.

A humiliated Dickins remained at the head of the British division. But he believed Morgado's actions had compromised him so severely that he couldn't run the company. "It's a basic rule of the workplace: you can't be held hostage by the people who work for you. I told him at the time, 'I think you're crazy. You could put Seymour [Stein] in at Elektra, me at Warner Bros., and someone else who wasn't part of the conspiracy at Atlantic.' But the fact that he just capitulated—he'd been the chief of staff for the governor of New York and was supposed to be a politician!—at that moment he was a lame duck."

Having won the war for control of Warner Bros., Morris and Goldberg now faced a conundrum worthy of a Shakespearean drama: how could Mo Ostin's enemies sit on his throne and rule? "Everyone was incredibly depressed," says a former senior executive, adding that the only positive was that few in Burbank had wanted to work for Rob Dickins, either. "But everyone knew this wasn't going to be the same company."

It didn't take Morris and Goldberg long to devise a strategy. Several key senior executives who had been Ostin loyalists received sweetened contracts, some at double their prior salaries. For select Warner artists, the payoff was even better. Neil Young—whose albums rarely sold big numbers but who was one of the most venerated and key artists on the company's Reprise label—re-upped with a rumored $25-million contract including the return of valuable publishing rights. Rod Stewart, whose manager, Arnold Stiefel, had been a Dickins booster, signed a similarly extravagant contract.

As he had at Atlantic, Goldberg was eager to put the new management's stamp on the Warner Bros. roster. He jumped feet-first into a bidding war for underground darling Jen Trynin, who was worried that moving to a major label would alienate her fans. Goldberg offered not to immediately release her more commercially promising album, *Gun Shy, Trigger Happy*. "Danny said, 'No problem, we'll let you release an EP first,'" recalled one Warner exec. When Trynin eventually signed for $1 million, Goldberg ordered *Gun Shy* released. "I reminded him what was said," recalls the executive. "He said, 'Hey, she got her money.'"

Goldberg doesn't recall saying that and doesn't believe he would have. But whatever the source of the machinations, it confirmed for the staff that Ostin's long-held view—if you believe in the artist and nurture his career, then success will come—was history. Managing for the long haul was an anachronism: no one could afford to care about anything but today.

"Record company presidents are always worried about this quarter's numbers and getting fired if they don't make them," says Goldberg. "They're less concerned about the big check they have to write in five years because, hey, they may not even be here."

With the situation at Warner in hand, Morris and his executives turned their attention back to Morgado. Though Morgado had once been Morris's champion, Doug was lobbying Levin to have him removed. Says Goldberg, "Dodge wasn't big enough for the both of them. It was over silly things: who signs the letter of stock options to record execs, Doug or Morgado? Everything just kind of melted down. In retrospect, nobody could be proud of how they behaved, me included."

None of this prevented Time Warner from granting new contracts to Morgado, Morris, Goldberg, and several of Morris's top lieutenants. More than lucrative, the new deals looked bulletproof. According to one insider, Goldberg wanted a special provision to be paid $5 million if "fired for cause"—turning on its head the standard clause that allows corporations to strip executives of options and other payouts if they are found to have acted improperly. In Morris's contract, the boilerplate language allowing Time Warner to fire an employee for a felony conviction was removed. Yet at the same time that Time Warner was rewarding Morris and Goldberg, its reservations about being in the record business—particularly the rap record business— were only increasing.

In November 1994, Interscope/Death Row artist Tupac Shakur was charged with sodomizing and sexually abusing a woman after a party in New York. Convicted on the sexual assault charge and sentenced to one and a half to four and a half years, Shakur was freed in early May 1995 on $1.4 million bail pending appeal.

Shortly thereafter, Danny Goldberg was at a dinner for Time Warner division presidents and board members and found himself seated next to Henry "Hank" Luce III. Luce had served as publisher of *Time* and *Fortune* prior to joining the board and took a dim view of the conglomerate's record companies. He was incensed over not just Shakur's arrest, but the fact that Atlantic Records, which had a 50 percent interest in Interscope, had guaranteed $850,000 of the bail. When Goldberg explained that Shakur was using his own money since Atlantic had booked it as an advance against his royalties, Luce wasn't mollified. "Why put out this junk?" he asked.

Goldberg explained that a record company ignored its buyers' interests at its peril.

Luce pondered that for a moment. "You've got what? A twenty-seven percent market share? Why don't you just get rid of this crap and go to a twenty percent market share?"

Goldberg was dumbfounded: a member of the board was suggesting the music division stop selling its biggest performers and chuck a market-leading position that it had taken over thirty years to achieve. Levin and Time Warner president Richard Parsons had overheard Luce and pulled Danny aside and apologized. Levin added that Luce would soon be retiring from the board.

That same week, Levin finally weighed in on the Morgado-Morris feud. On May 1, a rumor began circulating around Time Warner's cable company, HBO, that the division's chairman, Michael Fuchs, was about to be named head of the music group as well. Indeed, Morgado was summoned to Levin's office the following day and told he was out and Fuchs in.

Naturally, the Morris crew was delighted. But Levin had given Morgado quite a consolation prize—a severance package widely reported to be worth an astounding $50 million. Throughout Morgado's tenure, which coincided with the cash bonanza provided by the introduction of the CD, his loyalists had credited him with overseeing a dramatic leap in the division's revenues. His detractors saw him as an unqualified and insecure manager who'd engineered the exodus of the division's most talented executives. Here, at last, was something everyone at the record group could agree on: Morgado's exit deal was over the moon. Clearly, Levin could be counted on to pay an obscene price to wash his hands of a problem.

With Robert Morgado vanquished, Doug Morris, Danny Goldberg, and Jimmy Iovine saw smooth sailing ahead. Goldberg immediately called Fuchs and urged him to expand Morris's portfolio to include international. Fuchs assured Morris that as soon as things settled down again he would.

That same week, Bruce Roberts asked Morris to meet Edgar Bronfman at the Four Seasons. Over lunch, Bronfman talked about buying MCA and his recent troubles with Ovitz, then came to the point: would Morris run MCA Records? Doug turned him down cold. MCA was a chronically underperforming also-ran, and Fuchs had just promised him the power he wanted at the far larger Warner Music Group. "I said I'd just signed a new contract," Morris recalled.

In the end, the lunch would prove the overture to an extraordinarily productive eight-year relationship between the two men. At Warner, Fuchs had no intention of giving Morris more power and was simply stalling for time while formulating a plan for dumping the division's executives. Gerald Levin had suffered all the problems he would tolerate from the record division.

4

A Rising Tide

Gerald Levin had issued Michael Fuchs explicit marching orders: either clean up the record operation or clean it out. Like his boss, Fuchs didn't seem to care which way it turned out—or that he was setting in motion a chain of events that would send Doug Morris to Seagram, where he would build MCA Records into a powerful competitor whose greatest assets were the labels, artists, and executives Time Warner was about to discard. A few weeks into his tenure, Fuchs called Warner's senior management to a meeting at 75 Rockefeller Center to lay down the law.

"My nickname is 'the Principia,'"* Fuchs announced. "I'm the Michael Jordan of management."

No one was quite sure what principia meant, but Danny Goldberg whispered to Jimmy Iovine, "Yeah, he's Michael Jordan—the Michael Jordan of *baseball*."

Iovine loved the snide analogy. And since he was a coowner of

---

*The command quarters inside a fortress.

Interscope and not a Warner employee, he didn't care what the new boss thought of him. He repeated the crack for everyone's benefit.

Fuchs was enraged. "I'm going to evaluate everyone," he said, eyeing Iovine.

"I know how you got this job," Iovine said. "You bullied your way into it. If you give Doug this job, we're going to follow you like ducks. But if not . . ." He let his voice taper off.

Fuchs bounced him not just from the meeting, but from the building. The new regime was off to a flying start.

Fuchs had spent his career at HBO. As far as he was concerned, the executives in the record business were less polished, less loyal, and far greedier. "I couldn't figure out what they did," Fuchs later confided to an associate. "When I'd ask Doug what his plans were, how he was going to fix things, he'd say, 'All we need is more hits.'"

He thought Morris had mismanaged the record division and perhaps even misused his office. The ceaseless agitating for broader power and wealthier executive contracts and a restructured deal for Interscope that seemed to enrich its coowners while decreasing Time Warner's leverage were the most blatant examples. But if these arrangements appeared to be better deals for the executives than for the company, were any of them grounds for dismissal?

On Wednesday, June 21, Fuchs summoned Morris to his office and told him he was being fired for cause—meaning he was not entitled to a severance package or his stock options, worth a minimum of $5 million. Morris never saw it coming. "I thought I was going to see Michael Fuchs to be promoted," he says. When he returned to his office, he discovered it was already sealed and under guard. The following day Fuchs told the *New York Times* that "when I got here, I discovered that this place was becoming organizationally dysfunctional. My decision is not just based on my observations over the past six weeks. This is a situation that has been simmering in the music group for more than a year."

Morris was hardly going to accept a humiliating public firing that stripped him of millions of dollars in severance and options after Levin had just paid Morgado a reported $50 million. Within two days, he filed suit against Time Warner alleging he'd been dismissed without cause and seeking the full balance of his contract, which he valued at, coincidentally, $50 million. "They had just paid Morgado and didn't want to pay me," he says. "They said they fired me for cause, [but] they never revealed the cause." Time Warner counter-sued, stating Morris had been fired over the in-house theft and subsequent sale of thousands of promotional CDs by Atlantic executives. According to the affidavit of a Time Warner attorney, Morris had been aware of the problem but never informed his superiors.

The company's charge made ugly newspaper headlines, but within the industry the rationale was greeted with a roll of the eyes. Selling promotional CDs—those for free distribution to radio, reviewers, and retail buyers and on which artists receive no royalties—was illegal but also commonplace and generally ignored. Firing a record company head for that was tantamount to canning the secretary of defense because a military contractor received payment on an inflated bill.

The very public firing of Morris, who had spurned Bronfman just weeks before, presented Edgar with a unique second chance. As a songwriter and onetime film producer, he agreed with Morris's strategy of trusting proven record executives over professional business managers. "Record companies have just two primary functions," Bronfman would later say. "Editorial and marketing-promotion."

He called Morris the day he was fired. "Have you seen *The Shawshank Redemption?*" Bronfman asked. Alluding to the film's storybook ending in which two long-suffering prison comrades are reunited in freedom on the Mexican coast, he added, "I'm the guy who's waiting for you on the beach." By the time they met the next day for lunch David Geffen had already phoned Morris and urged him to go with Bronfman. But Morris didn't want Al Teller's job and he was already being wooed by Frank Biondi at Viacom and Alain Levy at Poly-Gram Records. More important, he told Edgar that Time Warner had left him leery of working for others. He wanted something he could call his own.

Edgar wasn't to be dissuaded. He wanted Morris at Universal even if he wasn't going to run the division. "How much money would it take to start a record company with a realistic chance?" he asked Doug. When Morris suggested a credit line of $100 million,

Bronfman didn't blink. "Okay," he said, "let's be partners," offering to finance a label in return for 50 percent of its equity. Then, taking a page from Geffen's playbook, he added one proviso: the deal had to be signed in forty-eight hours. Morris agreed, and they dubbed the label Rising Tide in tribute to *Shawshank*'s concluding scene.

It proved a shrewd move. Time Warner wasn't finished destroying its record division and creating openings for Bronfman. Having made available the record executive Edgar coveted, they were about to dump the hottest record label of the era, Interscope, in his lap.

Firing Morris compounded the problems at Time Warner's music division. The senior staff was packed with Morris loyalists, and his litigation was sure to be echoed and amplified when Time Warner dismissed them—unless they had nothing to complain about. Within six weeks, Danny Goldberg was bought out at a price reportedly between $10 million and $20 million. Attorney Ina Meibach, who'd functioned as Morris's consigliere but had only joined the company recently, was paid a ten-year severance deal, according to company sources. (Calls to Meibach for comment were not returned.)

But even more problematic was Time Warner's continuing fear that rap music would continue to be a hot potato and hurt the company, particularly its cable business.

In March 1995, just three months prior to his firing, Morris had paid $80 million for an additional 25 percent interest in Interscope, bringing Atlantic's total share and investment in the label to 50 percent and $100 million respectively. When the deal became public, critics had a field day. *US News & World Report*'s conservative essayist John Leo dubbed Time Warner America's "leading cultural polluter," while likening the Interscope deal to buying a mustard gas factory. C. Delores Tucker, the chairwoman of the National Political Congress of Black Women, and William Bennett, critics who had pressured Time Warner during the "Cop Killer" controversy, reappeared. At the annual Time Warner shareholders' meeting that May, Tucker held the floor for seventeen minutes and read particularly graphic lyrics from Interscope's rappers and the label's rock act Nine

Inch Nails. "How long will Time Warner continue to put profit before principle?" she asked, receiving a smattering of applause.

Later, the pair met privately with Time Warner executives. Tempers flared on both sides, and at various times both Tucker and Levin stormed from the room. Still, the critics found sympathetic ears on the board. Luce, who'd applauded Tucker during the stockholders' meeting, pressed the company to drop rap music. "Some of us have known for many, many years that the freedoms under the First Amendment are not totally unlimited," he told a reporter from *Time.* "I think it's perhaps the case that some people associated with the company have belatedly come to realize this." Former US trade representative Carla Hills and ex–baseball commissioner Fay Vincent reportedly urged Levin privately to do something.

In June, during a campaign stop in Los Angeles, Senator Robert Dole lashed out at Hollywood in general and Time Warner's music division in particular. "I'd like to ask the executives at Time Warner a question," Dole said. "Is this what you intended to accomplish with your careers? You have sold your souls, but must you debase our nation and threaten our children as well?"

Time Warner was caught. As a public corporation with broadcast interests it relied upon government approval in order to operate, and the Republicans' likely presidential candidate was characterizing them as a threat to the country and its children. Yet Interscope was clearly speaking to someone because it was the hottest label in the record business. Of its last nineteen albums, two had gone double platinum with sales of over two million copies; three were at platinum, or a million copies; and two more at gold with sales of 500,000 copies each. And with a winning track record—not to mention a 50 percent equity stake—Field, Iovine, and the Interscope staff staunchly maintained that they were not going to knuckle under the way Ostin had and tell their artists what they could and couldn't say. But to Time Warner, Interscope's next big release, *Dogg Food,* the explicit debut album by Los Angeles rappers Tha Dogg Pound, looked like another political nightmare. Within weeks of Morris's dismissal, Fuchs—at the urging of Levin and the board—ordered the sale of Time Warner's 50 percent interest in Interscope.

Since Fuchs had banned Iovine from Time Warner's offices, negotiations to sell the company's stake back to Interscope were conducted without him. Instead, Field and the high-profile attorney and industry wheeler dealer Allen Grubman represented Interscope; the Time Warner team, aside from Fuchs, included staff attorney Fred Wistow and Ed Aboodi, a longtime crony of Steve Ross's, who'd recently settled charges of insider trading in Time Warner stock by paying the government over $900,000. Interscope proposed a deal in which Time Warner would simply get its money back—$100 million—and the label would be free to seek a new partner. After initially agreeing, Fuchs suddenly got cold feet and yanked the deal. "I'm new on the job," he said, "and I'm not giving anything away."

Interscope—the most successful startup in recent industry history—would have no trouble finding a new home with one of his competitors, especially a foreign-owned major like Sony or PolyGram that could shrug off the objections of American politicians. But Fuchs's trepidation came largely from an unfounded fear that Interscope would sign a new deal with another company and then get out of the rap business, making Time Warner look even worse. Despite heartfelt assurances from Ted Field that he was committed to rap and was never going to abandon the music, Fuchs remained unconvinced. "He wanted a deal with schmuck insurance," says one participant.

In the midst of the negotiations, things took a bizarre turn when Fuchs agreed to participate in a secret meeting arranged by C. Delores Tucker at the Los Angeles home of singer Dionne Warwick. A critic of rap whose own career now centered around television infomercials promoting a psychic hotline, Warwick asked Death Row Records head Suge Knight to come to the meeting and listen to a plan Tucker had hatched in which he would leave Interscope and create a new rap label in conjunction with Tucker and Time Warner—one that would eschew gangsta rap and its violent lyrics.

It was a ludicrous move that betrayed both Time Warner's and Tucker's ignorance of the rap world. For starters, the notion of a self-censored rap scene was antithetical to the most basic notion of what rap, at its best, aspired to be: a straightforward account of urban culture. "Rap is CNN for black people," Public Enemy mastermind

Chuck D once said, in an analogy both succinct and expansive. And in purely business terms, Death Row had been wildly successful with Interscope, which, unlike Time Warner, really believed in both the legitimacy and commercial viability of rap. Fuchs should have read all he needed to know about the relationship between Death Row and Interscope three months earlier in a profile of Iovine in the *New York Times Magazine*. "Jimmy knows music, but what's really important is that he knows people," Knight told reporter Patrick Goldstein. "His background is U2 and Bruce Springsteen, and I'm a black guy from Compton. But if you're Jimmy's friend, he'll go with you 110 percent." Not surprisingly, Knight phoned Iovine as soon as he got the invitation from Warwick.

"Hey," he said, "who's that guy we hate?"

"Michael Fuchs. Why?"

"Well, he's coming to Dionne Warwick's house tonight and I'm supposed to go."

"Fuck that," Iovine said. Instead, Iovine and Knight met at Jerry's Deli in Westwood.

The next day an irate Warwick phoned Knight, demanding to know why he'd stood up Michael Fuchs and embarrassed her. Knight laughed. "You're supposed to be the fucking psychic," he said. "You tell me."

An incensed Field confronted Fuchs. "I'll never give this music up! Never!" he shouted. "It's political!" Field, who had recently lost three fingers in a racing accident, pounded his hand so violently that his bandages unraveled. His lawyer Allen Grubman insisted Fuchs leave the room while he calmed his client. A shaken Fuchs soon agreed to sell Time Warner's stake in Interscope back to them for terms less favorable than those he'd already scuttled in return for his "schmuck insurance," the guarantee that Time Warner would be further compensated if Interscope quit the rap business.

Less than six months earlier, Levin and Parsons had apologized to Danny Goldberg when Luce suggested Time Warner should dump rap music—and now they'd done precisely that. Goldberg, who'd been hired by PolyGram to run Mercury Records within a month of being fired by Warner Bros., could only shake his head.

"Selling Interscope was a huge mistake," he says. "As was the purge of Doug Morris. The Warner Records Group never recovered. When the smoke clears, the record operation is thirty percent to forty percent smaller."

Time Warner's decision to sell its interest in Interscope was a rare opportunity for any one of the record division's major competitors, PolyGram, Sony, EMI, BMG, and MCA. In one move Interscope would bring an interest in the industry's hottest label, bolster the buyer's own business by adding a steady source of hits for distribution, and—perhaps sweetest of all—add a sizeable gain in market share at the expense of Warner Music. But no one wanted to acquire Interscope more than Doug Morris. He knew Time Warner was making a drastic mistake by ignoring rap and, by extension, its own customers. "My pitch to Edgar was that I wanted to invest in black music and urban," says Morris. But it also was personal. From its inception, Morris had backed the label and Iovine, and his faith had been vindicated by their extraordinary success. And Time Warner had rewarded him with a firing and public humiliation! Nothing could please Doug more than sticking it to them by proving that both Interscope's and Iovine's best days lay ahead—or that Seagram could succeed where Time Warner didn't have the stomach to go. He told Bronfman that it was essential to acquire Interscope and Iovine if the company was ever to exorcise its Music Cemetery of America ghosts.

It was the moment Bronfman had been waiting for. He summoned Morris to his house in Malibu and told him that if he was going to take the Interscope plunge on Morris's say-so, then he should be willing to oversee it as chairman of MCA Records rather than as the head of a custom label. "He was very persuasive," says Morris, who negotiated a deal for himself in which he sold back to Bronfman the half of Rising Tide that Edgar had just given him.

Edgar's next task was to convince the Seagram board, and particularly his uncle Charles, to buy Interscope. "It was difficult," says Morris. "The music was very explicit in nature."

The big concern was Death Row. Although Seagram was a Canadian company and had a measure of insulation from US politics, both Edgar and his father were American citizens. More worrisome was how any controversy could affect the role the elder Bronfmans, Charles and Edgar Sr., were fashioning for themselves in Jewish politics and philanthropy. Edgar Sr. had recently been named chairman of the World Jewish Congress, a philanthropic umbrella organization. With the help of the Clinton White House and New York's Republican senator Alfonse D'Amato, chairman of the Senate Banking Committee, he'd wrested a landmark payment to Holocaust victims from Swiss banks. He and Charles were also staunch supporters of Labor and other progressive elements in Israeli politics. They did not want those interests or influences tarred with the "cultural polluter" brush.

Edgar Jr. set out to convince the Seagram board that Time Warner had responded incorrectly to rap's critics and that he could sidestep that minefield. "When we were still Time Warner shareholders, I had discussed with Gerry [Levin] that I thought his perspective was not right," says Bronfman. "It's not a First Amendment issue, it's a corporate responsibility issue." He told the board that while artists had the right to say whatever they wanted, Seagram would exercise its own right to decide what it was and wasn't going to distribute.

Bronfman's stance echoed a tack Geffen Records had successfully employed in 1990. After being criticized for releasing stridently homophobic recordings by the comedian Andrew Dice Clay, the label declined an album by Houston rappers the Geto Boys that included a track, "Mind of a Lunatic," which described murdering a woman and having sex with her corpse. "I'm not saying the artist hasn't got a right to make these records," David Geffen said. "I have a right to say I won't make money selling these messages."

The Seagram board debates were animated, particularly regarding controversial material. "We're going to handle it differently," Bronfman told them. He also suggested that rap was likely to become more, rather than less, mainstream. "I felt the genre would ultimately mature and that Jimmy Iovine is a very talented guy. The board, fortunately, went along."

On November 11, Morris replaced Teller as chairman of MCA

Records. That evening, Morris called Mel Lewinter, another old side-kick recently dismissed by Fuchs, and hired him as vice chairman.

At 7:00 a.m. the next day, an excited Allen Grubman called. "You're not going to believe this," the attorney said. "Fuchs is getting fired at three o'clock today."

It seemed inconceivable that Fuchs—having cleaned house and sold off Interscope as he'd clearly been instructed to do—was now being shown the door. But Grubman was right. Fuchs declined to comment on his firing, but he seemed finally to have been undone by a myriad of problems. He objected to Levin's acquisition of Turner Broadcasting, which would restructure the broadcast division and force him to report to Ted Turner. Perhaps more damaging was his ongoing feud with the cochairmen of Warner Brothers, Terry Semel and Bob Daly, over a variety of issues, including HBO's investment in Savoy Pictures and the high licensing fees Warner was charging HBO for its movies. The industry press was rife with gossip that the film executives had made Fuchs's departure a key point in their recent contract negotiations with Levin.

Semel and Daly were immediately named his replacements as co-chairmen of both Warner Films and Warner Music Group, for which each was rumored to be receiving over $20 million a year. They quickly disposed of any lingering business associated with Fuchs. "Semel and Daly want to know where you want your piano sent," attorney Bert Fields told Morris. His grand piano had remained sealed in his Warner Music Group office since the day he was fired. It was official: the fight was over. A severance deal was quickly hammered out for Morris that, while short on cash, gave him back all his Time Warner stock options, which were then worth over $20 million.

It cost Time Warner an estimated $150 million to get rid of Morgado, Fuchs, Morris, and their spate of loyalists. If government officials were to criticize Time Warner's senior management for anything perhaps it should have been for the way they wove stockholder money into their own golden parachutes.

Semel's and Daly's animosity toward Fuchs was matched by their unabashed admiration of both Morris and Mo Ostin. They were convinced that terminating the relationship with Interscope had been a major mistake. A few days after Semel assumed control of the music group, he ran into Jimmy Iovine in a Malibu clothing store. "Jimmy," he told him, "if I had this job three weeks ago you wouldn't be getting out of your deal."

The suggestion made Iovine's blood run cold: he was anticipating a big payday from reselling Time Warner's Interscope share. "I love Terry," he said. "But he *knew*. I mean, he looked me in the eye when he said it. I ran home to call my attorney and find out if [Time Warner] had signed off on the deal."

They had. There was strong interest in Interscope, particularly from PolyGram Records chairman Alain Levy, but there was really only one deal Iovine wanted to make. "I was always Doug's guy," he says, "and I hope to be until I die."

Having just reclaimed Time Warner's interest in the label for the $100 million the entertainment conglomerate had sunk into it, Interscope now wanted $200 million from Edgar for the same half. Morris pronounced it a good deal, but Geffen urged Bronfman to walk away. "He felt Jimmy was asking for way too much," Bronfman says. "When [Jimmy] didn't come down, David cautioned against the high price." Instead, Bronfman followed Morris's advice.

After he gained the approval of the board, Bronfman had one more group to sell on the deal: the politicians who had hounded Time Warner. In January, he met with William Bennett. Pointing out that Seagram's proposed relationship with Interscope would allow Universal to decline to distribute albums they believed questionable, he asked that Bennett and his colleagues, particularly Tucker and Connecticut senator Joseph Lieberman, hold fire until they could see how Seagram management behaved. "There are lines we will not cross," Bennett recalled Bronfman saying. "Watch us and judge us."

Interscope learned to tiptoe around public controversy. MCA released *Dogg Food* through Priority Records, the independent West Coast rap label that had taken in Ice-T when he became too hot for Warner Bros. The week Interscope closed the deal to sell a 50 percent stake to MCA for $200 million, the label released Tupac Shakur's *All Eyez on Me,* but MCA turned over the album's distribution to the Dutch-based PolyGram. Insulating Seagram in this way would prove an expensive insurance policy for Bronfman. If MCA had distributed the record themselves, the company would have reaped a fee from Interscope for handling shipping and ordering—generally 11 percent of a recording's wholesale cost. When Shakur's album debuted at number 1 on the *Billboard* albums chart and racked up sales of 9 million copies in the US alone, MCA lost nearly $10 million in distribution charges. It was the last time an Interscope rap record was distributed through another company.

On the rock side, Interscope's goth rocker Trent Reznor and his group Nine Inch Nails received close scrutiny. Their short video for the song "Closer" featured images of a crucified monkey, disemboweled and butchered animals, a naked and blindfolded woman, a child's skeleton, and a bound and gagged Reznor, which were severely edited before the video aired on MTV. Reznor also submitted a self-financed ninety-minute video that, over Iovine's objections, the company refused to put out. "There were images in it that were just incredible," says Bronfman. "We couldn't release it." Instead, the company reimbursed Reznor $750,000 in production costs and gave him back the video.

Still, the standards Bronfman created didn't quell the barking of the cultural watchdogs. Following Interscope's release of Marilyn Manson's *Antichrist Superstar,* Bennett and Senator Lieberman wrote to Seagram's directors and major stockholders, urging them to "clean up" the music. Unlike Time Warner's board, Seagram was impervious. Bennett publicly challenged Bronfman to a debate. When Bronfman didn't take the bait, Bennett got a measure of revenge at a Senate Commerce Committee hearing on marketing violence to children by singling out both Bronfman and Seagram and implying that Marilyn Manson had inspired the Columbine High School murders.

The Interscope acquisition paid immediate dividends for Seagram and invigorated MCA Records. In 1996, the first year under the MCA umbrella, the label followed up Shakur's *All Eyez on Me* with platinum albums by rockers Bush, Marilyn Manson, and No Doubt, R&B group Blackstreet, and rappers Snoop Dogg and Thug Life, as well as Shakur's second album of the year, *The Don Killuminati: The 7 Day Theory.*

There was also the old MCA label in Los Angeles and Universal Records—run by Morris—in New York. To shore up MCA, Morris turned the label over to Jay Boberg, who'd been the president and a partner in I.R.S. Records, the shoestring label that had launched R.E.M, the Go-Go's, and Wall of Voodoo. "They wanted a quantum shift: create an environment for the artists you'd want to have," recalls Boberg, who credits Morris and Bronfman with giving the label heads the freedom to run their own shops. "They stressed the entrepreneurial, and Doug did not call every three minutes. We improved quite dramatically by chasing the records we believed in." Even better for Seagram, Boberg had learned the business while running his own company, and he made spending decisions like they were still being financed out of his own pocket.

An encouraged Bronfman, who changed the company's name from MCA to Universal Studios, Inc., began thinking about expanding the record division even further and shifting the overall balance of the company. Taking a page from General Electric chairman Jack Welch, he had been wondering which of Universal's businesses could become a market leader.

Bronfman was discovering that one of the most attractive things about the record business was the way it produced better and steadier cash on a lower investment than films. For the cost of one moderately priced motion picture, a record company could sign and develop a roster's worth of performers. Plus, over 30 percent of the record company's sales came from catalog, while it looked to new artists for less than 10 percent of annual sales—a good hedge against weak signings. Even better, the recording industry, unlike films, was built on long-term contracts which, while they escalated in cost with artists' success, virtually tied performers to a record company for the life of their careers. Regardless of whether he'd paid a premium for Interscope—and the label's first-year performance suggested he hadn't—Bronfman was emboldened by its success to believe that Universal should emphasize music. It was also evident that whatever depth, chart muscle, and street credibility Interscope had brought to Universal, the company remained weak internationally, a serious flaw as overseas record sales grew quicker throughout the '90s than in the United States. Bronfman estimated that it would take thirty years to build a competitive international operation from the inside. A major acquisition or merger was a better remedy.

The obvious candidate was EMI, weak in the United States but with a significant international presence. Mike Ovitz had introduced Bronfman to EMI's chairman, Colin Southgate, around the time of the MCA purchase. A year later, emboldened by the success of Interscope, Edgar suggested to Southgate that they discuss a merger.

The talks got off to an inauspicious start. Accompanied by John Thornton, the co-CEO of Goldman Sachs International, Bronfman had dinner with Southgate in London. Bronfman had been told that Southgate was a wine collector and that he was born in 1937. That was a notoriously bad year for red wines and Bronfman instead bought a highly prized 1937 Château d'Yquem that cost over $3,000 a bottle. To Bronfman's surprise, Southgate barely acknowledged the wine—perhaps because it turned out he was born in 1938. It was all downhill from there. Bronfman, whose own musical tastes run to Ashford and Simpson, found little to say over dinner to Sir Colin, an opera devotee.

When Southgate did deign to make conversation, it was hard to tell whether his sense of conviviality was rusty or if he was going out of his way to be insulting. "I have nicknames for all you Hollywood guys," Bronfman recalls Southgate saying. "You know what my nickname for you is? Bootlegger."

Bronfman was dumbfounded.

Talks with EMI limped on for a year, and Bronfman eventually put out feelers to PolyGram. Unlike EMI, PolyGram didn't have as much to gain from a merger with Universal. The Dutch company's extensive American holdings included Mercury, A&M, Island, Polydor, and Verve Records as well as a 60 percent stake in the rap label Def Jam. But they had the international operation Bronfman craved. PolyGram's European and Asian affiliates boasted extensive rosters, and its Deutsche Grammophon label was the world's leading classical imprint.

To sound out PolyGram, Bronfman invited Cor Boonstra, the chairman of the record company's parent firm, Philips Electronics, to his Manhattan home for dinner. To Bronfman's surprise, Boonstra brought along Alain Levy, the head of PolyGram.

The French-born, Wharton-educated Levy was cocksure to the point of arrogance and had few fans within the industry—a fact he met with complete indifference. He had first solidified the company with the purchases of Island and A&M records, but recently strained its finances by starting a movie company, PolyGram Filmed Entertainment.

The dinner went poorly. Laying his cards on the table, Bronfman pointed to Universal's growing roster and prowess and PolyGram's first-rate international operation and wondered if a PolyGram-Universal merger wasn't a way for one-plus-one to equal more than two. But Philips was looking to slim down and refocus; it was not in the market to buy Universal. And Levy made clear one reason he had for not wanting to see Universal buy PolyGram. "Under no circumstance am I working for you," he told Bronfman. Stunned, Bronfman waited in vain for Boonstra to say something. "Alain," he finally said, "I don't know *what* the deal is."

With no interest from PolyGram, Bronfman returned to the lumbering negotiations with EMI. Finally, in January 1998, the companies agreed on a target price of £6.35 per share for EMI Music. But when Universal undertook due diligence on the British music group's financials, Bronfman discovered that EMI was in worse shape than he'd previously believed. He told Southgate that he couldn't recommend the deal to the Seagram board at the proposed price.

"Colin," he said, "we're not even at six."

Southgate barely shrugged. "It doesn't matter because there's no deal if it's less than seven."

Obviously, that wasn't going to happen. "Colin," Bronfman said, "it's one thing if we're negotiating, but I'm serious. We're not at six."

"We're done," said Southgate.

Bronfman left believing that a deal was still doable but much further away. A few days later, Cor Boonstra, who hadn't spoken with Bronfman in over a year, telephoned him from a yacht in the Bahamas.

"Can I come see you?" he asked.

"Is it just the two of us?"

"Yes."

When they met in February, Boonstra explained that he had agreed to let Levy speak for the company at their first meeting. Now Bronfman concluded that Levy, who had lost a lot of money trying to start a film studio, had fallen out of favor with Philips's management. Boonstra asked if Universal was still ready to make a deal to acquire PolyGram.

Unsure whether to make a deal for EMI or PolyGram, Edgar went looking for advice. The least helpful response came from Lew Wasserman, who had accepted a seat on the Seagram board but wasn't interested in counseling a chairman whom he viewed with evident disdain. "Why are you asking me?" he asked.

"Because I'm asking," said Bronfman.

Wasserman shrugged. "Buy both of them."

David Geffen proved both blunt and far more enlightening. "Do you know what the difference is between PolyGram and EMI?" he asked. "The first is chicken salad and the other is chicken shit."

As always, polling Geffen came with a risk. If you didn't follow his advice, you were certain to hear about it—and so was everyone else. It was a standing joke in the industry that there were three forms of mass communication: telephone, television, and tell Geffen. Indeed, around this time Bronfman was assiduously not asking his opinion about his pending merger with Barry Diller. Diller had specifically asked Bronfman not to consult Geffen, apparently fearing he'd either recommend against it or leak the proposal and kill it. In a complex deal, Bronfman sold Universal's television studio and its two cable channels, USA Network and the Sci Fi Channel, to Diller's company, Home Shopping Network (HSN), for $1.2 billion cash plus a 45 percent share in the bulked-up HSN for a total value of $2.9 billion. When the deal was announced, many in the media business thought Bronfman had committed a cardinal sin by giving up control and revenues in a group of bedrock assets—particularly the TV studio, whose *Law & Order* series would become a franchise—for a passive position. But the arrangement gave Bronfman two things he wanted: cash to help pay for either EMI or PolyGram and the services of the shrewd Diller. Along with Seagram's continuing 45 percent stake, Bronfman held veto power over large deals and—frequently overlooked by critics—the exclusive rights to buy back the stock. If Diller ever wanted to retire, he could sell only to Seagram. If he died without selling the company back, Seagram got it anyway. From Bronfman's point of view, he was paying Diller the steep price and equity position his reputation commanded—and granting him the illusion of autonomy—in return for getting his unique skills to beef up Universal's weak cable holdings.

Three months later, in May, Seagram and Philips reached an agreement in principle. Universal would buy 75 percent of PolyGram for $10.4 billion—slightly less than twice PolyGram's annual revenues—and Philips would receive a $2-billion stake in Seagram, a sizeable minority position of nearly 12 percent and second only to the Bronfmans'. Trading such a large chunk of Seagram stock—and letting in a powerful, vested voice—was not the kind of deal earlier generations of Bronfmans would have made. But it was precisely the kind of deal Edgar's idol, Steve Ross, had favored when he was building Warner Communications. Though it cost nearly twice the $5.7 billion Edgar had paid for MCA, which had held just a 6 percent share of the world record market, PolyGram instantly transformed Universal from a Hollywood also-ran into the dominant global player in the music business with a worldwide market share of 23 percent. It was no longer Sam Bronfman's swashbuckling liquor empire, or even the diversified investment portfolio masquerading as a corporation it had been during the days when Charles and Edgar Bronfman Sr. called the tune. It was Efer's now.

It had taken Edgar Bronfman Jr. just over three years to remake Seagram from a liquor company with an unrelated but profitable stake in the chemical industry into a music and entertainment company with an unrelated but profitable stake in the liquor business, which now accounted for less than 30 percent of the company's revenues. (The Tropicana operation was also spun off in a public offering to help defray the costs of the PolyGram acquisition.) When the deal finally closed in November 1998, a drop in the dollar and the inability to sell PolyGram Filmed Entertainment to defray the purchase price added over $1.3 billion to the cost of the acquisition, but Bronfman was betting that entertainment—and the record industry in particular—would prove an infinitely better business for the future than liquor. Satellites, high-speed cable, mobile phones, and computers—Efer believed that they spelled a multiplication of markets and a robust future for entertainment companies and intellectual property owners at a time when the prospects for Seagram's original business seemed limited. And he also believed he had to move fast. With the multimedia convergence typified by the Time Warner merger he fretted that the rules for the emerging market would be written by a handful of big players. Being the undisputed leader in the music industry was a way to make sure Seagram got a seat at that table. "The music business is now going to be the most important business to us," he declared the week after the sale was announced.

It was Doug Morris's job to make sure that happened.

5

Lansky and the Hustlers' House of Higher Learning

To sell the MCA merger to the Seagram board, Bronfman pledged to eliminate as much as $300 million in salaries and expenses, which meant laying off 20 percent of the combined music company's 15,000 employees and dropping over 200 acts. That was a huge order. At the record division, Doug Morris's plan was to integrate the PolyGram labels into the Universal Music Group (UMG) and structure the new company as a group of allied but competing record labels, distributed by one sales team. He wanted to combine the dozens of record imprints under four main labels: MCA and Interscope in Los Angeles, and Universal and an as-yet-unnamed company drawn from the remaining New York–based imprints. "I set Universal Music Group up like Warners," he said. "I know what a record company should look like, and it gives you separate pipelines into the market. You also get the benefit of different tastes and the opportunity to move executives."

Combining the Los Angeles labels was relatively straightforward. A&M and Geffen Records, which had previously operated as freestanding record companies within PolyGram and MCA respectively, would become parts of Interscope. MCA Records, which already had an extensive catalog that included such venerable specialty labels as Chess, Impulse!, and Decca, got PolyGram's jazz and classical imprints, including Deutsche Grammophon and Verve. In New York, Doug would run Universal Records, which would encompass Motown as well. There were also several PolyGram labels in New York, including Mercury and Island, but it was unclear how they should be organized.

Mercury seemed like the obvious choice to anchor the fourth group. PolyGram's primary pop, rock, country, and black music label, it had a fifty-year history and was run by Danny Goldberg, Morris's old Warner protégé and crony. Mercury boasted the country and pop singer Shania Twain, whose album *Come On Over* was in the midst of selling an astounding 20 million copies in the US alone, but Goldberg hadn't been able to build on that success. Having spent lustily on artist signings, he had nothing to show for it but the teen band Hanson, who sold 15 million copies of their debut album and then disappeared. Goldberg had spent heavily on A&R at Warner Bros., so his strategy was no surprise. What was surprising was that Morris, who had once championed and relied on Goldberg, seemed unenthusiastic about working with him again.

"Doug and I weren't that close at that moment," Goldberg offers. "He had hard decisions to make. Plus, I had a contract under which I would get a four-year lump payment if my job was changed— and obviously my job was going to change. My attitude was 'I'm happy to do it, but I want that check.'" Left unsaid was the fact that as Morris cemented his comeback at Universal, he'd worked hard to erase the stain of his Warner firing. Whatever was left was often portrayed as the result of Goldberg's own ambitions and bad advice.

Danny wasn't the only odd man out. There were no roles for Al Cafaro and Ed Rosenblatt, the chairmen of A&M and Geffen Records respectively. Those executive departures, along with all the accompanying rumors—employees who didn't know if they still had jobs and acts who feared they were about to be dropped—brought most of the new Universal Music Group to a halt. Loss of momentum was one of Morris's biggest headaches. He needed hits.

Morris did get one red-hot New York label from PolyGram: Def Jam. Founded in the early '80s by pioneering rap manager Russell Simmons, it had scored some of that decade's most influential hits with platinum albums by the Beastie Boys, LL Cool J, and Public Enemy. The label had gone cold in the early '90s, but it was now dominating *Billboard*'s black music charts with hits by Ja Rule, DMX, Foxy Brown, and Jay-Z. Morris surmised that the timing of the label's dramatic surge wasn't happenstance. PolyGram owned 60 percent of Def Jam and had held an option on the rest—an option that UMG now owned and would be obliged to exercise at a premium when it came due a few months after the merger was scheduled to close. Def Jam was holding all the cards. Morris desperately needed its hits and would look weak if he immediately lost his hottest company to a competitor. And the restructuring couldn't be completed until it was clear whether Def Jam was staying or going.

Simmons was the label's chairman and public face, but its well-timed chart run was created and directed by his unlikely protégé and partner, Def Jam president Lyor Cohen. Doug didn't know Lyor. But as he weighed Universal's best strategies for a Def Jam buyout, he had to admire the way Cohen had managed the timing of the label's hot streak.

Had Morris taken a close look at the hard-charging Cohen's rise, his role in the emergence of the rap business, and the way he'd re-fashioned Def Jam in his own image, he might have recognized the insatiable hunger for money, power, and respect that would make Cohen a godsend for Universal, a rival for Jimmy Iovine, and a challenge for him. "Lyor comes across almost like a fictional character," says Bill Stephney, who helped put together the group Public Enemy and worked with Lyor. "But on the other hand, he's a steely-hearted businessman—totally focused. More than anyone, he was emotionally and culturally prepared to deal with hip-hop as a business." Says Carmen Ashhurst, who preceded Cohen as president of Def Jam: "Lyor has a deaf ear to the world, which is what gives him his focus and self-assurance. He is never embarrassed or ashamed." If Morris had known that, perhaps he would have foreseen that Bronfman would want the pugnacious Lyor by his side in the fight to save both his reputation and the record business.

Lyor Cohen was born in New York to Israeli parents. His mother, Ziva, was the daughter of Zionist settlers, and his father, Elisha, fought in Yitzhak Rabin's Harel Brigade during the Israeli war for independence (he would name his first son Harel). The couple met in an Israeli hospital after Elisha suffered an eye wound in the fighting; Ziva was his nurse. Moving to New York, she served as consular aide to Abba Eban, Israel's first UN ambassador, and Elisha worked security at the consulate. But their stormy marriage did not last; Ziva moved to Los Angeles and remarried when Lyor was three years old. Her new husband, Dr. Phillip Shulman, was a psychiatrist and he adopted Lyor, changing his name from Cohen to Shulman. Though privileged—the family lived in a mansion formerly owned by Chico Marx—Lyor's relationship with his biological father was strained. "Lyor had an on-again, off-again relationship with his biological father, who didn't want children," said Ziva. "He did not relate to his children."

While Lyor was growing up he heard his stepfather talk about a large-scale psychiatric study of highly successful men that identified an instructive common denominator: each, to a man, could be described as a risk taker unfazed by earlier failures. Later, Lyor would claim it left a lasting impression. "When they failed, their first question was, what else can I scheme?" he recalled. Says Ziva: "He always thought big."

Ziva's second divorce proved as acrimonious as her first, and when Lyor's stepfather refused to pay his adopted son's college tuition, Lyor turned to Elisha. He agreed to pay, with two conditions: First, Lyor had to go to school east of the Mississippi, away from his mother; and second, he had to change his name back to Cohen.

On his second day of classes at the University of Miami in the fall of 1976, Lyor found a friend and like-minded hustler in Ovid Santoro, and the two were soon thick as thieves. Partnering to sell lemonade at the Coconut Grove Arts Festival, Santoro was startled by how focused and driven his friend became when it was time to do business. "Lyor would become like a slave driver," marvels Santoro. "'*More! Faster!* Squeeze those lemons!' We were buying hundred-pound bags of sugar and going to the fruit district to get enough lemons."

When a roommate whose grandfather was president of Ecuador told Lyor about the country's rich shrimp fishing, Cohen joined forces with a marine biology professor and after graduating he put together a proposal for an Ecuadorian shrimp farm. But he couldn't sell his business plan.

"He was crushed," says his mother. "He moped around for about three days, then concocted a résumé and sent it to two hundred banks. He said he wanted to know how an international bank operates and what they approve or disapprove."

When Cohen's banking résumé failed to generate any heat, his family's connections landed him a job in Beverly Hills with Leumi, an Israeli bank. But when the bank promoted him, Lyor promptly quit. "I don't want to be an employee," he told Ziva.

Cohen and Santoro, who was now splitting time between attending Columbia and hanging out in Los Angeles with Lyor, began looking around for prospects. At one point the absentee owner of the Ennis-Brown House, designed by Frank Lloyd Wright, placed an ad looking for a caretaker, and Lyor talked his way into the job. Cohen knew nothing about being a groundskeeper—but he hired day laborers off the street to do the work. What he did know was that the landmark home with an in-ground swimming pool had been used as a location for *Blade Runner* and that he was going to live there. He and Santoro were intrigued by Hollywood, but the industry drill of starting at the bottom wasn't attractive. "We saw really talented guys doing what you were supposed to—taking PA jobs—and winding up doing crappy jobs to climb the ladder," says Santoro. "Lyor didn't want to eat shit for ten years. He's in it to win it—whatever it is."

Motorcycling around Los Angeles one afternoon, Santoro's bike broke down in front of the Stardust Ballroom on Sunset. Borrowing tools from the ballroom's janitor, Cohen and Santoro learned that the enormous main room and a smaller room that held one thousand were largely unused. Lyor immediately called the owner and struck a deal to open a music club on the weekends. They borrowed several thousand dollars from Ziva and dubbed it Club Mix. "We took the door, they took the bar," says Santoro. "We paid for security and music, and they fronted marketing money."

They passed out business cards to girls in Westwood and Venice Beach. "We'd sign 'em on the back so they could get in for free. I'd work the door, and Lyor was on the phone or in the cash room."

The club booked some of Los Angeles's best young bands including the Red Hot Chili Peppers, Fishbone, Social Distortion, and the Circle Jerks, and hired the young Ice-T as their MC and the New York DJ Afrika Islam. *LA Weekly* soon picked Club Mix as one of the city's best nightspots. With lots of cash in their pockets, Cohen and Santoro started thinking about using the club to introduce New York rappers.

A frequent visitor to Disco Fever, the pioneering Bronx rap club, and a DJ at Columbia's radio station, WKCR, Santoro got to know several of the performers, offering them a chance to play and talk on the radio or make no-budget videos at the campus studio. The first rappers they wanted to bring to Los Angeles were Run-DMC.

Managed and produced by Russell Simmons, a City College sociology student turned budding rap entrepreneur who managed Kurtis Blow, the trio featured Simmons's younger brother, Joey "Run" Simmons; Joey's friend Darryl "DMC" McDaniels; and the DJ Jason "Jam Master Jay" Mizell. And while they were already celebrities in their Queens neighborhood and on the rapidly expanding New York street scene, it was all very local: they'd never even been on an airplane. Lyor had to fly to New York and go out to Hollis, Queens, to assure McDaniels's mother that he wouldn't let anything happen to her son. If he didn't really know what he was doing, you couldn't tell. "Lyor just stepped in and handled that," Santoro says.

Cohen brought his mother to Run-DMC's show. If Ziva believed in Lyor, she wasn't sure what to make of the music she heard that night. It was a threadbare performance: no band, no stage lighting, no lasers—just a DJ and two rappers in matching black leather coats and hats, shouting, bounding across the stage, and furiously pumping their fists to exhort the packed house. "It was just them, with scratching, walking back and forth," Ziva says. "They were doing 'You Talk Too Much' and the people seemed to like it." She wasn't so sure.

"What do you think?" Lyor asked proudly, putting an arm around his mother and shouting over the music. Ziva, struggling to find something to say, just looked at her son. "Mom," he said, "you just saw the Beatles of the '80s."

The Beatles? They don't even play instruments—and good luck finding their records!

None of that mattered to Lyor Cohen. Run-DMC had just put $36,000 in his pocket—more money than he'd ever made in a year. Cohen didn't care that rap was barely on the music industry map. He'd just make a new map.

But their next rap show, featuring another trio managed by Russell Simmons, Whodini, failed to attract an audience. In later years, Lyor would wax philosophic about "the truthfulness that comes with getting things wrong." "When I made thirty-six grand on Run-DMC and lost forty on Whodini—*oh!* The pain! What I'd do to avoid that!"

Whatever the financial ups and downs, meeting Russell Simmons would prove the watershed event in Lyor Cohen's life. Russell had a growing management company, a barely existent record label, and enough hunger and hustle to scheme of reinventing the entire music business. Though Simmons didn't know it yet, he and Cohen were a match made in heaven, or wherever it is that such partnerships are made.

Russell Simmons's aspirations made Cohen's look downright shabby. He imagined the nascent rap scene as a beachhead for an empire that could redraw American culture and capitalism. In the coming years, Simmons's vision and industry would translate into management firms, record labels, clothing lines, magazines, and film, television, and Broadway production companies. Like Motown Records founder Berry Gordy Jr., to whom he has invariably been compared, Simmons had a near-religious belief in the power and inevitable success of African American culture. But where Gordy polished and frequently prettified the soul music of the '50s and '60s to present it to white consumers as "The Sound of Young America," Simmons wasn't interested in sidling up to the mainstream and crossing over. He saw rap music and the urban culture that came to be called hip-hop as an unstoppable African American current redirecting the course of the mainstream. It was a monumental and audacious vision: the browning of America.

Simmons grew up in Queens, the son of college-educated civil servants who placed a premium on education. His home life was secure and stable, but Hollis, once a typical middle-class Queens community, was being transformed by white flight into a new ghetto outpost. Heroin snagged his older brother, Danny, for a time and Russell ran with a gang and did a little small-time hustling of nickel bags of marijuana and powdered coca leaf incense palmed off as cocaine. "It was a way to get the things I wanted," Simmons said. "Things that in retrospect were ridiculous and unnecessary. My goal at that point, and for much of my teen years, was simple—to get into clubs where the fly kids hung out and to own fly clothes."

His professional epiphany came in 1977 at Charles Gallery, a Harlem nightspot he frequented while attending City College. Charles always featured young DJs, but one night they also had an MC, Eddie Cheeba, who used simple rhymes and humorous boasts to exhort the crowd to dance. "Hearing Cheeba made me feel like I'd just witnessed the invention of the wheel," he'd recall. "I was standing there in a room full of peers—black and Hispanic college kids, partying and drinking—and it hit me: I wanted to be in this business. Just like that, I saw how I could turn my life in another, better way. All the street entrepreneurship I'd learned selling herb, hawking fake cocaine, and staying out of jail, I decided to put into promoting music. It seemed a lot less dangerous, more fun, and more prestigious."

Simmons's prescience about rap was dead-on. Presenting shows with DJs and rappers in clubs, it didn't take him long to land a recording contract for one of his more popular rappers, Kurtis Blow, at Mercury. Blow's first singles, "The Breaks" and "Christmas Rappin'," were hits, but there was a lot of industry resistance to rap and few executives—black or white—wanted to make the records. When it came time to cut a deal for Run-DMC, the group Russell organized around his brother, Joey, the best he could do was Profile, a small, independent downtown label specializing in dance music. And while Profile did a good job of launching and promoting the band, getting paid was another story. The entire budget for Run-DMC's debut album was $25,000—out of which $15,000 went for recording with the balance split five ways between the rappers, Russell, and coproducer Larry Smith. Even when the record sold, royalty payments were slow. Profile was a small operation and its ability to collect from its distributors was always predicated on having a good-looking list of upcoming releases. Simmons was confronted with the rules of independent record industry economics: he'd have to deliver a second album if he wanted to get paid for the first. His management company, Rush, was fast becoming the premier talent company for rap, but if he was going to become a force in the record business, he *had* to find a way to get the wealthy, powerful major record companies interested in what he was doing. The solution came in the form of a bratty NYU undergraduate named Rick Rubin.

Rubin was a well-off Jewish kid from Long Island who'd spent his high school years listening to punk and heavy metal and playing guitar in a band called the Pricks, but like Simmons he had been seduced by the excitement and possibilities of rap. He produced an independent EP by the group Hose when he was nineteen, and he'd begun DJing dorm parties and moving deeper into the emerging urban music scene. It didn't take long for him to notice that the way the music sounded on early rap records wasn't the way it sounded in the clubs, where the music was raw and much more exciting. DJs used beat boxes and "scratching"—manipulating the turntables to produce scratchy patterns on vinyl records—to give the rappers a rhythmic backbone. Wanting to record that live sound, Rubin convinced the DJ at Manhattan's Club Negril, Jazzy Jeff, and a young rapper, T La Rock, to make a record with him. The result, "It's Yours," was financed by Rubin's parents and sold to the small street-oriented Party Time label, but it carried Rubin's own logo, Def Jam Records. The record sounded just the way Rubin had intended—it hit the club vibe right on the head. "It's Yours" was only a modest commercial success, but it didn't escape Russell Simmons's notice, and he was flabbergasted when he met Rubin at a party in the summer of 1984 and discovered he was white. "That's the blackest hip-hop record that's ever been!" he gushed.

Before long the two were inseparable. Rubin introduced Simmons to a trio of white rappers he was working with and DJed for, the Beastie Boys, and Simmons began finding gigs for them. When Rubin played Simmons a new record he'd cut with a young rapper from Queens, LL Cool J, called "I Need a Beat," Russell loved it. Rubin, unhappy that he hadn't made any money on "It's Yours," begged Simmons to be his partner in Def Jam. Russell demurred at first, hoping to sign with EMI Records. But that deal never materialized and Simmons came on board.

The Simmons-Rubin alliance created the most potent and influential company in hip-hop, and its greatest strength was its two visionary founders. But two gurus and no administrator isn't a business plan. Lyor Cohen would provide the missing piece to make Def Jam a going business.

"Lyor moves to New York and just shows up," says Bill Adler, who was then the publicist for Rush. "I think Russell was surprised to find him on his doorstep."

Lyor's last contact with Simmons had been to book Run-DMC for a return appearance at Club Mix. Simmons also had booked the group at two other clubs that night and they showed up so late that Club Mix was empty. Lyor wanted his advance back. He didn't get it, but he began to worm his way into Simmons's business. When a feature on the front page of the *Wall Street Journal* in December 1984 trumpeting Simmons as "the mogul of rap" led to a meeting with the film producer Menahem Golan, Lyor got wind of it and convinced Golan's secretaries that the others were waiting for him to be patched in. "There's no such thing as 'no' to Lyor," says Adler. "He wasn't even working for the company and he just chewed his way through two secretaries."

Lyor became Run-DMC's road manager on the eve of the group's first overseas trip when a friend of the rappers handling those duties went AWOL. Cohen got the passports together, ferried them to their show in London, and—miracle of miracles—got them paid. "He'll get it done," says Adler. "He assumes responsibility and executes. He *will* get it done." Adds Santoro: "Lyor didn't know how to be a road manager. But he did know how to go in there like an Israeli tank commander and say, 'I'm here to get paid.'"

His determination immediately made him a power at Rush. Simmons was a master of networking and promotion, building relationships at clubs and radio that would become the core of Rush's and Def Jam's street muscle, but he was far more interested in being the architect of the enterprise than administering it. Similarly, Rubin—who was about to take tiny Def Jam platinum with hits by LL Cool J and the Beastie Boys—was interested in the nuts and bolts of the business only insofar as it allowed him to make the records he wanted. "Rick is an artist, and an artist wants control," says Bill Stephney, who worked for both Def Jam and Rush. "He wanted to be the visionary behind a great culture—and have as much autonomy as possible. The only way is as an entrepreneur."

It didn't matter that Lyor knew nothing about managing acts; he exuded so much self-confidence and presence that no one was going to call him on it. "He was certainly a workaholic—and he did not know a thing about the record business when he began," says Carmen Ashhurst, who joined Rush as a publicist and eventually became the president of Def Jam. "But his strong sense of entitlement carries him a long way. He's used to being around people who command respect." Lyor began buttonholing people in the business, desperately trying to go to school on them. He approached Alice Cooper's manager, Shep Gordon, unsuccessfully seeking to apprentice with him. He made a similar overture to Charlie Stettler, who managed the successful comedic rap trio the Fat Boys.

Relatively new to the business himself, Stettler had stumbled on to the Fat Boys when they won a Radio City Music Hall talent contest he'd put together as a product promotion. He signed the group to a recording contract at Sutra Records and one of his savviest moves was landing the group a $400,000 endorsement deal with Swatch

Watches—the first major brand endorsement for rappers. That got Russell's attention, and he dispatched Lyor to find out how Stettler had pulled it off.

"The secretary says there's a guy named Lyor outside," Stettler recalls. "I'd heard about him a bit from his club and knew that he was now with Russell—and I come out and he tells me, 'Russell says there's nobody better to learn from.' I'm thinking, 'What are you, crazy? I'm going to tell you what I've had to work to learn?'" Stettler politely declined, but it didn't take Cohen long to figure out how to do Stettler and the Fat Boys one better. When Run-DMC cut a paean to their favorite sneakers, "My Adidas," Lyor talked the shoe company into an endorsement deal reportedly worth over $1 million.

Nor was he finished going to school on Stettler. When the Fat Boys teamed up with three of Rush's acts for the Fresh Fest, rap's first national tour, Stettler supervised each night's closing ticket count, essential for getting proper payment from the promoters. "One night I look over and there's Lyor," he recalls. "'Russell said I'm supposed to learn how to do the count from you.'"

Cohen had a focus and approach that, to some of his coworkers, seemed almost perverse. "My strongest memory of Lyor is watching him conduct the settlements," says Ashhurst. "He would say to Big D, the tour manager, 'Tell this to the house manager, tell this to the promoter,' trying to get more money. He would get so into it, so psyched, that he would literally be walking around and physically pumping his hips. It was very sexual."

Simmons sent Rush's artists on a series of increasingly ambitious and successful tours run by Cohen. It wasn't easy: aside from being viewed in the business as an urban phenomenon unable to attract a broad audience, rap shows didn't *look* like concerts. For starters, where were the musicians? Promoters accustomed to working with black acts and rock bands dismissed the notion that people would pay to see rappers backed by just a DJ.

"Today hip-hop is used to advertise everything and everyone takes it for granted," says Lisa Cortes, a film executive who started her career as Cohen's assistant. "Russell and Lyor went from town to town with the music when there wasn't any scene. There were people who didn't want to pay, who didn't want 'em in their little town. Lyor went out there and was fearless and didn't care about hurting feelings. He's very proud of his grandfather being one of the original [Israeli] settlers. Like him, he was turning the desert into an oasis."

Put in charge of Rush Management, Lyor proved just as tough on employees as he was on promoters. Newcomers had to prove themselves, and the drill was simple: be ready to do anything at any time. Rubin hired Stephney to do radio promotion for Def Jam and on his first day Cohen told him he was going on tour with Whodini. Flabbergasted, Stephney reminded him that his job was radio promotion. Cohen was unimpressed. "Now, my friend, you are part of the team—you must do everything." Says Stephney: "I bitched to Russell and Rick, and I didn't go out with Whodini." He pauses—half a head-shake, half a chuckle. "But I did go out with other acts."

It was partly a reflection of how disorganized the company was. Simmons, who could talk a mile a minute about rap's inevitable triumph and generate an endless stream of ideas, was irresistible. He didn't mention corporations—instead he told the staff that Rush and Def Jam was "a confederacy of hustlers," and everyone, from Rick Rubin on down, wanted not just to hang with Russell, but to be part of his swashbuckling vision and win his affection. It was a charismatic draw, and it played a large part in attracting the people who would make Simmons's hip-hop empire into a reality. But in its early days, the office was barely functional.

"When I first got there it was nine people and three companies working out of one bank account," recalls Ashhurst. "That was my first conversation with Russell: 'You can't do that.' He was surprised. *'Really?'* It was a mom-and-pop bringing in a lot of money, but it wasn't clear where it was coming from. Only the tour money was clear."

"When Rush and Def Jam were getting started, there was so much work to be done," says Adler. "It wasn't parceled out scientifically. Russell was going to have artistic ideas and work with the artists and be a promoter. Yeah, he was out there playing but working very, very hard to make the machinery. He knew about radio promotion, tour promotion. He could call the right jock in Charlotte, and he knew record production. He knew artist management."

Cohen didn't have Simmons's and Rubin's artistic sensibility and vision, but he had one very valuable attribute they both lacked: the will and discipline to make the trains run on time. "Lyor would come in every day when Rick and Russell wouldn't," Ashhurst says. Adds Adler: "One of the things Lyor brought was business skills. He has a degree in finance, he'd worked at Bank Leumi. He can read a balance sheet." But his endless ambition, coupled with a crude, dictatorial manner, hardly endeared Cohen to anyone.

"He would leave the bathroom door open during meetings," says Ashhurst. "He was like that all the time. And originally Lyor was hated because he was after money: he was hellbent on being big—he was *going* to run a big company."

As Rush's publicist, Adler even tried to keep Cohen away from the press. "He was not charming. He was a brute. I've seen him change his demeanor in the last ten years—there's a soft-spoken Lyor now. But back then he almost didn't believe in a free press. The idea that he couldn't dictate what the press said pissed him off. He was just a Doberman, and I didn't want him talking. It wouldn't have helped anyone."

"Lyor makes it so fucking hard," says Sean Carasov, who became friendly with Cohen in 1985 while road manager for the Beastie Boys. "He's sentimental, but one of the least sensitive guys I ever met. Like, he's abusive to waiters—and this is a character flaw that goes way back—and abusive to the people he's closest to. I had to create a special category for him. He's family; he lent me $25,000 when I had legal problems. But he's also a lifetime member of the bad friend hall of fame."

While his coworkers found working with the rapacious Cohen like trying to wrest a scrap of meat from a panther, he had a completely different effect on the rappers, whose up-from-the-streets business credo was unapologetically mercenary. They gave Cohen a street handle: Lansky.

"He had incredible rapport with artists," says Stephney. "Think about how hip-hop developed: the promoters, the store owners, the guys with their hustle going on. It was a direct street business, and you sold your records through urban retailers and Syrian-Jewish electronics dealers. I think Lyor embodied by perception the street guy with his hustle on, and many artists respected him. He's trying to get the money, and that's their ultimate goal. Public Enemy went on tours, and he would spend real time on the road with us. Lyor was a deal maker—fearless in a rough industry, fearless about collecting. That gained him the respect of the young guys and they watched his back. And you can't minimize the imprimatur that Russell put on him."

Record executive Aaron Fuchs, whose Tuff City Records has been recording and releasing rap records almost as long as Def Jam, says Cohen is one of the few people in the business with a real hip-hop sensibility. "He's a music executive who didn't have to call the cops when a rapper raised his voice." Observes Cortes: "He never did it with a liberal mentality, which I admire. There's a blinding truth in hip-hop—or there was at the time. You had to come at them with their truth. He could speak from one side of his mouth and encourage and let an artist know that someone cared—and from the other he could scold them. And from still another side of his mouth he could lock a deal. He was the first guy I'd seen who'd argue heatedly and then say, 'Okay, let's make the deal.' He gives tough love. He doesn't give compliments easy."

Lyor forged personal relationships with the people most important in his artists' lives, such as LL Cool J's grandmother and Russell and Run's father. When Rubin wanted to record the brilliant but elusive and troubled rapper Slick Rick, it was Cohen who found him in a mental hospital and worked to get him released and signed to Def Jam and Rush Management. Lyor's in-your-face style won him few friends outside of Rush. As the manager of two acts on Tommy Boy Records, De La Soul and Stetsasonic, Cohen would pop by the New York label's offices and berate anybody and everybody, and even threaten to have them fired. Eventually he was barred from the office and the receptionist stopped putting through his calls. Lyor didn't care; his scorched-earth tactics played extremely well with his clients. Bill Adler walked into Cohen's office one day—Lyor had only a leather couch and a speakerphone—to find him with rapper Posdnuos of De La Soul. Cohen was hunched over the speakerphone and yelling at the top of his lungs at Tommy Boy owner Tom Silverman's assistant. Adler recalled, "He's screaming into the box, 'Tell Tom, "Fuck you, *FUCK YOU!*"' And Pos is sitting there with his head down, rocking back and forth, quietly saying, 'Yes. Yes. *Yes.*'"

Rapper Ja Rule, who joined the label in 1999 and scored a series of platinum albums, found Cohen bracingly honest. "He was kind of gangster, man, and that surprised me. He was so up, and the shit he told me, he held no punches. Lyor gonna let you know straight out what it is—it's tough, it ain't a game; they only mark the hot ones."

"What makes Lyor run?" asks Bill Adler. "His father. He disapproved of Lyor. I went with Lyor to his father's house in New Jersey for Passover: I remember walking into the den, the father is there and the TV is on to a football game. And he's holding up a siddur (a Hebrew prayer book) and asking Lyor if he knows what it is. I don't even think his father was particularly religious, he was just giving him a hard time."

"Lyor's father was threatening to disown him," says Ashhurst. "First, because he hated the business. And there may also have been something racial about it—there was a vibe that he didn't like him working with all these black people." Worse, Lyor wanted to marry EK Smith, a model he'd met when she appeared in a Beastie Boys video, and his father refused to give his blessings. "He was crying on the phone with his mother over this," says Ashhurst. "So much of what he was doing at Def Jam was proving to his father that he could make it on his own. It wasn't hidden; he would talk about it."

Elisha did not attend the wedding when Cohen married Smith in 1988 in an April Fools' Day ceremony in Sosúa, Dominican Republic—a town chosen because it had welcomed Holocaust survivors. But then, the bride herself was nearly a no-show. Says Adler, "They'd found this little synagogue down there, and I'm in the shul with Chuck D, who's wearing a yarmulke, and Flavor Flav, who won't. And we're waiting, and waiting, and waiting—two hours. Finally, they had the ceremony." The scuttlebutt was the bride was down on the beach with a bad case of cold feet, which was borne out a few months later when the marriage broke up. Lyor couldn't have relished admitting his father was right.

Elisha had his own troubles. Moving to Nigeria in the 1960s, he told friends and family he'd struck it rich in the country's booming oil business. But an Israeli newspaper account portrayed Cohen as a military contractor who made his fortune building bases for both sides in the Biafra War and said that one of his partners was General Olusegun Obasanjo, who later became Nigeria's president; Ovid Santoro would meet Obasenjo years later at Elisha's home in New Jersey. In a bid to attract business, Cohen led the Nigerians to believe he was an Israeli spy. "He let it be understood that he was connected to the Mossad and the Shin Bet intelligence services or maybe even represented them in Nigeria," an acquaintance told *Haaretz* reporter Yossi Melman. "Among other things, he related that he worked on behalf of the Mossad in North Africa. Most of the Israelis were not very impressed by his hints and most of us understood that this was just fake showing off. But on the Nigerian army officers this made a great impression. They believed him."

As a result, the country's ruling junta hired Cohen in 1984 to find and bring back Dr. Umaru Dikko, the former transportation minister who'd fled Nigeria following the recent coup with reportedly as much as $1 billion. The country's military ruler, General Muhammadu Buhari, intended to bolster the junta's legitimacy by making Dikko the center of a show trial. Cohen took the job, for which he was reportedly paid between $3 million and $5 million.

To bring Dikko back, Elisha assembled an Israeli crew—including an anesthesiologist—and led them to believe that this was a Mossad job rather than a kidnapping-for-hire. Tracking the former minister to London, they tried to lure him to a phony television interview by having one of the Israelis pose as an American producer and renting a London apartment as a studio. But when Dikko wouldn't bite, Cohen cooked up a scheme to snatch the former minister off the street into a waiting van, drug him, and smuggle him back to Nigeria.

The kidnapping quickly went awry. When the abductors grabbed Dikko in front of his home at noon on July 5, 1984, his secretary witnessed it and immediately called the police. Believing diplomatic immunity could shield them, the men sped the drugged Dikko to the airport and placed him and the doctor in a wooden crate sealed by a Nigerian military intelligence officer attached to the embassy and stamped "Diplomatic Mail"; two of the other kidnappers were sealed in a second crate. Two hours later, British customs officials alerted to Dikko's disappearance opened the crates. Dikko, drugged but unharmed, was released, and the three Israelis were arrested and received prison sentences of between ten and fourteen years. Cohen was not in London for the kidnapping, but British investigators soon learned he'd been the mastermind. Charges against him—and his coconspirators—were never filed, reportedly because the British government feared a diplomatic rupture with Nigeria. Still, Elisha Cohen made it a point to never set foot on British soil again.

This was the man Lyor Cohen could never impress or please. By winter of 1987, the approval-starved Cohen and Rick Rubin were waging a full-blown battle for power and for Simmons's affection. Bill Adler remembers finding an agitated Simmons sitting in the recording studio one night. "Bill," Simmons said, "my Jews are fighting." Says Adler: "Today Rick is a fan of Lyor. But they're both very strong figures, and at that point there wasn't room for both of them at Russell's side."

In just two short years, Rubin had made himself into the enfant terrible of the record world and Def Jam into one of the hottest record companies in the industry. LL Cool J's *Bigger and Deffer* went platinum and the Beastie Boys' debut, *Licensed to Ill,* sold 4 million copies in 1987. Still, a rift was growing between Rubin and Simmons, and Cohen became the person Russell relied upon.

Differing views of how Def Jam should structure its deal with CBS's Columbia Records were at the heart of the split. Rubin wanted a joint venture, where CBS would divide the profits on Def Jam down the middle. In that arrangement, an outside label receives about 25 percent of the profits after the major charges them for distribution and other services and expenses. In order for that to work, Def Jam needed hits. Simmons wanted Def Jam's relationship with CBS structured as a more modest, but surer, override deal, with CBS paying Def Jam "points," or a percentage, on each record sold. The advantage of the override deal was that it put money in Def Jam's pocket immediately and allowed Rubin and Simmons to take a cut off the top. CBS's deal wasn't with Def Jam's artists—it was with the label for whatever Simmons and Rubin wished to deliver. Simmons won out, but because they were relative newcomers, they'd been forced to take a low override: 16 points compared to the 20 many of CBS's more established performers received. At first, it didn't feel so bad. LL Cool J and Public Enemy were selling extremely well, and a healthy chunk of that stayed with Simmons and Rubin. But when the Beastie Boys album became a runaway hit, it was obvious that Def Jam would have made a lot more money on a joint venture.

The Beastie Boys were equally unhappy with the accounting they received from Def Jam. After three years, much of it spent on the road touring in support of *Licensed to Ill,* the band desperately needed a break. But Simmons wanted a follow-up record, and he made it clear that the band's royalties would be withheld if they didn't get back into the studio. The band thought that was a smokescreen and wondered aloud if Def Jam had spent the money due them—a charge Simmons adamantly denied. The rift soon degenerated into opposing lawsuits. In the end, Def Jam lost the Beastie Boys to Capitol Records.

Def Jam stumbled. Simmons's attempts to produce more traditional soul and R&B artists like Alyson Williams and Oran "Juice" Jones proved a costly misstep, and Rubin spent Def Jam's money on a studio he would never use or even complete and produced disappointing sellers by the controversial heavy metal band Slayer and the offensive comedian Andrew Dice Clay. By 1989, Rubin severed working ties with Def Jam and started his own Def American Records out of Los Angeles. But he wouldn't relinquish his financial interest in Def Jam for several more years.

"It was the longest divorce on the planet," says Ashhurst, who adds that Simmons was running up a tab at Sony Music, which had purchased CBS Records in 1988, by taking repeated advances. "Some of it was to buy out Rick, who then wouldn't leave. Rick, he was fucking horrible."

Cohen continued to run Rush, the talent side of the company, but by 1992, with the concert business in a slump, he took the reins of Def Jam. The label was not in good shape. Cohen clashed frequently with the pugnacious Columbia head Don Ienner; at one meeting the two executives had to be physically separated. Worse, all those advances had come home to roost and Def Jam now owed Sony $20 million. Quietly, Simmons and Cohen looked for a new distribution partner—someone, ideally, who could pay off Sony.

With the help of attorney Allen Grubman, they found that—and more. In June 1994, PolyGram purchased 60 percent of Def Jam for $33 million, allowing the label to pay off and leave Sony, and Simmons to realize a nice profit. Cohen was now adamant that Simmons make him his full partner in Def Jam. He was running the company on a day-to-day basis while Simmons focused on the HBO show *Def Comedy Jam,* chasing movie deals, and his new clothing company, Phat Farm. Just as important, PolyGram had an option to buy the remaining 40 percent of Def Jam, and Cohen wanted a piece of any cash-out.

The negotiations between Cohen and Simmons proved a tight-rope walk: both were eager to maintain their friendship, but neither wanted the other to get the better of the deal. But once the deal was done, Cohen played one game: make Def Jam hot and sell the remaining stake to PolyGram.

Things got off to a good start. The first release through Poly-Gram, *Regulate . . . G Funk Era* by Warren G, the younger brother of Dr. Dre, sold 3 million copies, and the following year the label scored hits with LL Cool J's album *Mr. Smith* as well as a more mainstream sound, including Montell Jordan's "This Is How We Do It," and "I Got Him All the Time" by the female trio MoKenStef. But the rough-and-tumble Death Row was far outselling them, and upstart Sean "Puffy" Combs was stealing their thunder with his New York–based Bad Boy Records, featuring Brooklyn rapper Biggie Smalls. Simmons complained to Cohen that all he saw on newsstands were magazine covers of Death Row and Bad Boy. "Why don't we get covers?" he asked. Cohen, who later admitted the company was "tanking," told

Simmons he'd call him back with an answer in three days. When he did, it wasn't what anyone had expected.

"We're going to become AAMCO," Lyor announced. He explained that Def Jam's best bet would be to forget magazine covers and do the grimy under-the-hood work required to build careers. "Our work is under the transmission," Cohen later said, poking fun at both the stylish Combs and Suge Knight, the muscular and thuggish head of Death Row, after their companies became embroiled in a violent rivalry. "Bad Boy wouldn't get under there in their suits. Those bulked-up guys wouldn't get under there. That's how we avoided the East Coast/West Coast beef—who wants to be AAMCO?"

In Cohen's estimation, Def Jam had never been able to replace Rick Rubin as a creative force. But the company still had two key calling cards: its history and Russell Simmons. Def Jam was the label aspiring rappers grew up listening to, and Simmons was the original hip-hop entrepreneur, its Henry Ford. In his wake came a new generation of ambitious inner-city dreamers who recognized that hip-hop culture held the means to a sweeter life.

As Cohen solidified his position at Def Jam, a cadre of trusted lieutenants formed behind him, most notably promotion executive Kevin Liles, marketing executive Julie Greenwald, and attorney Todd Moscowitz. "Lyor was always very good about saying 'Everyone fucks up,'" remembers Greenwald. "But he'd also say, 'If you keep making the same mistake, I'll put you out of fucking business.'" And along with the stick came the carrot. "Lyor said to me at a very young age—I was twenty-four—'If you stay, I'll give you a piece and it's going to be worth millions,'" says Greenwald. "I said, 'Millions? Millions is good.'" Adds filmmaker and journalist Nelson George, who has worked with Russell Simmons and been his close friend since the earliest days of Def Jam and Rush: "Even though Lyor's got a brusque demeanor and a reputation for being rough, he's a relationship guy and he gets incredible loyalty from his people. Execs say Lyor intimidated them at first, but that it also motivated them. It led to a corporate culture. Lyor rebuilt that staff in his image."

Def Jam refocused itself on its roots, signing deals with Newark rapper Redman as well as Method Man from the Staten Island rap collective Wu-Tang Clan. The next step was beating Sean Combs to the female rapper Foxy Brown, which Lyor accomplished by sitting on the stoop of her Brooklyn brownstone in order to keep Combs and other label execs away. More important, Lyor offered to set up joint ventures for new labels with aspiring producers and entrepreneurs. It was a way for Def Jam to remain current, and for up-and-coming hip-hop executives to learn the ropes as part of Simmons's storied "confederacy of hustlers."

Two of those ventures would produce hits and profits dwarfing those from the company's early glory days. One was a $1.5-million deal for a fifty-fifty partnership in Roc-A-Fella Records, which boasted a young Queens rapper named Shawn "Jay-Z" Carter and would eventually produce Kanye West. The other was hiring a DJ turned A&R man from Russell Simmons's old Hollis neighborhood, Irving "Irv Gotti" Lorenzo. Gotti signed and produced hits for Ja Rule, the Queens-based rapper he brought with him from another label, and DMX, the tough, scratchy-voiced rapper from Yonkers who would become Def Jam's answer to the West Coast gangsta sound of Death Row. Def Jam ultimately bankrolled Lorenzo's own imprint, Murder Inc., as a $3-million joint venture.

But finding the right product was only half of the equation. To break its new artists and score hits, Def Jam needed the backing and clout of strong marketing and distribution. Sony had known how to get records in the stores and on the radio, and the fact that Def Jam received a comparatively low royalty rate acted as a further spur because Sony got to keep a bigger slice of the profits on a Def Jam record than on a hit by one of their own superstars like Billy Joel or Bruce Springsteen. But at PolyGram, Def Jam was having a hard time getting its records treated as a priority from the sister label handling its marketing and promotion, Island Records.

"Island had all the incentive in the world to work their records and no incentive to work ours," Simmons said. "If one of our records came out on June 1 and one of theirs on June 2, which do you think got maximum effort? We lost a lot of hit records."

The relationship with Island's chairman, Chris Blackwell, quickly turned poisonous. Already at loggerheads with PolyGram chairman Alain Levy, Blackwell would soon quit the company, and he asked Danny Goldberg to take Def Jam off his hands. "I hate these guys, Russell and Lyor," he told Goldberg, who was now heading PolyGram's Mercury Records Group. "Why don't you take them?" Goldberg welcomed the additional billing. But it didn't take him long to find out what Blackwell was complaining about. Cohen was relentless when it came to getting Def Jam and its artists what they needed to succeed.

"I told Lyor to go fuck himself a couple of times," Goldberg says. "But if he wasn't always pleasant, he wasn't wrong. The things we would argue about—the areas where he was pushing for more control—were largely promotional. Day in and day out it was Lyor who was running Def Jam and making it into a success. He just worked harder than anyone, including me."

Cohen and Simmons became so frustrated that they decided they'd be better off selling the rest of Def Jam to PolyGram and starting over somewhere else—despite the fact that the company still wasn't hot enough to command top dollar. "We felt PolyGram was actually killing Def Jam instead of saving it," Simmons said. In late 1997, Alain Levy offered Def Jam attorney Allen Grubman $50 million—not an awful sum considering how deep a hole the label had been in only a few years earlier at Sony. But PolyGram wanted to subtract a variety of advances and other items from the deal, making the actual figure significantly lower, which Simmons could live with but Cohen couldn't. Cohen thought Goldberg was trying to cow them into accepting it. "Danny put a tremendous amount of insecurity in the company," Cohen says. "He started putting it in some of my people's heads that I was going to sell and they should be concerned for their futures. I didn't like the fact that the clock was about to run out and the anxiety being created—or the price. I went into a depression."

Grubman, however, urged them to take the deal. One Sunday morning in March 1998, he tracked Cohen and his young son, Az, to Barney Greengrass, the famous smoked salmon emporium on Manhattan's West Side. The lawyer grabbed the boy by the arm. "Tell your dad if he doesn't accept the $50 million, he'll never see it again," Grubman said. A few days later a deflated Cohen agreed to sign off on the sale.

The following week he got an unexpected call from Grubman. The lawyer was apoplectic. "You fuck! I told you this would happen! The deal is off!" Grubman had just heard that Boonstra and Bronfman had agreed in principle to sell PolyGram—including the 60 percent stake in Def Jam—to Universal; all other deals were frozen.

To Cohen, the news was a godsend. Def Jam was beginning to find its groove again and, given a few extra months, would likely fetch a better price than the one he had just been saved from taking. Instead of Levy and PolyGram, Lyor would try to cut a new deal with their successors—Morris and Universal.

6

Hurricane Shawn

One of Cohen's first and most intelligent moves was to create a special incentive agreement for his key executives, including vice presidents Julie Greenwald, Kevin Liles, Chris Lighty, and Wes "Party" Johnson. Cohen told them that when they sold Def Jam, the first $50 million would go exclusively to him and Simmons but that they would split the next $25 million dollar for dollar with the senior staff. "It kept everybody focused," says Cohen.

Beyond that his strategy was straightforward: stack the release schedule. The rule of thumb in the record business was to wait at least a year—and sometimes much longer—between new albums by hit acts in order to protect and extend their careers. But Def Jam was far more interested in hiking its sales numbers. Just six months after Yonkers rapper DMX scored a hit with his album *It's Dark and Hell Is Hot,* Def Jam put him back in stores with *Flesh of My Flesh, Blood of My Blood* for the all-important Christmas shopping season. Albums by Jay-Z and Ja Rule were also ready to go.

Still, when Cohen was summoned to a meeting in October at

Doug Morris's Universal office on West Fifty-sixth Street, he had no idea what to expect. A smiling Morris greeted Cohen like a long-lost cousin. "Lyor, I want you to be the Ahmet Ertegun of your generation. I'm going to buy your company, you're going to be the president of Universal and sit in the office next to me. I want to give you a hug in the morning and a high-five at night." *How did Hanukkah come in October?* Cohen wondered.

Morris wanted to buy the remaining 40 percent of Def Jam and integrate the label into Universal. He would continue as chairman of Universal Records with Lyor as president, responsible for the expanded company's day-to-day operations.

Cohen was ecstatic. Not only was he going to get his Def Jam payday, he was getting a new five-year contract and a bigger company to run. Familiarizing himself with the Universal roster and staff, he met with Mel Lewinter and Universal's restructuring advisors from Boston Consulting Group, who were being paid $50 million. In early November, when a story leaked in the *Los Angeles Times* outlining the expanded roles planned for Cohen and Jimmy Iovine, Morris wanted to hurry the deal for Def Jam along.

Lyor wasn't sure he wanted to close a deal right away. He was already troubled because Morris had rejected any Def Jam executives he had tried to include in the new Universal staff. "What about my people?" he asked.

Morris made it explicit: the deal was for Lyor to come to Universal, along with the Def Jam artist roster and logo. "Son, I'm bringing you, not your people. I want you to be president of Universal Records."

"I don't understand. I like my people." Aside from the fact that they were *his* people, Cohen fretted that moving on at the expense of his employees—from whom he'd always demanded total commitment and fierce loyalty—would destroy his reputation. "I didn't want to get my bitch card punched," he says.

Lyor later admitted that he still might have accepted if he hadn't thought that accelerating the move to Universal would impact the sale price of Def Jam. Letting the Def Jam staff go and moving from Mercury to Universal in the middle of the Christmas season—which frequently accounted for 40 percent of a record company's annual sales—would stop his hits dead. "All of my singles were out—they were in play with great momentum. I had to make sure these albums came through." Suddenly Cohen found himself ascribing ulterior motives to Morris. "I know I'm gonna sell for a good price and then I get a phone call from the head honcho—who never once called me before."

Though fearful he would be making an enemy of Morris, Cohen decided he couldn't accept the offer. Def Jam *had* to fetch a better price if he continued to work his records right up to the buyout date. "I didn't think Doug was going to take me out," he says, "but here's the chairman I have to work with and I'm going to go directly at loggerheads with him."

Morris took the news badly. "You're making the worst mistake of your career," he told Cohen. But he was far too driven and professional to nurse a grudge against someone making money for him.

Part of the reason may have been that Lyor's instincts and maneuvering proved spot-on: while the other PolyGram labels foundered, Def Jam had a red-hot Christmas. The two DMX albums sold over 5 million copies, Jay-Z's *Vol. 2 . . . Hard Knock Life* sold 4 million copies, and Ja Rule's *Venni Vetti Vecci* went platinum. Cohen's subsequent boasts that Def Jam booked $100 million in sales in one month may have been an exaggeration, but not by much.

Morris's unsuccessful attempt to woo Cohen had failed to gain Universal any leverage in its buyout negotiations with Def Jam, but he never balked. The PolyGram deal was only eight months old, and the last thing Morris wanted was to lose his hottest label. Though willing to give Doug free rein, Bronfman was not happy. "You're telling me I have to buy *more*?" he asked when Morris raised the looming 40 percent buyout. But Def Jam's hot Christmas did everything Cohen hoped it would: negotiations began in earnest in February, and by July Universal acquired the remainder of Def Jam for $130 million. Cohen, who had nearly been forced to sell for $50 million just a year earlier, was euphoric. "From the prior June to that July I made $80 million," he crowed.

The deal gave Lyor a tremendous new cachet in the business. PolyGram's offer valued the company at $325 million. No one had thought Def Jam was worth that much money, and now Lyor was the genius of the month. Morris recommended to Bronfman that they tie up Cohen to run Def Jam with a five-year contract and a bigger berth. Several executives including Zach Horowitz, Universal Music's powerful COO, argued against expanding Lyor's role, but as usual, Bronfman followed Morris. "Everyone else in the industry told me I was insane—'Lyor's rough, he's never handled administration,'" Bronfman recalls.

Morris made Island/Def Jam/Mercury the fourth Universal label group and largely deactivated Mercury. Under the new arrangement, Island, whose biggest act, U2, had been poached by Jimmy Iovine at Interscope following the merger, would get a shot in the arm with the transfer of several Mercury acts including Bon Jovi. Lyor was cochairman of the new group along with Island's top executive, Jim Caparro.

Cohen was suddenly very popular and people wanted to work for him. "At Island Def Jam he became like Tony Soprano," says his longtime friend Sean Carasov. "Everybody loves him even though he kills people."

In July 1999 Lyor Cohen may have found himself the happiest man in the record business, but Edgar Bronfman Jr. was not. The Poly-Gram purchase was not well received. It initially drove down Seagram's stock, and the business press continued to criticize him as a crown prince who'd spurned business school for Hollywood. But it was just as true that he'd breathed the oxygen of big business since the cradle and had worked hard to understand the nuances of the entertainment industry. His desire to move the company in a different direction wasn't being helped by family politics, particularly the ever-present whine emanating from his uncle Charles.

Charles never seemed to miss an opportunity to remind anyone that he viewed the DuPont sale as a huge mistake. "Yes, it's well known that I was not in favor of moving into the entertainment business, that I considered the DuPont holdings to be a wonderful position," Charles told the *Jerusalem Post*. "My concern was not only for the family, but all the Seagram shareholders, to whom I feel we have a fiduciary responsibility. But you don't always win every argument. The only reason I finally said yes was, one, I wanted the family unified, and two, I knew we weren't endangering the security of Seagram's core business. Even if things don't go well, we're not imperiling the fundamental value of Seagram, because you can always sell these entertainment companies. Maybe you take something of a hit, but not a serious one."

Hardly a ringing endorsement. Charles couldn't resist taking a dig at the studio, opining that the movie business "is not actually a 'business' at all." And naturally, none of his remarks should be taken to mean he wasn't pulling for Efer. "I really hope my nephew, whom I am very fond of personally and is such a bright person, will prevail over his critics."

By the summer of 1999, fifteen months after the PolyGram deal, the company's shares were hovering around 55, an increase of nearly 35 percent, but Edgar hadn't kept pace with the bull market. He'd doubled the value of Seagram's stock in his five years as CEO, when the stock price of most S&P 500 companies had tripled. Trading at a multiple of 12 and continuing to rise on the internet boom and media merger speculation, Seagram nonetheless felt earthbound. Worse, as Edgar watched the media mergers that were breeding ever-larger conglomerates, he worried that he wouldn't be able to navigate a course for Seagram in their wake.

In 1996, Disney acquired Capital Cities, which owned ABC, for $19 billion. In September 1999, Viacom—begun nearly three decades earlier as a spinoff of CBS's syndication arm and expanded by Sumner Redstone to encompass Paramount Pictures, MTV Networks, Blockbuster Video, Simon & Schuster, and nineteen television stations—announced it was merging with its former parent, CBS, in a deal valued at $35 billion. The matchup—which created a company that could not only come up with its own programs but broadcast and syndicate them on its owned-and-operated stations and make a good deal of money at each phase—was heartily embraced by Wall Street. Everywhere in the industry the watchword was *synergy:* massive, vertically integrated media companies.

That summer the Bronfmans had suffered a personal tragedy when Edgar's wife, Clarissa, miscarried. Edgar put business on the back burner to be with her.

It would prove a particularly poor moment for the head of the world's largest record company to suffer a loss of focus. The music business was about to be blown off its foundation by an unforeseen development that would take billions of dollars out of it and change it irrevocably. The first rustlings came from a small office in Silicon Valley.

Shawn Fanning grew up in a working-class family in Massachusetts. In another era—say, two years earlier—a scrappy, creative, blue-collar kid like him might have sought his personal and financial salvation in a rock and roll band. But his uncle, John Fanning, a hustling college dropout who'd run several financially troubled computer firms, gave him an Apple Macintosh to do his homework. Mesmerized, Shawn discovered a new world of possibilities in the intricacies of programming. By the time he entered Northeastern University in the fall of 1998, it was clear that school was going to take second place to his passion for computers and the rapidly evolving internet.

One of the internet's main attractions for Fanning was the increasing availability of music. Since the earliest days of the World Wide Web, the music industry's lobbying and trade group in Washington, DC, the Recording Industry Association of America (RIAA), had been discussing home delivery of music and the soon-to-debut high-speed systems like DSL. But for most consumers the files were unwieldy and transmission speeds too slow. Then, as the '90s progressed, internet bandwidth—first on campuses with large servers and then for the general consumer—grew dramatically, and programs to compress information became more advanced. For music, the key programming breakthrough was the German-developed Moving Picture Experts Group (MPEG) Audio Layer-3, which came to be known as MP3. Capable of compressing CD-quality sound into a file just one-tenth the size of the original with a marginal loss of fidelity, MP3s meant computer users could now convert, or "rip," a

50MB CD track into a 5MB MP3 computer file. And the availability of high-speed connections made it easy to email those compressed files. Player software like Winamp, developed by Justin Frankel, a nineteen-year-old, made it even easier to listen to MP3s and to convert CD tracks into computer files.

By 1998, "MP3" became one of the most popular searches on the internet, a fact that may have gone unnoticed by most senior record executives but not Michael Robertson, an aspiring internet entrepreneur in San Diego. For $1,000, Robertson purchased the domain name MP3.com and started a site where people could post their own original music for others to download. Though MP3.com attracted a few tracks from established musicians like David Bowie, it was almost completely devoid of recognizable names or recordings and quickly became the world's largest repository of garage bands, aspiring professionals, and weekend warriors. With hundreds of thousands of tracks, the very occasional gem was buried beneath ten tons of junk. As far as the major record labels were concerned, MP3.com was commercially irrelevant, provided its users didn't post any of the majors' recordings. But Silicon Valley investors were sufficiently impressed by the millions of people interested in trading MP3s that they pumped $11 million into Robertson's company.

To record executives, digital downloads were downright alien; it certainly wasn't the business *they* were in. "The heads of the record companies tended to view this as a technology issue," says Hilary Rosen, then president of the RIAA. "They pushed it aside for a good long time."

They could afford to feel that way. CDs were selling as well as they ever had. And if converting CD tracks to MP3s was simple, finding and downloading them from the internet was often more trouble than it was worth. The primary problem was locating the songs you wanted and connecting with the people who'd posted them. The sender and receiver had to be online at the same time, and even if you could find someone who had what you wanted, the links to songs were often broken or required specialized knowledge of File Transfer Protocol to download. Those shortcomings were a major annoyance to computer-literate music fans like Shawn Fanning. To make it easier to find and download MP3s, Fanning proposed a real-time index to show the available music files of online MP3 traders. More experienced programmers derided the idea, which Fanning took as a personal challenge. He became so obsessed with solving the problem that he never finished his freshman year. By the spring, he and his friends had worked most of the bugs out of the MP3 file-sharing program that he named Napster, his hacker chatroom handle. He released an early version of the program online June 1, 1999. It was an immediate internet sensation.

"Napster is not revolutionary," Fanning said with earnest modesty. "The technology itself is very simple, but it's something that was needed—there was a huge demand for it and it was going to exist regardless of whether I made that effort at school or not. If, after using a computer for three and a half years and programming for two years, *I* was able to write something like that, then, really, it was sitting there waiting to be done." That this thing waiting to be developed had been obvious to a computer geek in a dorm room and yet missed by executives of billion-dollar record companies should have alarmed them. A new world was coming that they did not comprehend.

Shawn set up a company to promote and manage Napster as an internet service and turned the day-to-day running of Napster over to his uncle, John, along with 70 percent of its stock. He and a growing coterie of online programmers focused on the continuing technical aspects and the development of an attractive online interface. Almost overnight Napster became one of the most sought-out sites on the web. By September, the Fannings had enough backers to rent offices in the Silicon Valley town of San Mateo, California. They hired an acting CEO and started shopping for venture capital partners. Two months later, Napster was regularly logging 150,000 simultaneous users, accessing 20 million MP3s. One veteran industry executive, Warner Music Group's new chairman and CEO, Roger Ames, was terrified by Napster. The simplified file-sharing technology looked like the death knell of the record business. "I already thought the record industry was a train wreck waiting to happen," he says, citing runaway spending. "But the first time I heard about Napster I fell off my chair. I thought, 'Oh my God—this is the end of the world!' "

At RIAA headquarters in Washington, DC, repeated samplings of the music being offered on Napster showed that, unlike MP3.com, virtually all of the music being swapped was ripped from commercial recordings, with the most traffic on the best-known artists. This wasn't garage bands; this was the record industry's bread and butter.

By mid-November the RIAA announced that it was bringing a copyright infringement suit against Napster, with all the major labels as coplaintiffs. "Our urgent requests for a meeting were not taken seriously," said RIAA spokeswoman Lydia Pelliccia. "We really had no other option but to file litigation."

The case that was filed in San Francisco's US district court on December 6, 1999, was straightforward: Napster had infringed record company copyrights and constituted itself to trade on their unauthorized use.

The lawsuit did nothing to spur Napster to a settlement. Making their case directly to the public, the company positioned itself as the avatar of internet freedom, a ragtag band of piratical programmers and free-market scallywags with the intellectual courage to help evolve the PC into what it was intended to be: the medium at the center of life. Compared to Napster's dazzling promise of free instant music, the traditional record industry was about as appealing a concept as high school. It didn't hurt Napster that the major record labels—who had been alienating their customers with overpriced and generally uninspired CDs—had an abysmal reputation with the public.

The record industry also faced a serious problem with the way it dealt with its artists. Up-and-coming performers and their representatives had long complained about the standard recording contract—a nearly hundred-page marvel of brain-deadening legal boilerplate and conditions that generally tied a performer to the label for life. But now established, successful artists began to grumble as well. This was new. Record companies were accustomed to renegotiating a higher royalty rate for performers when they became stars, and successful performers had generally contented themselves with the knowledge that they could become rich—sometimes fabulously so—if they had hits. Naturally, in return for renegotiating, the record company always asked for something back, usually an extension of the contract. For the labels, these extension options had long been one of the business's most appealing aspects. As CBS Records chairman Walter Yetnikoff remarked in 1988, "Steven Spielberg will make his next movie for whomever he wants. I have had Barbra Streisand under contract for more years than she would like me to say." Indeed, with contracts often giving the label as many as seven options on future albums, it wasn't unusual for even the most successful and veteran performer to make all of their recordings for one label. But the notion of being tied to a company for life had begun to rankle. One of the most vocal critics was Don Henley.

A member of the Eagles and a successful solo performer, Henley was far from a starving artist, and just as far from a happy one. Well spoken and savvy, he knew that no matter how well he'd done, he should have done better. "I don't think you could find a recording artist who has made more than two albums that would say anything good about his record company," Henley said. "I am responsible for my success. You know, my partners and I wrote those songs. We busted our butts touring for years and years before we made any money. Most artists don't see a penny of profit until their third or fourth album because of the way the business is structured. The record company gets all of its investment back before the artist gets a penny. It is not a shared risk at all. It doesn't matter how well I've done, or how well anybody else has done. The point is the business is simply not fair and people are getting ripped off."

To promote their interests, Henley and a group of artists including Sheryl Crow, the Dixie Chicks, Beck, and Billy Joel cofounded the Recording Artists' Coalition (RAC) as a professional and lobbying organization. Meeting with lawmakers in Sacramento, they urged the repeal of the record industry's special exemption from California's seven-year limit on personal service contracts. "Artists never get a chance to go out and compete in the open marketplace to see what their true worth really is, like all other working people," said Henley.

Next, they went to Washington, DC, where the RIAA had long been the sole voice of recording industry interests. Simultaneously with suing Napster, the RIAA snuck an amendment into an unrelated bill reclassifying sound recordings as "works for hire"—meaning that performers would lose the right to reclaim their work from record companies after thirty-five years. Further tarnishing its image, the RIAA then hired the congressional aide who'd written the amendment. When the organization's actions came to light, the law was quickly reversed, but they provided just the spur RAC needed.

Record industry greed made it easy for Napster to argue it was an antidote to a corrupt and terminally unhip industry. To stoke grassroots support, it provided clandestine financial aid to a supposedly independent student website, Savenapster.com, and coached its earnest founder, Chad Paulson, on speaking points. Paulson, a free speech advocate who thought Napster was a potentially powerful tool for exposing new and unsigned artists, spoke extensively on the company's behalf but soon came to believe they were less interested in new bands than cynically manipulating the issue. What really spurred Paulson's change of heart were the actions and arguments of the unlikeliest of crusaders, the heavy metal band Metallica.

Napster caught the band's attention in early 2000 when an unfinished version of a new song, "I Disappear," popped up on the web, and radio stations downloaded and aired the unreleased track. The band went ballistic. "We were still trying to figure out which chorus to use," says drummer Lars Ulrich. "All of a sudden the song is on the radio and it wasn't even fucking done! That just brought a different reality to it."

Band managers Cliff Burnstein and Peter Mensch immediately recognized that Napster could undercut the entire music business by making the site attractive not just to internet users but to Silicon Valley venture capitalists who wouldn't care whether it was stealing, only whether it was a winner, and use it to cherry-pick the music industry's assets. Their fears proved well founded. In May, the Silicon Valley venture capital firm Hummer Winblad bought a 20 percent stake in the company for $13 million and a partner, entertainment lawyer Hank Barry, became Napster's CEO.

"Other than maybe Shawn himself—who came up with a brilliant idea and who I certainly have respect for—Napster's anonymous investors are not looking at this for the benefit of mankind," Ulrich said. "They're looking at this like one day there'll be a major IPO or an AOL-type company is going to come and buy Napster out for a gazillion dollars. One of their major arguments is the record companies are so greedy. Fair enough. Record companies are greedy—we can agree on that. But you cannot sit there with a fucking straight face and tell me you want to take it away from the record companies and then give it to all these other organizations who are gonna be less greedy."

In April, Metallica filed a federal suit in San Francisco against Napster, charging not only copyright violations but racketeering. Napster responded that it had no control over what its users did and pointed out that the website carried a standard disclaimer urging users not to engage in unlawful copying. They also made the seemingly coy and unachievable offer to remove any users Metallica could identify as having copied their music.

Three weeks later, on May 3, Shawn Fanning was scheduled to pose for the cover of *BusinessWeek* and hang out with an MTV film crew documenting life at Napster when the legal battle spilled into the streets. Burnstein and Mensch, proving far more resourceful than Napster had imagined, hired a British computer firm to identify 335,000 Napster users who had downloaded and posted Metallica recordings. After giving the press a heads-up, Lars Ulrich and the group's lawyer, Howard King, were greeted by a crowd and four rows of television cameras when they pulled up in front of Napster's offices at 10:00 a.m. in a pair of SUVs loaded with thirteen boxes of printouts from their user search. It was pure theater: the entire list would have fit handily on a disc.

A group of protesters clad in black Napster T-shirts, many of whom appeared to work for Napster, held up an anti-Metallica banner. Just before Ulrich's arrival, a man with a typed list of talking points approached reporters. Though he wouldn't give his last name and claimed to be afraid Metallica would sue him, he sounded more like a coached provocateur than a fan, particularly when he hyped an anti-Metallica website and stomped on one of their CDs.

But Ulrich was the main event. "I write music and I record it and pay for the recording, and I feel that I have the right to do with that what I want," he said. "I can put it on the radio, I can sell it—and ob-viously, the internet is the future of that. Ultimately, we feel we have the right to control who downloads it. So this horseshit that Napster is just providing a service—that's very kind of you. But maybe next time you could ask first."

The protesters were unmoved.

"Is Metallica the internet police?" shouted one woman in a Nap-ster T-shirt.

"Music should be free!"

"*Fuck you*—you're rich enough!"

Ulrich wasn't fazed. "Napster is trying to make this an issue with Metallica and its fans," he told them. "It's not—it's about Metallica and Napster. This is something that's clearly illegal. If people want to steal our music, why don't they go into Tower and put the album under their shirts instead of hiding behind their computers?"

At the restructured Warner Music Group, Napster wasn't Roger Ames's only nightmare. WMG's operation had been hobbled by the one-two punch of casting off its best executives and selling Inter-scope, and its international operations were severely outmatched.

During the '90s, when the foreign record markets expanded as the American share—traditionally 60 percent—began to shrink, WMG's competitors had outspent it overseas. Its current worldwide market share was now only 15 percent to 18 percent. At the Universal Music Group, Bronfman had already responded to the shift by merging MCA with PolyGram and creating a record company that was nearly twice WMG's size; Ames didn't think his company could compete. During his first meeting with his new boss, Time Warner president Richard Parsons, Roger suggested that WMG get out of the record business—an idea that sounded strange coming from the division chairman. "It's a mess and too small outside the US," Ames said. "We should either sell or double down by merging with EMI."

Born in Trinidad, Ames made his mark in the British music business, largely at PolyGram Records. He was highly regarded throughout the industry and considered a lot savvier about the wider corporate and business world than most record men. "He's one of the few people around who really has a grasp of the overall business structure as well as someone who can judge records and hear hits," said Chris Blackwell, founder of Island Records.

Ames had a flair for deal making. As part of his executive package to run WMG, he sold his new employers London Records, a not particularly successful label that he coowned, for $200 million—far more than it was worth. Even more impressive, he made it sound like Time Warner executives held him down and forced him to take the money. "Ted Turner insisted that there was a conflict of interest in my owning the company," Ames said. "It was just stupid, the whole deal. And they overpaid!" Within three years London had effectively vanished as an imprint and the Warner Music Group wasn't even carrying it on their books.

In his first week at Warner, Ames took Parsons to London and met with Ken Berry, the president and CEO of EMI Records. Like Bronfman before them, Parsons and Levin liked the idea of an EMI marriage. David Geffen might have considered it "chicken shit," but the London-based record company was strong in the UK and had a much broader international operation than Warner Music. And it was weakest in the United States, where Warner was strong. A combined Warner and EMI, while not quite as large as Universal Music Group, would still be a behemoth with a roster of thousands of artists on over a dozen labels including the Rolling Stones, Madonna, Radiohead, R.E.M., the Spice Girls, the Red Hot Chili Peppers, Metallica, and Neil Young. EMI had the Beatles, and between them, Warner Bros. Records and EMI's Capitol owned most of the significant recordings by Frank Sinatra. Berry was gung-ho for a deal, and by the end of September, Eric Nicoli, who had replaced Colin Southgate as chairman of EMI's parent company, EMI Group PLC, had agreed in principle to the proposed merger.

Even after the merger with PolyGram, Bronfman still fretted that his company wasn't big enough to dictate its own fate, especially on the internet. He believed that a handful of larger entertainment, communications, and tech giants such as Time Warner, AT&T, Microsoft, AOL, News Corp., and Disney were better poised to define and dominate the online entertainment business and place Seagram at a competitive disadvantage. He wanted a seat at that table—and he didn't think he could get it on his own.

Then there was Napster. Unlike Ames, Edgar didn't believe it was the end of the record business, but he did view it as a serious problem that could impact the industry for several years. He wondered if a larger corporate umbrella could help there, too. "The PolyGram purchase was good," Bronfman says, "but clearly a bumpy ride was coming in the music business."

Something more personal was also nagging at him when he returned to work in the fall of 1999 after a six-month absence. Edgar had grown weary of the family politics that governed Seagram.

In the seventeen years since joining the company, he had harbored no illusions about how the world was likely to view him. "I made a decision when I came to Seagram that it had to be okay that my public persona would be bad," Edgar said. "It's the downside of a family business: anything good is because I'm somebody's son; otherwise, I'm a schmuck." But he found it impossible to grow up and leave home. Edgar's father and uncle still controlled the family's shares, and he couldn't make a move without their approval. Whatever love he felt for his family, he dreamed of being free of them. "I didn't want to go through another five years of the conflict with my father and uncle," he admits. "I had no support from my uncle, and I didn't have the strength to continue that way."

One move held the answer to all of Edgar's problems: sell Seagram. "It was clear to me that if we were going to get bigger we needed to be acquired," he says. In January 2000, he broached the subject to his father for the first time. "He asked if there was any rush and I said, well, no, but the market is going crazy and our competitors are likely to do something," Edgar recalls.

Three days later, Bronfman's instincts were confirmed. AOL announced it was acquiring Time Warner. The $165-billion blockbuster merger, funded with inflated stock trading at 55 times cash flow, left Wall Street and the financial press at a loss for superlatives. The marriage of the cable, publishing, film, and music powerhouse with the world's preeminent internet service suggested a new era had arrived in which electronic delivery of all media was right around the corner. "The leaders of the net economy will become the 21st century establishment," *BusinessWeek* crowed in a cover story that declared Gerald Levin and Steve Case "Men of the Century."

The EMI executives who were finalizing the merger with the Warner Music Group were delighted by the news. The prospect of having exclusive access to AOL, a company virtually synonymous with the internet to many Americans, made them even more eager to merge with Warner Music. "The timing of this agreement could not be better as our industry embraces the digital revolution," Nicoli said. But Time Warner management feared European regulators wouldn't approve both the AOL deal and a record company merger, and soon abandoned the record deal. But despite its size, the AOL–Time Warner merger wasn't going to make the record operation any bigger. A frustrated Ames found himself back at square one.

The merger had two immediate consequences for Bronfman: First, the stock of Seagram rose 11 points on speculation of a deal for them. Second, it solidified his belief that Seagram, despite owning the world's largest record company and a Hollywood studio, could not control its destiny. "AOL Time Warner made me nervous," he says. "We wouldn't have those marketing opportunities." And if selling also got him out from under the weight of family politics, well, that was more than a bonus—that was freedom.

Edgar put out feelers to media and telecommunications companies from Disney to AT&T. But despite the overheated market, he attracted meaningful glances from only one potential suitor: Jean-Marie Messier of Vivendi.

A year younger than Bronfman, Messier grew up in Grenoble, the French alpine resort and university town. He attended the prestigious École Polytechnique and later the École Nationale d'Administration, France's incubator for the government officials and business leaders who form its ruling class.

After serving in Jacques Chirac's finance ministry he joined Lazard Frères bank. Among his clients was Compagnie Générale des Eaux

(CGE), the giant, privately owned water and sewer utility. Founded in 1853, the firm was a nearly ubiquitous utility providing heating, school and hospital administration, cable television, and theater management. It also owned France's second-largest construction company and had extensive commercial and business real estate holdings in Paris. Messier helped CGE gain control of a 49 percent stake in the French cable and film company Canal Plus and was named chief executive in 1993; two years later he became its chairman, just the ninth in the company's 143-year history. Like Bronfman, Messier seemed far less interested in the world he was in than in the one he could envision. He sold off CGE's troubled real estate holdings and refashioned it into a media and telecom company, which he renamed Vivendi. He purchased a €10-billion stake in Rupert Murdoch's British Sky Broadcasting, and to make Vivendi a major player in the emerging internet and mobile world, he bought a stake in French mobile provider SFR.

Messier responded to the AOL–Time Warner merger much like Bronfman did, arguing that Vivendi was in a race for survival that hinged on internet access and control. "AOL and Time Warner are the first to understand that the new and old economy must merge," he said. Less than three weeks later, Messier teamed with Vodafone, the British-based mobile phone giant, to form Vizzavi, an internet service provider. Using Vodafone's and Vivendi's 75 million new mobile phone and cable subscribers as a base, the aim was to take on AOL, Yahoo!, and other American internet firms. With an announced startup budget of €1.6 billion, it looked like a serious contender.

The markets continued their speculative frenzy for all things internet. Analysts and investors loved the new Vivendi, especially the Vizzavi venture. When Vivendi's shares skyrocketed to €142 by March, a leap of 130 percent in just four months, Messier had the financial resources to make a big acquisition.

Messier believed Vivendi needed content to attract customers to its internet, mobile, and cable operations. Vivendi's publishing holdings were far-ranging. Canal Plus had a growing film library, but an American studio and a record operation would put them on a global footing to match the films, music, television programming, and magazine content that AOL Time Warner could offer its online customers. A few months earlier, in October 1999, Bronfman had had a breakfast meeting with Messier in Paris that turned into a wide-ranging two-hour conversation. The two found they shared the same expectation and fear that entertainment on the internet would soon be dominated by a handful of global players.

On February 9, just ten days after Messier's Vizzavi deal, Seagram's board of directors authorized Bronfman to retain Goldman Sachs for potential sales and merger opportunities. By the end of the month, Messier and Pierre Lescure, the chairman and CEO of Canal Plus, were in New York for a series of financial presentations. Bronfman and Messier discussed a variety of possible combinations, including a three-way deal in which Vivendi would acquire not just Seagram but the outstanding 51 percent stake in Canal Plus.

In March, Messier and his top executives made their pitch directly to Edgar Sr., Charles, and the rest of the family in New York. It was the kind of presentation at which Messier excelled. Marrying Vivendi's telecom holdings with Seagram's entertainment assets sounded like a match made in heaven. "He was absolutely calm, clear, and utterly convincing," Pierre Lescure noted later. "I had never seen him articulate his vision so convincingly." On April 24, Messier proposed a stock swap that valued Seagram at $72 a share—a 12 percent premium over the stock's $64.50 peak of the prior month. The family was willing to sell, but Bronfman thought the price was too low and was confident that Messier—flush with internet funny money and a reputation for overpaying—would be back. Bronfman was right. By May 5, negotiations were on again, and by the start of June a general framework was in place.

A three-way merger between Vivendi, Seagram, and Canal Plus to create a new firm named Vivendi Universal was announced June 14. For their stake in Seagram, the Bronfmans would receive 106.5 million shares of Vivendi Universal. Valued at $77.35 per share—a 53 percent premium over Seagram's market price before the company was rumored to be in play—that translated into a $12.4 billion cash-out for the family. And in keeping with their preference for minimizing their capital gains taxes, the entire sale—$33 billion plus the assumption of $6.6 billion in Seagram debt—was structured as a stock swap.

The swap made the Bronfmans Vivendi Universal's largest shareholders, with roughly 8 percent of its stock. They received five of the company's eighteen board seats—more than they'd had at DuPont when Seagram controlled 25 percent of its stock—and Edgar Jr. was named vice chairman with responsibility for the film, music, and internet operations. Seagram's liquor holdings were immediately put on the block. Despite Charles's professed interest in the liquor business, he backed out of an investment group attempting to bid for Seagram's brands. He had a representative, attorney Samuel Minzberg, on the Vivendi Universal board to watch out for his interests, but the sale finally allowed the family members to go their separate ways. By all appearances, Charles was at least as happy to be rid of his brother and nephew as they of him, and to have as little as possible to do with Vivendi Universal and the worlds of entertainment and media.

Edgar Jr. believed he'd pulled off a perfect triple play: Universal now had the size and internet access it needed to compete with AOL Time Warner; he'd negotiated an eye-popping price for his family's holdings in Seagram; and he'd shed the personal albatross of the Seagram name and family politics. It was also the end of the great family empire.

At the June 20, 2000, press conference at Vivendi Universal's Paris headquarters Edgar announced the formal closing of the merger. "Today is my father's birthday," he declared. "And I can think of no better present to give to my father, his children, his grandchildren, and his great-grandchildren than this world-beating company that we are creating today."

7

Turf Wars

At the Universal Music Group, the business of making and marketing records was unaffected by the sale of Seagram. With the PolyGram labels integrated into UMG, the only important question about the recently minted world's largest record company was whether it could live up to expectations and benefit from its heft.

Doug Morris's design for UMG mimicked the competing fiefdoms he'd known at the Warner Music Group. So far the only obvious beneficiary was his protégé Jimmy Iovine's company, Interscope. The Los Angeles label's already powerful rock and rap roster had been bolstered by having two very successful West Coast labels, Geffen and A&M, folded into their operation. But Interscope wouldn't remain unchallenged for long, and Morris, who liked to foster competition between his executives, was about to learn that UMG wasn't big enough for his two most ambitious label heads, the shoot-from-the-hip gunslingers Iovine and Cohen.

As cochairman of Island Def Jam, Lyor discovered that while he liked being rich, he still had something to prove. "I had a real anxiety that I would be known strictly as a rap guy," he said. Despite the genre's mainstream success, it was, incredibly, still viewed condescendingly by many of the executives who'd come up during the underground rock movement. Twenty years after "Rapper's Delight" took the music industry by storm, rap remained its bastard child, and Cohen, as much as he loved and fought for the music, was desperate to prove that his talents transcended genre. The roster he'd inherited from Island and Mercury was bloated with a surfeit of artists signed during Danny Goldberg's tenure. The one that wasn't there was U2, far and away Island's biggest, which had gone to Interscope. Cohen began whittling down the rosters and organizing. He put rap and soul at Def Jam, rock at Island.

One of the more promising acts was Dru Hill, a young soul quartet from Baltimore whose first two Island albums had produced several Top 10 pop hits. In 1999 the group caught a big break when it sang backup for actor Will Smith on "Wild Wild West," a single from the soundtrack that went to number 1 on the *Billboard* Hot 100 Singles Chart. The accompanying video prominently featured only one of Dru Hill's members, SisQó, and when the clip went into heavy rotation on MTV he suddenly found himself a star. Cohen soon heard rumors that Iovine was trying to sign SisQó to Interscope as a solo act. He called the executive.

"Five months before I got here you took U2," Cohen fumed. "I got dealt a shitty hand. There need to be *rules*. I need you and [MCA Records president] Jay Boberg trying to help me, not breaking up one of the only platinum acts on the roster."

Iovine was unimpressed. "He's going to leave anyhow," he told Cohen.

For support Lyor turned to Doug Morris and Zach Horowitz, Universal's COO. "Let's try to impose some rules," he said. "No poaching on each other's acts." Morris heard him out and said he'd call back. When he did, the answer surprised Cohen. "Jimmy doesn't want any rules," Morris told him. Lyor wasn't sure why Morris wouldn't referee. Was this really supposed to heighten competition and improve the company? Or was it personal—payback for spurning his offer to become president of Universal? Maybe it was because

Jimmy was his fair-haired boy. If Cohen didn't know the reason, he recognized that he was being tested.

An invitation to a brawl? No one had to ask Lyor twice. He called Interscope's hottest act, the Detroit rapper Eminem, and offered him his own label through Def Jam with the freedom to sign and produce whomever he wanted. It didn't take long for Lyor's phone to ring.

It was Morris. "You can't do this."

"What do you mean? There are no rules."

"Okay. Jimmy understands. He wants rules."

That satisfied Cohen, who figured he'd made his point. But two months later, with SisQó still talking about leaving for Interscope, he called Iovine to remind him of their agreement.

"I changed my mind," Jimmy told him.

Convinced that Morris was tacitly encouraging the intercompany squabble—"Doug loved having a counter to Jimmy, and Jimmy was telling everyone that he was going to get Doug to put me out of the building"—Cohen took the offer he'd made to Eminem to Fred Durst, the lead vocalist for one of Interscope's biggest bands, Limp Bizkit.

The raucous Jacksonville, Florida, band, which had combined elements of hip-hop with metal, scored their commercial breakthrough with 1999's *Significant Other,* which sold 7 million copies. Durst also had a wide entrepreneurial streak and an eye for talent, facilitating deals for several bands including Puddle of Mudd and Staind.

If the Eminem gambit had been a warning shot, Cohen aimed this one for the heart: he would sign Durst and win the turf war. Meeting at a conference room of the Beverly Hills Hotel, Cohen and Durst spent six hours hashing out a deal that would give the rocker his own Def Jam label along with the freedom to sign acts. "Do me a favor," Cohen said as they parted. "Don't tell anyone."

A month later Limp Bizkit was headlining a show in New Jersey and Cohen reserved the Vivendi helicopter to take the contract to Durst. That afternoon Cohen played golf in Ridgewood, New Jersey, in a foursome that also included Tom Whalley, the president of Interscope Records, who had convinced Ted Field to sign Limp Bizkit to their original $2-million deal.

Whalley, like Cohen, was growing increasingly unhappy with how powerful Morris had allowed Iovine to become. But whatever strains existed between Iovine and Whalley, Cohen wasn't going to tip his hand. A fiercely competitive golfer, Lyor hooked a shot into the woods to give himself time to phone the attorneys and check up on the contract.

The subterfuge was a waste of time. "Are you going to sign Fred Durst?" Whalley asked Cohen as he dropped him at Island Def Jam's Manhattan offices. Lyor admitted that he was. By the time he'd reached his office, Zach Horowitz was on the phone with a warning. "Don't sign this deal tonight."

Morris was next. "Lyor," he said, "your deal isn't done. I strongly advise you, *don't sign Fred Durst.* I promise you, this will never happen again." With that, Cohen relented. Iovine got to make the label deal with Durst and keep him in the Interscope fold—which meant any hits Durst came up with would count toward Iovine's bonus, not Cohen's. Morris brought his weight to bear on behalf of Iovine, but he kept his word to Lyor that Jimmy would be tethered. The war was over.

Iovine later admitted it had been a mistake to pick a fight with Cohen. "Our fighting was over something stupid," he said, though still smarting at Lyor's tactics, which he viewed as "a little rough. He decided to show me he could double down. Maybe I did do the wrong thing. At the time I was a guy who would take on a fight."

And a guy who always seemed to have Morris watching his back. In November 1999, Universal financed a new subsidiary to find talent through the internet—and it bore their names.

Dubbed Doug and Jimmy's Farm Club, the multimedia startup was a record industry twist on websites like MP3.com, which aggregated unsigned talent, and Garage.com, which sought to evaluate, sign, and promote acts. Iovine was the chairman and CEO, and though company press releases avoided spelling out Morris's role, it was no secret at the record company that he had a piece of it. Ted Field, who'd founded and cofounded Interscope but received a smaller equity share in the company than Iovine when Interscope moved to Universal, was fuming at being left out of the Farm Club deal. He would soon leave the company. (Field, though unwilling to be specific regarding why he left Interscope, said he "didn't like the corporate environment. I'm an entrepreneur. For Jimmy, it's a great home." But he added: "Don't underestimate Jimmy as a businessman. He's very shrewd.")

At Farm Club, acts would be encouraged to submit demos online, posting them for listener and executive feedback. If promising, they'd be given the chance to compete for a recording contract and to perform on a weekly cable show on Vivendi Universal's USA Network. The program was also a showcase for signed and established artists on the Universal labels like Dr. Dre and Gwen Stefani. Indeed, very little of the show's airtime was given to unknown bands.

As head of Farm Club, Iovine had to clear the use of videos and artists for the show from the other Universal labels, including Def Jam and Island. Swallowing his pride, he called Lyor during a visit to New York and asked him to meet with him.

Over breakfast in his suite at the St. Regis Hotel, Iovine suggested they bury the hatchet. Then, in a show of what Cohen took to be goodwill, he dispensed a little advice. He went into the bedroom and came back with a pill bottle.

" 'I truly feel if you use Prozac like I do,' " Cohen recalls him saying as he handed him a pill, " 'your life will be beautiful.' " Pretending to oblige, Lyor palmed the drug.

Iovine remembers the offer a little differently. "I was pissed," he says. " *'You need Prozac—you're a fucking lunatic!'* "

Whatever the tenor and intention, it marked a real truce. "From that moment on, Jimmy and I were cool," says Cohen. Adds Iovine: "I didn't want him to leave. He makes hits."

Indeed, both Lyor and the entire Vivendi music operation were posting big numbers. By the end of 2002, the Universal Music Group was selling more than 30 percent of all the albums in the US—far more than any other company. If Morris had intentionally played Iovine against Cohen to stoke their competitive manias, it worked like a dream. Whatever numbers Island Def Jam posted, Interscope could match or beat: Iovine's roster was wide and deep, with Eminem alone selling 20 million albums that year. It was almost enough to make a company not worry about downloading, and apparently Morris didn't. "Our strategy is we need to get more hits!" he said, echoing the refrain he'd heard Ahmet Ertegun use with Steve Ross nearly twenty years before. "Everyone thinks so much has changed in the record business; the way I perceive it is nothing has changed."

Industry sales figures told a different story, and Bronfman, unlike Morris, was concerned. In 2000, recorded music sales dropped for the first time in over twenty years, in large measure because singles sales had evaporated. The labels immediately pointed a finger at Napster and the other downloading sites like Limewire, Kazaa, and Grokster that had sprung up in its wake. The following year the decrease spread to albums. Industry shipments fell 10 percent, with sales dropping more than 4 percent. What UMG really had was a bigger share of a steadily decreasing market.

In June 2000, as the Vivendi sale closed, Napster investor and board member John Hummer asked Edgar if he could get the major labels to take a stake in the file-sharing company. The fact that no one knew how to monetize Napster and turn it from a popular pirate into a legitimate but still appealing music service troubled Bronfman, but he thought a deal was worth pursuing. "Here was an opportunity to maintain a large customer base, potentially, and over time migrate it into a commercially viable system," he said.

On July 13 at investment banker Herb Allen's annual Sun Valley, Idaho, retreat for media moguls, Bronfman met with Hummer, Napster CEO Hank Barry, Sony Corp. co-CEO Nobuyuki Idei and his top US executive, Howard Stringer, as well as Bertelsmann CEO Thomas Middelhoff. By the end of the meeting, Bronfman believed they were close to a deal for the record companies to take a stake in Napster. But a week later negotiations collapsed when Hummer told Bronfman he'd been offered $2 billion for Napster. Edgar was skeptical. He knew the record companies wouldn't pay anywhere near that and he doubted anyone would.

The possibility of a big payday for Napster evaporated on July 26 when US district court judge Marilyn Hall Patel granted the record industry's request for a preliminary injunction and ordered Napster to halt operations. Though an appeals court stayed the order, the handwriting was on the wall. Without an agreement with the copyright holders, Napster was probably breaking the law.

Bronfman, expecting Napster would now want to reach a settlement with the labels, also assumed Hummer Winblad would be more receptive to selling them a meaningful stake in the company. But Intel chairman Andy Grove had convinced Hummer that irregardless of Patel's injunction, copyright would not be protected in cyberspace, and Hummer now saw no advantage in making Napster into a label-sanctioned pay service. Bronfman was unpleasantly surprised when Hank Barry proposed the record companies take a 50 percent stake in Napster but have nothing to say about how it was run. "Things went backward from there," he said. Indeed, John Hummer's pronouncements became strident rather than conciliatory. "I decided I was willing to lose my whole $13-million investment rather than change Napster," he said after talking with Grove. Rather than make a deal with the copyright owners, the venture capitalist now spoke exclusively to Napster's boosters, referring to himself as the record industry's worst nightmare. "Before they close Napster they'll have to pry it from my cold, dead fingers."

On February 12, 2001, the US Court of Appeals for the Ninth Circuit unanimously upheld Judge Patel. "Napster, by its conduct, knowingly encourages and assists the infringement of plaintiff's copyrights," Judge Robert Beezer wrote in the decision, adding that the service was capable of policing its use.

The ruling was a huge win for the record companies because it suggested that cyberspace was not an endless, untamable frontier where recordings, like so many head of cattle, should roam free. The labels went back to business as usual; they believed it was only a matter of time before barbed wire went up, herds were consolidated by brand, and they were back in the saddle. For Napster, the decision had immediate ramifications: it couldn't be a legitimate business without licensing agreements, so it was now eager to make deals with the labels. But most of the major companies weren't interested. Indeed, now that the courts had upheld their rights, they didn't seem to want to make any deals for online music.

For the labels, it wasn't only a question of legal versus illegal downloads. With physical product, the record industry controlled how consumers got and used songs as well as what they paid—all factors that helped the labels preserve and maximize the market for recordings—and they wanted to do likewise on the internet. The biggest hammer in their technical toolbox was Digital Rights Management (DRM), a program code applied to songs offered for online sale. The code dictated how that music could be played, stored, and copied.

Intended to block unlimited copying, preserve future sales, and pointedly remind users that the work was copyrighted, DRM encoding also made tracks less mobile and utilitarian than the same song ripped from a CD and posted online, and therefore less desirable. MP3.com entrepreneur Michael Robertson, whom the labels first sued and then partnered with, correctly noted that DRM penalized paying customers. "If you can get music from file-sharing networks and pay nothing, and then get it from the record guys with a pair of handcuffs attached—I think it's awful." But in the wake of the court's ruling, any legitimate music service had to strike a deal with the major record companies—and that meant they had to agree to DRM.

Liquid Audio, a leading developer of music management software, was eager to do that. The company had a promising program that seemed made-to-order: for a fee, customers could download twenty songs per month, burn each song three times, and copy it onto five devices. The service had internet deals to provide software and backroom support to several big-name retailers including Amazon, Best Buy, Barnes & Noble, CDNow, and the Sony Music Club. But Gerry Kearby, Liquid Audio's president and CEO, discovered that even with DRM the record companies would license only a sliver of their catalogs and at royalty rates virtually no startup could afford. Music publishers, who also had the right to refuse the use of a song, were even worse than the record companies and proved completely unyielding in their demands, unwilling to develop an affordable, easy-to-obtain blanket license. Testifying before the Senate Judiciary Committee, Kearby railed against Napster for conditioning consumers to expect music for free and then lit into the labels for dragging their heels when it came to striking deals for legitimate, wide-ranging online music sites.

"The stage is set for a competitive marketplace that will serve the needs of music fans, artists, and their record companies," Kearby testified. "Why, then, are tens of millions of users turning to unauthorized sites on the internet to obtain digital music? The answer is simple: the music most people want is not available for purchase through legitimate websites . . . The problem before us does not involve a failure of the copyright system, but a failure in the marketplace. It's time to address this failure before the damage is irreversible." Likewise, Napster's now-contrite CEO, Hank Barry, begged the committee to make the record companies play ball. "Where are the internet businesses with clear and complete recording and music publishing licenses?" he asked. "There are none. Where are the emerging digital media companies with negotiated agreements with all rights holders? There are none." The following year Liquid Audio—on the verge of liquidation—sold its digital rights management patents to Microsoft for $7 million.

Record stores, at first opposed to online music, also became desperate to carve out a niche as physical sales slowed. But even the biggest retailers, who were used to receiving preferential treatment from the labels, now found them unwilling partners who doled out licensed songs in dribs and drabs and wouldn't allow music sites with broad selections. "We're starting to worry that maybe all the talk and activity about protecting the music is not about controlling copyright infringement, but is really about controlling lawful use and hiding plans for cutting retailers out of the marketplace," said a frustrated Mike Farrace, senior vice president of the 189-store Tower Records chain. "A lot of the deals the record companies seem most interested in pursuing are with each other, or with companies that they all buy a piece of."

Farrace was right: instead of licensing much of their catalogs to third parties, Universal and Sony were building their own jointly owned service, Pressplay, and the other major record companies had similar plans. Warner Music, EMI, and BMG made an exclusive arrangement with RealNetworks' subscription program, MusicNet. Bertelsmann, whose BMG music operation included RCA, Arista, and Jive Records, also bought the financially strapped Napster for $8 million in May 2002.

After the industry won its suit, BMG was the only major record company willing to strike a music licensing deal with Napster. Bertelsmann CEO Thomas Middelhoff liked the notion of building the pirate into a bona fide music service. Many of Napster's former users had already migrated to a host of other illicit free music sites, but Middelhoff believed Napster still had the name recognition to become a popular legal site if the major labels all participated.

"I thought what Bertelsmann did in getting Napster was right," says David Pakman, a veteran of several internet music operations who sold his online music storage site, Myplay, to Bertelsmann. "Middelhoff wanted to change Napster to a monthly ten-dollar fee with split ownership among the labels." The other majors were initially receptive to the idea. At Universal, Bronfman was convinced that Napster could still be a game changer and was willing to strike a sensible deal. "Edgar really got it right around the time of Vivendi," says former RIAA head Hilary Rosen. But Morris didn't want to make an internet deal with Napster or anyone else. He wanted to keep it all, championing homegrown services like Doug and Jimmy's Farm Club and Pressplay. When Middelhoff pitched Napster, Universal suggested that they deserved the largest piece since they were the largest record company. "They said, 'We should have prorated market share,'" says Pakman. "At that point everyone else said forget it."

In July, Middelhoff's scheme became moot when he was fired. Two months later, after Napster had filed for Chapter 11, attorneys for other record companies and music publishers challenged Bertelsmann's status as a creditor by characterizing the company as an investor, and the bankruptcy court killed the sale altogether.

In interviews, Morris could appear technology averse and unapologetic about it, an impression he later sought to dispel. "I'm not anti-technology," he said. "I'm anti-piracy. I'm trying to get the companies to be legitimate." When Universal's executives proved lukewarm to Napster, Edgar shrugged. His unwillingness to override them may have been philosophically admirable, but it was encouraging the record industry—the business he'd bet his money and his reputation on—to slide inexorably toward disaster. "They thought they were going to be the retailer with operations like Pressplay," says Rosen. "We should have worked more closely with the tech industry on the consumer experience and less on piracy."

Middelhoff's plan for Napster might have created a service with the wide-ranging selection of a record store; the other label-owned services didn't even try to do that. Pressplay offered only recordings from Universal and Sony, and for $15 a month subscribers could download fifty songs, burn ten of them to CD, and listen to five hundred songs while online. MusicNet charged $10 a month for one hundred streaming songs and one hundred downloads from EMI, BMG, and Warner Music, but they expired at the end of every month and had to be repurchased. Both services were unappealing and lightly subscribed—especially after Napster had set the bar at everything you want for free.

Napster had been created as a tool for internet users but without a thought for copyright or artists; when the record companies responded, they erred in exactly the opposite direction and didn't think like customers. Pressplay and MusicNet were designed to protect the record business and preserve the sanctity of its copyrights and contracts, not to help people find and enjoy music. It wasn't only that record companies didn't understand the internet—which they didn't—but that they were huge, often publicly owned corporations with entrenched business models and contractual obligations. Compared to spry and simple internet startups like Napster, they were lumbering dinosaurs.

"The big record companies can't move with speed," said music executive Laurie Jakobson. Between 1997 and 2003, she had worked for a succession of internet music startups. "They've got real lawyers, real issues, and real stockholders to think about. You can't just whack out your P&L to go down a different alley. There's no way to be as nimble as Shawn Fanning."

One of their biggest concerns was getting artists to agree to be part of the services. Musicians might speak glowingly about Napster and MP3s to their fans but then say just the opposite behind closed doors. Says former RIAA president Hilary Rosen: "It wasn't just the record companies. I sat in so many meetings with retailers, artists, managers—even the ones saying they liked downloading in public—saying, 'You better not fuck us. Don't let them do this.'" Jakobson, who joined Sony Music in 1999 and worked on Pressplay, says they fretted that a failure might give artists grounds for voiding contracts. "What if you put this stuff up and it flops?" she asks. "Will we be liable? The lawyers said we have a fiduciary duty to the artists. What if nothing sells and the artist says, 'You put it up—you steered me wrong'? There are tremendous ramifications."

Instead of winning consumers with appealing services, industry executives sought to control online music by putting teeth in the Napster ruling. Simultaneous with discouraging legal startups that they didn't own, the industry used the RIAA to litigate infringing sites vigorously. A second generation of file-sharing services that sprang up in Napster's wake, including Limewire, Kazaa, Grokster, and Morpheus, attempted to sidestep that company's legal problems by using a different technology. Instead of uploading music to central servers, the newer services helped users find and download music directly from other users' computers—dubbed peer-to-peer, or P2P, file sharing—and so claimed to have no role in any illegal copying. But in November 2001, the record companies and the movie studios filed suit against several of the American-based P2P music services including Grokster and Morpheus.

The original Napster and its boosters had suggested that cyberspace should exist as a largely unfettered public common, but resulting free music sites were clearly looking to become commercial concerns and make money. To venture capitalists, music sites were an online gold rush. Investment funds pumped money into numerous startups and frequently encouraged users to act as if the music that artists and labels had produced and marketed was not property they had created, invested time and money in, and owned, but nuggets found lying on the ground.

A particularly shameless spiel came from Silicon Valley venture capitalist Tim Draper, who backed Streamcast's P2P music site

Morpheus. Draper cast himself as a public hero out to bust the copyright oligarchs for the benefit of the little guy. "I really love things that change the whole game, where a big monopoly was in place and suddenly it's a whole new game and everyone gets to participate," he said. "So in some ways that makes me an iconoclast, in some ways a monopoly buster. I go up against government in certain situations where government isn't making it as great for business as it should be. I get a kick out of my work."

It was easy to understand why record companies would fight the startups and fortune hunters intent on eating their lunch. A far more controversial and problematic strategy were the illegal downloading suits they brought against individuals to discourage file swapping. Essentially, the record companies were suing their own customers without giving them a decent legal alternative. When the courts affirmed the validity of copyright in cyberspace, the RIAA asked the Justice Department to prosecute individual downloaders for copyright infringement. They refused. "The government didn't want the grief," says Rosen. "The attitude at enforcement was 'Yeah, you have the rights. You just have to prove it.' So the law is fine, the issue is enforcement. The labels didn't care what kind of grief *they* got." The RIAA would bring its own civil actions against file sharers.

In April 2003, as part of a broader effort to pressure colleges to block music downloads on their computer systems, the RIAA filed copyright infringement suits against four college students for allegedly creating and operating file-swapping services on their schools' networks. Some file-sharing advocates had argued that downloading would stimulate record sales, but the evidence coming out of campuses—where internet-savvy students were among the first to have ready access to high-speed campus networks—was just the opposite. A striking example was seen in the college town of Ithaca, New York, which had supported as many as five record stores. Rene Baum, who owned and operated Rebop Records in the shadow of Cornell University for nearly twenty years, saw business drop precipitously with the advent of music-swapping sites. "Students would come in and rifle through the new release bin and say, 'Look, there's a new Wire album. Let's go back to the dorm and get it.' The attitude was 'Why should I pay for it?'" Baum sold her store in March 2000, and it went out of business the following year. By the end of the decade there was one record store in Ithaca.

The RIAA action got quick results: each student settled the charges by agreeing to take down his site and pay a fine of between $12,000 and $17,000. But the suits had sought $150,000 for each act of direct and contributory copyright infringement—the legal limit—and left the industry open to charges that it was using the courts to terrify students. "The RIAA really wants to send a frightening message," said David Dobkin, chairman of the computer science department at Princeton, where one of the litigants was enrolled. "These students are being set up to scare others away from doing this."

That was exactly what the record companies wanted to do. Two years later, during the road show for WMG's initial public offering, Bronfman suggested to potential investors that the strategy had paid dividends. "When you sue one kid in the school, you sue the entire school and the parents," he said.

That was highly debatable. Even record company–financed research consistently showed that the vast majority of people agreed copyright was necessary and said they were willing to pay for music on an easy-to-use service. (Nearly ten years after Napster, over 85 percent of consumers still said they would pay for music, according to a 2008 research study conducted by Bain Media Partners for WMG.) But filing lawsuits was a conscious decision on the part of the labels to treat downloaders like rustlers instead of frustrated would-be buyers. And the industry offered no apologies.

"I was a big advocate in 2000 of suing consumers," said music business attorney Peter Paterno, whose clients included Metallica. "Everyone was saying, 'How can you sue our customers?' I said, 'They're not your customers; they're stealing your product.'"

That placed the industry squarely at odds with a growing internet culture where the tantalizing freedom and possibilities of cyberspace were loudly and romantically trumpeted, often as a world unto itself, beyond the laws of government or economics.

In "A Declaration of the Independence of Cyberspace," a missive first published in 1996 that would become an oft-quoted credo against the record companies, John Perry Barlow wrote, "Your legal concepts of property, expression, identity, movement, and context do not apply to us." A libertarian from Wyoming, Barlow served as a campaign manager for Dick Cheney's 1978 congressional race but was best known as a lyricist for the Grateful Dead and a cofounder of the Electronic Frontier Foundation (EFF), a respected advocate for an unfettered cyberspace. He characterized media companies as self-serving relics of a bygone era working against the public interest. "Your increasingly obsolete information industries would perpetuate themselves by proposing laws in America and elsewhere that claim to own speech itself throughout the world. These laws would declare ideas to be another industrial product, no more noble than pig iron. In our world, whatever the human mind may create can be reproduced and distributed infinitely at no cost. The global conveyance of thought no longer requires your factories to accomplish." Though the EFF would later develop a file-sharing policy that recognized the right of creators and copyright holders to be paid, Barlow's libertarian leanings endured as grist for a tenacious pirate minority—particularly on college campuses and in the tech world—whose pronouncements sounded progressive but were as self-serving as anything the record companies were up to. Not paying artists and copyright owners was presented as a moral stance against exploitive media conglomerates.

Whatever Barlow argued, the US courts ruled in *Napster* that copyright law applied on the internet. On the heels of quick capitulations by the first four students they sued, the RIAA aggressively expanded its actions. In September 2003, litigation was brought against 261 alleged file swappers who, unlike the four students originally targeted by the RIAA, had not created sites for others to use but simply engaged in posting and downloading recordings on existing sites. As in the first cases, the cudgel was potential liability of $150,000 per infringed file—millions of dollars in most cases—although the RIAA encouraged defendants to make a quick admission of guilt and accept an average fine of $3,000. "Our goal is not to be vindictive or punitive," said Cary Sherman, who succeeded Rosen as RIAA president. "It is simply to get peer-to-peer users to stop offering music that does not belong to them." The RIAA would ultimately file or threaten legal action against a reported 28,000 individuals, going to court when they refused to settle and sometimes winning judgments in the hundreds of thousands and even millions of dollars.

In the end, suing consumers was a public relations disaster and it hardly provided the quick victories the initial cases against students running university share sites had. The EFF, some of whose most active members were business and law professors at Harvard and Stanford universities, jumped into the battle as an advocate for those being sued. One of their chief objections was that the tactic was overly broad and possibly targeted the wrong people. "You have to assume that the recording industry actually got the right person," said EFF attorney Fred von Lohmann. "It's Mom and Dad's name on the ISP account, for example, but that doesn't mean it's Mom and Dad using Kazaa." Over the coming years, record industry spokesmen would repeat the mantra that they didn't want to be punitive—just make the public aware of copyright. "Virtually no one can claim not to know that the online 'sharing' of copyrighted music, movies, software, and other works is illegal," the RIAA later declared, adding that they had made "great progress . . . in deterring many individuals from engaging in illegal downloading behavior."

It was hard to know how the RIAA was measuring that progress. In 2008—five years after the first suits were filed—the record industry's own research suggested that just 5 percent of music downloads were paid for. Suing individuals made the record industry look more like a bully than a victim, and it became an object of outrage and exceptional vitriol from even mainstream commentators. "There might not be any bigger scumbags in the corporate world today than the Recording Industry Association of America," declared the popular liberal blog *Daily Kos*. Clearly, suing file sharers wasn't bolstering copyrights and it was costing the record industry the public's sympathies. Regardless of whether it could be legally justified, it was simply bad business. "The people who made decisions were lawyers, and their sole intent was to parse the law," said Pakman. " 'Let's sue the kids.' A lawyer says that. No businessman would say that."

In fact, many businessmen in the industry—including Bronfman, who was an early hawk on suing file sharers—did say that. "There are those who believe that because technology can access property and appropriate it, then somehow that which is yours is no longer yours," he wrote in an op-ed piece published in the *Los Angeles Times* two weeks before the June 2000 Vivendi merger. The folly of trying to sue consumers into compliance would be amply and embarrassingly demonstrated a few years later when Bronfman admitted he was "fairly certain" that his own children had illegally downloaded music. While stressing that he'd addressed the situation as a parent— "A bright line around moral responsibility is very important," he said; "I can assure you they no longer do that"—bloggers had a field day wondering why Bronfman hadn't sued his own kids after pursuing legal action against tens of thousands of other music fans for the same thing.

The sorry fact was that record executives had no personal financial incentive to be forward-thinking. In an industry where bonuses were based on chart performance and market share, incentives were tied to creating hits and not to addressing the fact that the CD business was being rendered unnecessary and needed to be reinvented. With a lethal myopia, the industry went about its day-to-day business and made sure all its windows and doors were locked, completely indifferent to the fact that its house was on fire.

Like his boss Doug Morris, Lyor Cohen had just one goal at Island Def Jam: get more hits. He was now sole chairman and CEO of Island Def Jam, and by the spring of 2002 his division was looking good. For the first time since he'd taken the reins, Island Def Jam outperformed Jimmy Iovine's Interscope, grabbing a 9.35 percent share of the *Billboard* Top 200 Albums Chart over the first half of the year. Some of it had been luck. He'd projected sales of 40,000 copies for the soundtrack to *O Brother, Where Art Thou?* and the record sold 9 million. But he deserved a lot of credit for the homegrown success of Def Jam artists like DMX, Ja Rule, Jay-Z, and Ashanti, all of whom habitually topped the charts and sold millions of albums. Maintaining that lead over his rival would be a challenge since Iovine had a stronger, deeper roster. If Lyor was going to do that, he'd have to develop Island's weak pop and rock roster while keeping Def Jam hot. An unexpected chance to bolster Island came in the sudden availability of the singer Mariah Carey.

Carey had been an enormous star at Columbia Records, where her meteoric rise from an unknown backup singer to the pop diva who had racked up fifteen number 1 singles in the US and sold over 90 million albums worldwide had been orchestrated and policed by her husband, Tommy Mottola, then chairman of Columbia's parent company, Sony Music. But when the couple separated in 1997, Carey was eager to prove she could direct her own career. When sales of her next two albums slipped, Carey complained that she could no longer get a fair shake at Columbia and decamped to EMI's Virgin Records.

The label was more than eager to have her. Bought by EMI from Richard Branson in 1992 for $1 billion, Virgin, like its parent company, was bigger in the UK than in the US. To help remedy that, the company had signed up global superstars the Rolling Stones and Janet Jackson. When Mariah Carey came calling in 2001, Virgin offered the singer her own label and $80 million for three albums plus options—far more than anyone else was willing to pay.

The first project, *Glitter,* was a train wreck. It was the soundtrack to a film featuring Carey in her first starring role, a semiautobiographical musical that was impossible to watch and seemed to close before it opened. Virgin tried to save the soundtrack by offering the first single, "Loverboy," at a deep discount, but the album became the first unequivocal bomb of Carey's career.

Distraught, the singer quickly spun out of control. At one point she walked onto the set of MTV's afternoon show *Total Request Live,* began an impromptu partial striptease, and handed out ice cream to the studio audience. "I just want one day off when I can go swimming and eat ice cream and check out rainbows and maybe learn how to ride a bicycle," she said. A few days later Carey was hospitalized in Connecticut for a nervous breakdown.

EMI beat an expensive retreat. Having paid Carey over $15 million for *Glitter,* the label forked out an additional $28 million to void the remaining contract.

But Doug Morris believed in the commercial potency of brand-name pop stars. He thought Carey could get the radio play she needed to rebuild her career if she had the right record. Morris gave her a deal and once again Carey got her own vanity label, MonarC—but it was for $12 million instead of $80 million.

Island was the natural place to put her, but radio hits weren't Lyor's forte. Def Jam came of age when radio wouldn't play rappers and the label had marketed careers, not records, in the belief that once the career and fans were in place the hits would follow. At Columbia, Carey's career had been built on exactly the opposite approach. The label had paired her with proven songwriters and established hit producers, and her sound and image were carefully crafted long before she ever set foot on a stage as a concert performer. Returning Carey to the top of the charts would require repeating the strategy, and to do so Cohen would need to become an expert at pop production and promotion.

Marketing *Charmbracelet* as a comeback album, Cohen picked "Through the Rain," a semiautobiographical song about Carey's struggles, as the album's first single and put the singer on TV, where she talked about her recent troubles on *The Oprah Winfrey Show, The View,* and her own MTV special. The album debuted at number 3 but quickly sank and failed to produce any Top 40 singles. By touring steadily, the singer ultimately sold over 2 million copies of *Charmbracelet* worldwide—nothing to sneeze at, but hardly a comeback for an artist who had routinely sold 10 million albums.

Lyor's inability to turn Carey's career around wasn't his only dilemma. He was renegotiating the contract of one of his key producers and A&R executives, Irv Gotti.

Gotti's history at Def Jam was instructive of the way Cohen liked to do business. A certified hit maker and a headstrong customer, Gotti could be hard to deal with, but had contributed as much as anyone to Def Jam's recent success and Lyor couldn't afford to lose him. He'd either discovered or helped break Ja Rule, Jay-Z, DMX, and Ashanti, and produced many of their records. Originally a DJ from Russell Simmons's old Queens neighborhood, he had been working as an A&R man for TVT Records when Cohen saw a video for the song "Get the Fortune" by a trio Gotti had signed, the Cash Money Click, that featured the then-unknown rapper Ja Rule. Cohen asked Gotti and the group to drop by his office, but Gotti explained that the group was signed to TVT. The following year Gotti popped up on Cohen's radar again, working with the rapper Jay-Z as a DJ and radio consultant. "Jay-Z couldn't get his records on the radio," Gotti recalled, "and I was having success getting records on [New York station] Hot 97. So he asked me to help him out." In 1996, when Cohen got Jay-Z and his partner, Damon Dash, to bring their Roc-A-Fella Records to Def Jam as a partnership, he suggested that Gotti leave TVT and join Def Jam.

Gotti got out of his TVT contract and the label also released Ja Rule. Irv quickly convinced Def Jam to sign him as well as the Yonkers rapper DMX. Acting as their producer, he scored big hits for Def Jam with both—not only helping to stem Def Jam's late-nineties cold spell, but also providing much of the commercial firepower that Cohen used to jack up the label's sale price.

"It was a unique time because Lyor had nothing," Gotti said. "Basically the guy just ran with me. He let me do what I wanted to do."

"Irv Gotti was the best thing to happen to Def Jam since the '80s," Russell Simmons said. "Lyor and Kevin Liles managed the label, but Irv made the records. He made a lot of money for us."

Yet Cohen—with his eye on the bottom line—wasn't in any hurry to reward his new star producer and talent scout. Even after several multiplatinum records, Gotti's annual salary didn't top $60,000—pauper's wages for a proven hit maker. When Tommy Mottola tried to woo Gotti to Sony by offering him his own label, Lyor finally told corporate they'd have to improve his deal.

In 1997, Gotti received $3 million and his own label, Murder Inc. Though it was Gotti's label to run as he saw fit, Murder Inc. was a fifty-fifty partnership with Def Jam, with the latter providing funding, promotion, and marketing and taking half of any profits. Lyor controlled Murder Inc.'s purse strings, but the increasingly successful and self-assured Gotti was not easy to mollify or control. The first thing he did after moving into Murder Inc.'s new offices at Universal's midtown headquarters was to complain to Doug Morris that they were too small.

Handling Irv was a full-time job. "Every time you say no, his conviction is to prove you wrong and do the opposite," Cohen complained. Indeed, when Cohen refused Gotti permission to work with the singer Jennifer Lopez, who was signed to Sony's Epic, Gotti ignored him. The record—a remix for the song "I'm Real"—became a hit. Eventually, Lyor adopted the strategy of distracting rather than dissuading Irv. "He wanted to sign Michael Jackson," Cohen recalled, "and I said, 'Listen, I don't know if that's a very good idea.' Because had I said *no,* his next phone call would have been from Never Never Land." (Jackson's California compound was dubbed Never Land Ranch.)

If TVT founder Steve Gottlieb now regretted letting Gotti and Ja Rule leave, he didn't say. In the summer of 2001 he learned that Chris Black, an incarcerated member of Rule's old trio, the Cash Money Click (CMC), was being paroled and saw an opportunity for TVT. Approaching Gotti, he suggested that the group re-form and make an album using a combination of new and unreleased older material. As Gottlieb pitched it, a CMC album could provide Ja's fans with an important glimpse into his development; at the same time, it would be a way for his old partners to earn some money and get back on their feet—a calculus that could only help the star's street credibility. He offered $400,000 to get the project going, and Gotti agreed.

Cohen viewed the offer as little better than a shakedown. Def Jam, not TVT, had succeeded with Ja Rule. Why should Gottlieb get a payday just because he had some old tapes and a contract for a group that didn't exist anymore? But he didn't want to rile Gotti and Ja—especially since Gotti's Murder Inc. deal was coming up for renewal within the next six months and he could easily leave and go to a competitor. When Gotti came to Cohen about the CMC album, Lyor was coy. He told Irv he thought releasing an album with old material was a bad idea that could upset Ja's career, but stopped well short of refusing to let them work on the project.

Mindful that it would be their best shot at having a big hit during the all-important Christmas season, TVT began planning a fall '02 release. But Gottlieb got his first indication that things might not go smoothly when Gotti, who'd originally told him that Cohen wanted a 10 percent override for Def Jam, informed him that Cohen wanted to make it a three-way split, giving Def Jam a bigger slice of TVT's shares.

Gottlieb was annoyed—"I'm putting up all the money in that proposition"—but nonetheless agreed. Then Cohen asked that net profits for Def Jam be calculated differently than for Murder Inc. "We thought it was a little odd, but we created it," Gottlieb said later. And when Cohen subsequently learned that TVT, which was already distributed outside the United States by Universal, was in separate negotiations for a US distribution deal through Interscope, he also asked that all CMC copies be counted toward Def Jam's yearly totals, rather than giving the TVT share of the count to Interscope, an arrangement that, if the album was a hit, could help Cohen reach the sales benchmarks he needed to earn his annual bonus from Universal while diminishing his rival, Interscope chairman Jimmy Iovine.

Gottlieb saw little reason to fight Cohen and agreed to the terms but complained about them to Iovine. "I told Jimmy that I couldn't understand how Lyor is doing these deals for his own benefit." The following week at the MTV Video Music Awards, Cohen told Gottlieb, "It's going to be great." But TVT had never actually received a signed copy of a contractual waiver from Def Jam allowing Gotti and Ja Rule to work on an album for TVT.

In August, with the Cash Money Click slated for a fall release, Gottlieb heard an unsettling rumor from an executive with Universal's Canadian distribution company: Def Jam had slated its own new Ja Rule album for the fourth quarter and pushed the CMC collection back into the first quarter of the next year. Panicked, Gottlieb called Gotti, who assured him that everything was as planned. "You've got the lane," Gottlieb recalled him saying. But a few weeks later when Gotti played the record for Gottlieb, he said there was "a problem with Lyor."

That Friday night, Gottlieb made sure he was on Cohen's seaplane flight out to the Hamptons. Sitting next to Lyor, Steve asked what was going on with the project. Cohen put him off with the excuse that the turbulence of the flight was making him too nervous to talk. "I'm scared to death," he said. "Please, let's speak over the weekend."

The next morning he tracked Cohen to a Hamptons baseball field where his son, Az, had a game. Cohen finally told Gottlieb that business at Def Jam had been slow and that in order to avoid layoffs he was releasing a new Ja Rule album, *The Last Temptation,* for Christmas rather than the TVT album on which Def Jam stood to receive a smaller share of any profits. Incensed, Gottlieb said TVT had spent over $1 million on the album and was banking on it for *their* fourth quarter—and had nothing to replace it with on such short notice. "He was very, very upset and frustrated," Lyor later recalled.

A few days later, Gottlieb met with Gotti in Los Angeles and urged him to live up to their agreement. "Irv, we have a contract," he said. "Deliver the record and let me worry about Lyor." When Cohen got wind of Gottlieb's attempt to go around him, he was apoplectic.

"Did you say I can't stop you?" he yelled when he got Gottlieb on the phone. "Did you tell Irv to deliver? You're going to hear from my lawyer!" He slammed down the phone and Def Jam's attorney dropped the bomb, informing Gottlieb that the agreement to allow Gotti and Ja Rule to work on the CMC album had never been executed.

Contractual squabbles between labels are commonplace and are invariably settled, but the CMC dispute had become far too personal. Breaking with industry convention, Gottlieb sued not just Def Jam and Universal, but also Cohen in a wide-ranging complaint that included charges of fraud and sought at least $30 million—meaning Cohen would have to pay a share of the damages if TVT won.

Despite such hardball tactics, Gottlieb still saw an out-of-court settlement as his only road to getting the CMC album out for Christmas. When asked during a preliminary injunction hearing in October how quickly TVT would need a decision if they won, Gottlieb suggested the trial needed to be over by November 1. Instead, the case was postponed until December, forcing Gottlieb—who was counting on money from the album—to look for a quick settlement. "I'm in trouble with my financial institutions," he said. "It's gonna hurt and I'm feeling fucked. At the hearing I go up to Lyor, but he disputes our offer to settle. He sort of gives me a 'fuck you.'"

A jury trial finally began in March 2003 in the US district court in Manhattan. Lasting nearly two weeks, it proved a disaster for Cohen. On the stand for several days, Lyor's recollections under questioning were uniformly vague on nearly every point—with the noticeable exception that he'd always believed that the CMC album was a really, really bad idea. Worse, some of his testimony was contradicted by his own executives. Gottlieb, by comparison, proved a sympathetic figure, a small businessman who'd spent over $1 million in pursuit of an album that he alleged Def Jam had never intended to let him have. In the end, the jury found Def Jam and Cohen guilty of fraud, tortious interference, and copyright infringement for releasing CMC recordings on a Murder Inc. compilation.

A few weeks later, when the penalty phase began, Lyor—who'd been represented by Universal's attorneys—had a new independent counsel and a new contrite tone. Still maintaining that he'd never agreed to let Ja Rule or Gotti work on a CMC album, he now said his "ambivalence" had been a mistake. "I messed up," he said. Backpedaling wildly, Cohen told the jury that he now believed he'd been unfair to Gottlieb and hoped he'd have a chance to give him an album.

If Cohen meant it, he couldn't sell it: the jury—as well as Judge Victor Marrero, who termed the inconsistencies in Cohen's testimony "morally reprehensible"—found his new explanations awkward and hard to believe. In May, the jury awarded TVT $131 million in damages, with Cohen personally liable for $56 million.

Cohen and Island Def Jam immediately announced that they would appeal the verdict and award. They also spurned a settlement offer from Gottlieb that would have required Cohen and Island Def Jam to pay TVT's legal fees and the marketing costs of releasing the CMC album. "I'm not paying you a nickel," Gottlieb recalls Cohen barking during a meeting.

Neither Gottlieb's suit nor Lyor's failed first attempt to revive Mariah Carey's recording career had damaged his stock in the industry: just prior to the start of the TVT trial, Roger Ames offered

Cohen a job running the Warner Group's American operation. It was a very tempting offer, and Cohen, though ambivalent about leaving Def Jam, began negotiating with him—perhaps hopeful that Ames's competing offer would get Universal to give him the kind of money they were paying Iovine, then believed to be making $10 million a year. Instead, it blew up in Lyor's face. Morris had already lost Interscope president Tom Whalley to Ames in a drawn-out wrangle, and he viewed Cohen's play as a betrayal. Universal threatened not to indemnify Lyor against the damages in the TVT case unless he signed a new contract.

Morris wasn't the only one feeling betrayed. Cohen was being forced to lay off staff at Def Jam and he didn't like it. "I had a five-year obligation to work for them after I sold Def Jam," Cohen said. "Every month I would deliver heads and money on time. I'd walk into Doug Morris's office and lay them on his desk. I thought what Universal did was gratuitous."

He told friends and associates that he feared Gottlieb would ruin him. "Every night I would walk to this tree in the park and rehearse the speech to my family about why I'm going bankrupt," he said. And when Cohen learned that his infant daughter, Bea, was deaf and would require a cochlear implant it was too much.

"He was crying as we were driving back from the Hamptons," recalls Sean Carasov. "The Gottlieb thing is going on and he'd just found out that Bea needed an implant. He was definitely more concerned about Bea, but it was both. Lyor is saying, 'I fucking *hate* this business. I've been missing out on my kids growing up, ignoring my wife. These people are fucking with me and look what I did for them!'"

Cohen received a good deal of breathing room in September when Judge Marrero reduced his $56-million punitive damage award to $3 million. There was no question of Cohen's ability to pay: aside from the money he'd made in the record business, he was about to receive over $20 million for his 16 percent stake in Russell Simmons's fashion company, Phat Farm. But no longer worried about going bankrupt, he became even more adamant about not dropping his appeal of the verdict or settling with Gottlieb.

With the Phat Farm money in hand and the extension of his Universal contract still up the air, Cohen began wondering what it would be like simply to leave Def Jam and start over. Speaking on a *New Yorker* panel on the music business in December, he found himself envying another panelist, Robb Nansel of Nebraska's small Saddle Creek Records. "Did you see that guy?" Cohen asked Carasov. "He's *happy*. I want to start an indie label–I'm sick of this shit. I wouldn't get these corporate dicks fucking with me and I could be with my family."

He yearned for a clean slate at home. Lyor and his wife, Amy, had drifted apart. She went with a friend to a poetry reading at a club in the Village and was stunned when, in the middle of the program, Lyor came onstage and read a poem he said he'd written for her. "Amy's jaw hit the table," says Carasov, who was just as surprised. "I didn't think Lyor had this in him." Asking Amy to renew their wedding vows, Lyor pledged that he would seek a new career away from the world of major record company politics and that it would be a rebirth for their marriage and family. Even with a $3-million judgment in the TVT case hanging over his head, Cohen seemed eager to change his life.

8

Le Divorce

Edgar Bronfman Jr. thought the Vivendi-Universal merger the answer to all his prayers: in a single move he'd become part of a global media behemoth, get out of the liquor business, and shed his relatives—all while receiving a premium for Seagram's stock. Yet just a few months after assuming his new role as vice chairman of Vivendi Universal, Edgar felt the first pangs of misgivings. He hadn't changed his mind about where the business was going, and he didn't regret selling Seagram. But he was beginning to wonder if he had taken an accurate read of Jean-Marie Messier, into whose hands he had entrusted the fate of his business and much of his family's financial future.

Having a boss—a real boss and not someone employed or bankrolled by his father—was a new experience for Edgar. Whatever criticism had been leveled at him in the past regarding the sale of DuPont, the humiliating negotiations with Ovitz to run the studio, or his deal to give Diller day-to-day control of Universal's television and cable assets, he'd at least had the freedom to make those moves. Throughout the merger discussions, Messier had assured Bronfman that that wouldn't change and that as vice chairman of Vivendi Universal his voice and vision would be key. That wasn't proving to be the case.

In December 2000, just two weeks after shareholders formally approved the $60-billion purchase of Universal and Canal Plus, Messier announced that he had spent $2.7 billion for a stake in Maroc Telecom, an African telephone company. The deal was a surprise to everyone, Bronfman included. "I was furious," said Bronfman, who had just spent six months on the road explaining the vision behind the Vivendi-Universal merger to the financial community. To Bronfman, making an acquisition without digesting Universal completely undercut the new company's credibility. "In terms of the message we were trying to send to investors it was disastrous. In that context, Maroc Telecom made no sense. Why did he do it? I have no idea."

It was a reaction that Bronfman was to have again and again over the coming months as Messier went on a binge. He spent over $400 million on the music websites MP3.com and Emusic.com, and shelled out $2.2 billion for US book publisher Houghton Mifflin. The latter deal particularly irked Bronfman, who'd taken Seagram out of book publishing in 1996 by selling MCA's Putnam Berkley to Pearson, and he argued against it to no avail. Messier was adding debt at the rate of $1 billion a month and seemed to think that Vivendi's internet and mobile platforms would make *any* intellectual property more valuable. "When I see a great book, I think movie rights, interactive games, and so on," he said. "The digital broadband revolution is going to make all content accessible across all platforms and devices."

What Jean-Marie was doing with the balance sheet was a shock to Bronfman. "I think anybody who worked for the company, invested in the company, should feel betrayed," he said. "He lost his head, and because he did, people got hurt."

None of Messier's moves concerned Bronfman more than his decision to buy Barry Diller out of his stake in USA Networks. Bronfman had structured the USA Networks agreement so that all Messier had to do to gain control of the company was wait for Diller to retire. But when he tried to tell Messier that negotiating a deal now would be a colossal waste of money, he got nowhere.

"Up until the USA Networks transaction, he had at least done me the courtesy of asking my advice," Bronfman said. "But when I wanted to discuss Barry Diller with him his eyes would just glaze over." Believing he could have no effect on the direction of the company and that Vivendi Universal was a ship whose captain had lost his bearings, Edgar resigned as vice chairman. He remained on the company's board but started his own investment group, Lexa Partners, to fund leisure and entertainment companies.

Largely a family affair, Lexa's initial investors included Edgar, his father, and Edgar's brother-in-law, Alex Zubillaga. However, the situation at Vivendi Universal soon took on a new urgency. Sam Minzberg, the attorney in charge of Charles Bronfman's investment firm, Claridge, Inc., and his representative on the Vivendi Universal board, was the first to raise the alarm.

Messier was presenting a relentlessly upbeat portrait of the company's finances at board meetings. Skeptical of the rosy picture, Minzberg ran the numbers and concluded that Messier was misleading them about the company's true financial condition and failing to disclose major expenditures.

The most shocking omission was Messier's $6.3-billion purchase of 104 million shares of the company's stock in order to prop up the price. Vivendi's CFO, Guillaume Hannezo, normally a Messier loyalist, had opposed the stock buyback plan, then discovered that Messier had ordered two of Hannezo's subordinates to execute the purchases without telling him. On the verge of announcing a 2001 loss of $12.7 billion, the largest in French history, Vivendi Universal was quickly running out of cash. An immediate crisis was averted by the sale of 9 percent of the company's utility firm, Vivendi Environmental, and the receipt of $8.15 billion from the sale of Seagram's liquor holdings. Though he never warned the board and continued to back the chairman in public, Hannezo was so distressed by Messier's spending that he sent him a handwritten plea. "I've got the unpleasant feeling of being in a car whose driver is accelerating in the turns and that I'm the death seat," he wrote. "All I ask is that all of this not end in shame."

Minzberg's warning got the Bronfmans' attention. The company—

and the Bronfmans' stock, which still totaled 6 percent of its shares—was in a lot of trouble. "He just did his homework," Edgar Bronfman Sr. said of Minzberg. "I suddenly realized, 'Oh my God, we've got to get this guy out.'"

It was a tall order. As part of the Seagram sale, the Bronfmans had agreed not to seek Messier's ouster as chairman. Even more problematic was Messier's relationship with the French directors who comprised the majority of the board. For a French director to challenge his chairman simply wasn't done. Besides, Messier was a heroic figure in France, the corporate swashbuckler who'd planted the Tricolor on the global media map. When Minzberg accused Messier of deceiving the board and mismanaging the company, the French directors rushed to defend Messier's honor. Anonymous Messier loyalists were soon playing on national sympathies, complaining in the press that the chairman was the victim of a vicious rumor campaign to destabilize the company and slander it as "the French Enron." If Messier was to be replaced and the company salvaged, someone other than Minzberg would have to make the case.

Messier remained unwilling to acknowledge the looming financial disaster and spent much of his time in New York, where the company had purchased a $17-million apartment for him. After a two-week Colorado ski vacation, he returned to Paris for a March 5 press conference, where, looking tanned and relaxed, he declared that "Vivendi is in better-than-good health."

Behind the scenes Hannezo was desperately trying to meet the company's obligations through a bond sale. At his invitation, bankers from Citigroup pored over Vivendi's books for three days and concluded that the runaway media conglomerate wouldn't last more than a few months without a major cash infusion. The bank suggested a standby credit line of between $2 billion and $3 billion, but discussions fell apart over terms.

Not surprisingly, neither Messier nor Hannezo informed the board of their discussions with the bank, and it was nearly two months before Bronfman learned of Citigroup's analysis from Fehmi Zeko, head of the media group for Smith Barney. Edgar phoned Hannezo, who denied there was a problem. And when a front-page story in the May 14 edition of *Le Monde* questioned the company's financial stability, Messier responded with a €1-million libel suit against the newspaper.

A week later at the May 29 board meeting in New York the French directors raised concerns over their own personal liability under French law. The moment seemed right for the Bronfmans to push for Messier's removal, but Minzberg spent the better part of the eight-hour meeting haranguing Messier. Grilled like a witness, Messier bristled in righteous indignation and the French directors who hours before had seemed ready to desert him rallied to his side. By the end of the meeting, Edgar had managed to get only board approval for a financial review by outside analysts.

Bronfman formed a new corporate governance committee with French director Marc Viénot and brought back Goldman Sachs to analyze Vivendi's immediate cash situation for the next board meeting, scheduled for June 25. On June 24, with the press reporting the company's desperate attempts to raise cash, and Vivendi Universal's stock plummeting 23 percent to €18—the company's lowest price in thirteen years and €5 lower than it had been trading as Compagnie Générale des Eaux when Messier took over—the bankers gave Vivendi executives and directors a preview of their report. Goldman Sachs held out little chance of the company floating a new bond and warned that Vivendi could be bankrupt in three months. Speaking privately with Messier, Bronfman suggested he resign in order to restore the company's financial faith.

The next morning at the board meeting it was clear that Messier was not willing to step down. Locking horns with Minzberg, cutting off the Goldman Sachs presentation at every opportunity, he managed again to hold the support of his loyal directors, who ignored one-on-one pleas from Bronfman to find a replacement for Messier. With financial ruin staring it in the face, the board was still more concerned with protecting the honor of the sinking conglomerate than saving the shareholders. Messier adjourned the meeting confident that he'd thwarted the Bronfmans and their allies. A formal request for his resignation could be made only at a board meeting, and the next one wasn't until late September. As chairman, only Messier could schedule additional meetings. And he let it be known that he was not going to do that.

Messier's victory lasted only a few hours. That evening, news broke that WorldCom, the American telecommunications company that owned MCI, and its chairman, Bernie Ebbers, had engaged in an enormous accounting fraud. The news had ramifications for Vivendi, as any hope of floating the bond financing ended in the wake of the scandal. Over the next business days, two of Vivendi's primary lenders, BNP Paribas and Deutsche Bank, informed the board they would not give the company any more money as long as Messier was chairman.

Desperate, Messier raised €353 million by unloading the remaining stake in Vivendi's old construction division and burned up the phones looking for a new line of bank credit. But WorldCom had taken the last air out of the Vivendi Universal balloon. Less than two years after VU had hit its market high of $79.70 (on September 12, 2000) on the hype and hysteria of an endless internet and telecom boom, the company was a smoldering, nonfundable wreck. All that remained was for Messier to resign and let the board pick a replacement who might instill enough confidence in the financial community to facilitate Vivendi Universal's restructuring.

Finally forced to act, the French board members informed Messier on Sunday, June 30, that they would release a public statement of no confidence unless he called a board meeting and resigned. At that point Messier had to agree—but he had a proviso, informing Bronfman and Viénot that there would be no board meeting unless the corporate governance committee signed off on a €21.7-million severance package. Bronfman was enraged but agreed, believing that such blackmail wouldn't stand the light of day.

"His attitude was, 'Unless I get my money, I'm not going to call a board meeting,'" Bronfman said. "But we couldn't wait until September. The company would have been gone by then. My view was, however repugnant it may be to give that cocksucker anything, it was more important to save the company. It was €20 million or so to save a company with a €13-billion equity value. I take that deal any day."

Bronfman's thinking proved sound. Following his resignation,

Messier was investigated by the SEC for fraud and agreed to return the severance and pay a $1-million fine to settle the charges. But a more pressing problem for incoming Vivendi Universal chairman Jean-René Fourtou was the company's lack of liquidity. "If Mr. Messier had stayed, the company would have gone bankrupt within ten days," he later told a French parliamentary hearing.

Vivendi's debt was downgraded to junk status, and its credit lines had all been severed. Working with Fourtou and new director Claude Bébéar, chairman of insurance giant AXA, Bronfman searched for short-term financing to keep Vivendi alive long enough to restructure. "I flew to Paris with Edgar during the ouster weekend and spent eight or ten days there," recalls Michael Klein, then Citibank's European head of markets and banking. "He and Claude took my passport away."

Pledging a fire sale, Vivendi's new management cobbled together €1 billion from the banks. Says Klein, "Edgar had a sense of calm and the ability to see the issues. It's clear to me that Vivendi would not have survived—certainly not as it is—without him."

With Vivendi in ruins, Bronfman's first two goals were to rebuild some of the value in the family's remaining shares by getting the company back on its feet and to repurchase any Universal assets spun off in the restructuring. But while the company was shedding many of its operations, sometimes at fire-sale prices, the board would not consider selling him the US studio and the record business. After Vivendi accepted reduced prices for its publishing properties, environmental division, internet company, and stake in EchoStar, he exploded. In an interview with journalists Jo Johnson and Martine Orange, Edgar lashed out, laying the company's unwillingness to sell him Universal to French xenophobia and a deep-seated anti-Semitism.

"There's an anti-American tinge to the desire to keep the Hollywood assets," he said. "It's odd there's no similar sentiment in France about selling Vivendi Environment at knock-down prices or selling Houghton Mifflin cheaply or Canal Plus or Telepiu. It's the fact that Hollywood is Jewish, that the Bronfmans are a Jewish family. It's a fear not just of selling it back to the Americans but of selling it to

Jews. I feel this undercurrent of anti-Semitism. It's in the water. That Hollywood is a Jewish town has a lot to do with all this."

Bronfman had helped rid Vivendi Universal of Messier and set the company on a road to respectability. But whatever prudence he'd shown in the closing minutes of the saga was dwarfed by the monumental failure of the merger, the family's loss of Seagram and several billion dollars, and the humiliation of championing a deal that now looked idiotic. The normally evenhanded *New York Times* left open only the barest possibility that he would ever be taken seriously again as a businessman. "His reputation as a financial steward," the paper declared, "has been the butt of jokes ever since he sold his family's liquor empire, Seagram, to Vivendi in 2000, only to watch the whole thing nearly implode."

Years after Vivendi Universal went down in flames, Edgar continued to defend the logic of the original deal. Defensive and self-righteous, Bronfman refused to second-guess himself for making the deal and still argued that it would have been spot-on if only the megalomaniacal Messier hadn't destroyed everything. "My biggest mistake? The fact that Messier so misled Vivendi," he said. "It obfuscated the successful job I'd done." He certainly didn't see the inflated price Messier offered for Seagram as *his* mistake or allow that the strikingly similar collapse of AOL Time Warner suggested there hadn't been any advantage in such a merger. Indeed, Edgar's biggest regret was not selling his Vivendi holdings. "If I had anything different to do, I should have sold all our stock."

Strenuously objecting to the idea that he'd destroyed the family fortune, Edgar claimed that whatever losses the Bronfmans had suffered hadn't touched their core wealth. "The piece we lost was the money I made," he said. But spinning events didn't change the fact that he had presided over a deal that lost a monumental amount of money and traded the family's signature business for a chimera.

9

Redemption Song

Edgar's protestations that he hadn't damaged the core of the Bronfman fortune impressed no one. In the eyes of the American press his makeover of Seagram had been the act of a "ludicrously vain pretender," a lamb who received the shearing he deserved. Humiliated, Edgar was driven to prove Vivendi an aberration, and he was still willing to put up the Bronfman bankroll to do it. He didn't make an auspicious start.

Bronfman's primary investment vehicle was his own Lexa Partners and he found one deal, in the spring of 2002, while Vivendi Universal was reaching the apex of its financial crisis. He put up over $150 million to acquire 32 percent of the British luxury goods company Asprey & Garrard from Prince Jefri Bolkiah, the brother of the Sultan of Brunei. The remainder was purchased by Tommy Hilfiger founders Silas Chou and Lawrence Stroll, the TAG Group—the private holding company for Lebanon's Ojjeh family—and Morgan Stanley Private Equity. The new owners' game plan was to modernize and expand both operations without sullying their exclusive image and then take the company public. Jade Jagger, the daughter of Mick and Bianca Jagger, was hired as Garrard's creative director, and Asprey Jewelers spent a reported $60 million on a Fifth Avenue flagship store at Trump Tower meant to presage a major American expansion. By 2006 Bronfman lost virtually all of his $130-million investment.

In August, one month after Messier's removal, Edgar invested in Accretive, a small New York private equity firm founded by J. Michael Cline, a former partner at the international equity group General Atlantic. Bronfman knew Cline because their children attended school together. The Accretive investment that most interested Edgar was the movie ticketing service Fandango. As an Accretive general partner, Edgar took a seat on Fandango's board.

Vacationing in Anguilla over the Christmas holiday, Bronfman ran into publishing executive Richard Snyder and invited him to bring Lexa any proposals he deemed promising. The two were only casual business acquaintances, having served together for a year on the board of Barry Diller's USA Networks. Coincidentally, Bronfman's primary contact with Snyder, as with Cline, was through their children. Though Snyder never invested heavily with the partnership, he joined Lexa and moved into the Manhattan office the firm shared with Bronfman's financial advisor, Gary Fuhrman.

Bronfman next saw an opportunity when Columbia House, the mail-order music company jointly owned by Sony and Time Warner, was put on the block, but by the time he jumped in a sale to the Blackstone Group was already well along. In February 2003, Prestige Brands—the health-care and cleaning products company whose brands include Comet, Spic and Span, Prell Shampoo, and Compound W Wart Remover—was shopped and Bronfman was interested enough to fly to Florida with Snyder and meet with the company's bankers. Prestige ultimately opted not to sell, and it was hard to imagine Bronfman hawking scrubbing pads and eyedrops. Edgar's primary interest remained the entertainment business, and Universal was the company he really wanted. But even in his continuing role as a member of the Vivendi Universal board he remained unable to convince the new management team to sell it back to him.

A few weeks after the Prestige talks, his father mentioned that Ted Turner had suggested over lunch that Edgar Jr. contact Time Warner's new CEO, Richard Parsons, and make an offer to buy the Warner Music Group.

It was no secret that the debt-riddled AOL Time Warner was looking for money. The blockbuster merger with AOL, which Bronfman and Messier had mimicked, had proven an even bigger bust than Vivendi Universal. Almost as soon as the deal closed, the internet bubble began to lose air. By the fall of 2000, the NASDAQ was down 40 percent. The predicted boom in internet advertising—on which the AOL Time Warner merger had made hay—was not in the foreseeable future. AOL Time Warner was a listing ship and everyone onboard—including Roger Ames and the record division—was madly bailing water. "The parent company had to shed unbelievable costs," he recalls. Despite the growing problem with downloads, the Music Group was under orders from corporate to show market and revenue growth for Wall Street. It was an impossible mission. The company's stock, once trading at $58.51, plunged to a low of $8.60.

By 2003, Parsons, like Fourtou at Vivendi, was casting himself as a caretaker and healer trying to clean up the financial mess Gerald Levin had left behind, including reducing Time Warner's $29-billion debt by at least a third. Among those burned the worst was Ted Turner, who had quit the Time Warner board in January but was still the company's largest shareholder with 10 percent of its outstanding shares. "So I picked up the phone and called Dick Parsons," says Bronfman. "We talked—I think I even signed a confidentiality agreement—but he decided to sell pieces of the music operation first."

The person urging Parsons to break off and sell bits of the record group was Ames. The AOL merger had cost Roger his deal with EMI. "Instead of being a public music company reporting to a board, now we're part of AOL Time Warner with fucking idiots—*lunatics!*—running the asylum," Ames fumed years later. "*God!* Imagine how different the world would look now if the European Commission had killed the Time Warner–AOL deal. EMI Records and Warner Music Group would have merged, and Time Warner would have wound up losing $1 billion instead of $100 billion."

In 2002, Ames tried another music merger, this time with Bertelsmann Music Group (BMG), the German-owned record company whose labels included RCA, Arista, and Jive records. It wasn't as promising a match as EMI. BMG ranked last in worldwide sales of the five major record companies. In a stunning example of the company's ineptitude, Clive Calder, a music publishing and record executive, had recently forced them to pay a staggering $3 billion to buy out his Zomba Music and Jive Records as part of a deal they had undertaken years earlier. Though Jive boasted Britney Spears, 'NSync, the Backstreet Boys, and R. Kelly, the price was silly. "You could buy the EMI Group right now for about that," one industry analyst complained. Ames took a more philosophic and mercenary view. "They got some great assets with Zomba," he said. "They overpaid, but in a merger, why do I care?"

BMG's parent company, Bertelsmann, was in as much turmoil as AOL Time Warner. Under chairman and CEO Thomas Middelhoff, it had rapidly expanded its holdings to include not just the record company but over four hundred magazines, two of the largest American book publishers, Doubleday and Random House, and twenty-two European television stations. Middelhoff's global dreams required money. But his solution—taking the company public—was derailed by the descendants of company founder Reinhard Mohn. After 160 years, the Mohns still controlled Bertelsmann through a family foundation and feared the dilution of their power. In the summer of 2002, they fired Middelhoff.

The deal had other problems. A proposed $400-million sale of Time Warner's book publishing division to Bertelsmann had already fallen apart, so no one at AOL Time Warner trusted them. And Roger's immediate boss, Jeffrey Bewkes, chairman of Time Warner's entertainment and networks group, didn't see much upside to staying in the record business, telling associates Warner Music was "the hair on the tail of a dog" and a business that produced a lot of head scratching from analysts. Bewkes preferred to sell the whole operation. As far as he was concerned, the only thing the cash-strapped AOL Time Warner needed from the record industry was cash or cost-savings—and the BMG merger didn't promise enough of either.

The deal would likely cost Warner $300 million to $400 million in salary expenses for layoffs and, though it had the potential to increase the value of AOL Time Warner's music holdings by 50 percent, it would probably take four years to get the two music companies integrated and up to speed. That kind of timetable didn't interest Bewkes. "There's no emotional attachment to companies at Time Warner," says Ames. "Actually, there's no emotional attachment to companies anywhere."

In early 2003, when Ames's original merger target, EMI, came calling with a $2.5-billion offer to buy the Warner Music Group outright and take the expanded EMI Music public, Roger was cool to the idea. If he didn't like any deal in which he was likely to lose his job, he also thought Time Warner could do better by selling off ancillary parts of the Warner Music Group. He urged Parsons to sell the publishing and CD manufacturing operations and merge the record labels with EMI. This way, Ames suggested, they could raise $3 billion selling assets and still wind up as part owners of the world's second-largest record company. "You'll look like a genius," Ames told Parsons. In October the CD manufacturing company was sold to Canada's Cinram for $1 billion. Ames hoped to sell the music publishing division, Warner/Chappell, which boasted a massive catalog ranging from standards like "Happy Birthday" to the songs of Madonna, Led Zeppelin, and Bruce Springsteen, for $2 billion. "Goldman Sachs was ready to provide financing for [music publishing executive] Charles Koppelman," he says. Investor Ted Forstmann and Israeli entertainment mogul Haim Saban were also said to be interested.

It was a clever plan—or would have been. But later in the year Bertelsmann took the merger plans it had developed with Warner and proposed combining BMG with Sony Music. The European Commission might be ready to approve one big record company merger, but it certainly wasn't going to approve two of them in rapid succession. Cash-strapped Time Warner was back to being a seller.

• • •

During the same period, Vivendi finally came around to the idea that selling off Universal Studios and the record division was its best shot at financial stability. For Bronfman, the question wasn't whether to bid, but how to structure the offer. For a man whose business acumen had been officially decreed a joke, Bronfman had surprisingly little trouble finding partners.

The Carlyle Group, Washington, DC's, largest private equity firm, called him. But Bronfman knew he could make a more competitive bid by marrying Universal Studios with an existing network and instead approached James Dolan at Cablevision. The New York cable company owned several networks including American Movie Classics, the Independent Film Channel, and Women's Entertainment, and Bronfman convinced Dolan to contribute the networks to a combined company in return for a stake of between 25 percent and 33 percent. Edgar planned to become chairman of the expanded company, and he and his father resigned from the Vivendi Universal board so Efer's offer could be considered. Along with his own group, Lexa, and Cablevision, Bronfman's investors included two leading private equity firms, the Boston-based Thomas H. Lee and New York's Blackstone Group. Debt financing would be handled by Wachovia Securities and Merrill Lynch.

The competition was stiff. Viacom, DreamWorks, Liberty Media, the General Electric–owned NBC, and Barry Diller were all tagged as potential buyers, and the Carlyle Group joined a group led by billionaire Marvin Davis that opened the bidding with a $15-billion offer. Most of the deal gossip focused on Universal Studios, but Bronfman was also keen to reacquire the Music Group, which he'd built into the world's largest record company. Unauthorized downloading was an increasing drag on earnings, but Edgar had come to believe the problem would either be resolved or factored into a new business model. In April 2003, Apple launched the first commercially viable internet music store with iTunes, and Bronfman believed other services would follow. He also saw a huge, untapped market in selling music to cell phones. When that happened, whatever he paid now would be a bargain.

Vivendi came to the same conclusion that Edgar did. After a nine-hour meeting on July 1 to weigh the first round of bids, the board opted not to include the Music Group in the sale. "They figured the business was going to get better," said Bronfman. Though disappointed, he still believed his group had the edge on getting the studio. "The bet—which was almost correct—was that no one was going to be there because the other equity groups didn't have a Cablevision." As it turned out, Vivendi rejected Davis and his group—which had no similar property to pair with the studio—out of hand. Two of the parties invited to submit second bids, NBC and Viacom, appeared way behind, offering letters of interest instead of first-round bids. "I didn't think the new GE CEO [Jeffrey R. Immelt] would let [NBC chairman] Bob Wright get it." He smiled ruefully. "Like I said—*almost* correct."

Bronfman's intimate knowledge of Vivendi's finances made him confident that he knew better than anyone what kind of a deal the French board members were looking for and how to optimize Universal's assets. Vivendi was $13 billion in debt, so Bronfman saw a cash-oriented bid as the best bet: his group offered $12 billion for Universal—a 20 percent equity proposal that also included debt assumption and $8 billion in cash. It was clearly a serious bid aimed at addressing Vivendi's stated concerns. But to Edgar's frustration, the auction dragged on for four months. His partners, particularly Lee and Blackstone, grew restive at having their money tied up.

As late August approached, the field had narrowed to the Bronfman group and GE/NBC, but Edgar could feel the Vivendi board tipping inexorably against him. Desperate, he upped the offer to $13 billion. In press interviews, he argued that because NBC had never run a studio, an entertainment cable network (in fact, its cable holdings included at least one network, Bravo), or a theme park, they were "exactly the wrong outcome." In addition, their proposal, which included a 25 percent stake in the company but significantly less cash than the Bronfman group was offering, wasn't the kind of big debt-reduction deal Vivendi had said it was looking for. "I don't think it's a particularly attractive approach," he told British reporters.

Lobbying in public won him no champions in the Vivendi boardroom. It was increasingly clear that, talk of debt reduction notwithstanding, the company would much rather enter a partnership with NBC than with Cablevision and Bronfman. And by the beginning of September, Vivendi was exploiting the Bronfman bid to milk a few final concessions out of General Electric. "GE's the apple in their eye," a Vivendi executive said of the board. "They're able to come back to their shareholders and say, 'See, we're in business with one of the premier companies in the world.'"

It was a gut-wrenching moment for Bronfman, whose family was still Vivendi's largest shareholders. During a last-stab negotiation on September 1, Edgar was offered the thin solace that while he wasn't going to get his company back at least he'd helped Vivendi wring a better deal out of NBC. "I'm going downstairs to see GE," Fourtou told him. "Unless they give me what I want, this is yours. But if they do, know that you made Vivendi billions of dollars."

Edgar's hard-fought losing bid for Universal hadn't been a complete failure. The *New York Times,* while wryly noting that it's "not easy to feel sorry for a billionaire who gambled and lost much of his family fortune," admitted that Bronfman had regained a good deal of the financial community's respect and won over initially skeptical partners with the way he assembled and managed the consortium. "For a guy who certainly doesn't need to work for a living, he went about this as relentlessly and professionally as anybody has ever approached a deal," said investor Steve Rattner, who had a front-row seat to the negotiations as a key shareholder in Cablevision. Added Richard Snyder: "The most important part of it was that Edgar gained his credibility back on Wall Street and with the private equity groups. It was not easy."

He wouldn't have to wait more than a few weeks to put that public reassessment to the test.

In mid-October Bronfman, still smarting from having lost Universal, heard the rumors that EMI was going to buy Warner Music. He telephoned Scott Sperling, the managing director of Thomas H. Lee Partners, one of the private equity firms he had teamed with on the

Universal bid. "I don't know if they're going to sell," Bronfman said, "but let's bid."

Lee Partners' eschewal of hostile takeovers in favor of using a mix of debt, institutional investors, and its own funds—usually in concert with existing management—was atypical in an eat-or-be-eaten business. Like Bronfman, Sperling had a passion for the music industry. He was preparing to invest in two leading music management firms, Irving Azoff's Front Line Management, whose clients included the Eagles, Christina Aguilera, Van Halen, and Velvet Revolver, and Jeff Kwatinetz's the Firm, whose roster boasted Korn, Ice Cube, Linkin Park, Jennifer Lopez, Snoop Dogg, Kelly Clarkson, and actress Cameron Diaz. Lee Partners, along with another equity firm, Bain Capital, pumped approximately $20 million into the two companies, apparently with hopes of rolling them together and going public. A merger never happened, no doubt in part because Azoff and Kwatinetz detested each other, but Sperling justified the investment as a way to get Kwatinetz and Azoff as advisors on other entertainment deals.

Unbeknownst to Edgar, Kwatinetz also suggested to Lee and Bain that they bid for Warner Music Group. According to one executive privy to those discussions, Kwatinetz—whose own ambitions didn't end with running a talent agency—had even presented the investment companies with a plan for buying the labels, which he wanted to run. (Jeff Kwatinetz declined requests to be interviewed for this book.) But Bronfman saw himself running Warner Music Group—and the fact that he would be coming in as an equity player clearly trumped Kwatinetz.

An unsuccessful bidder for Warner Music's manufacturing operation, Sperling had stayed in touch with Time Warner's senior vice president of mergers and acquisitions, Rob Marcus. On October 28, Bronfman, Sperling, and Marcus, along with Jeff Bewkes and Dick Parsons, met in Parsons's office in Rockefeller Center.

Acknowledging that EMI had the inside track, Bronfman and Sperling suggested Time Warner could gain a lot by allowing them to bid on the Music Group since a sale to US investors could be both lucrative and a good deal easier than selling to EMI. For starters, there was the issue of Warner/Chappell, which owned or administered over 1 million songs. The European Commission would likely allow EMI to buy Warner Music, but it was almost certain to frown on including the publishing divisions, since EMI Music was already the largest music publisher in the world. Sperling knew that Morgan Stanley had lined up several potential buyers for Warner/Chappell, but a Lee-Bronfman group would be prepared to make one bid for the whole operation.

"We knew the EMI deal [for just the record labels] was like $800 million to $1 billion plus equity," says Bronfman. "But there were also regulatory stipulations, and we made the point to Dick that in that period he couldn't sell the publishing in a separate deal—so what if the record deal fell apart? He'd have to hold the publishing until the end of the regulatory hurdles. Our pitch to Dick was, 'Why *wouldn't* you want to see what your alternative is? We—Lee and Bronfman—will have the most money and expertise; we'll be the highest, most aggressive bidder.'"

Parsons proved willing to entertain a competing bid, but on a very tight schedule. The company's board was going to review EMI's offer at its November 20 meeting, less than a month away. That meant that a competing bid would have to be made without a thorough financial review. That didn't bother Bronfman or Sperling, who knew that a well-managed record company would throw off enough cash to finance its own buyout, even with the pressure from downloads.

"If you looked at the price as a multiple of free cash flow, it was still attractive," Sperling says. "I think that's one of the things that happened to the record industry: the cash flow led to excesses. It spits out *so* much cash—there's no comparison to the film business, which consumes rather than generates cash. You just had to believe piracy wasn't going to jam us down to zero. And we'd just looked at Universal Music Group and had a lot of understanding of how the banks would look at it." Throw in Warner/Chappell Publishing, whose income hadn't been nearly as impacted by downloading as the record operation and might fetch as much as $2 billion if spun off, and the partners believed it unlikely they could make a bad deal.

Bronfman and Sperling signed a confidentiality agreement and met with Ames and his senior executives, who urged Bewkes and Parsons to make a deal with the Bronfman-Lee group rather than EMI. "I thought it was crazy to go to the EU with two deals in front of it," says Ames. "If you're Time Warner, why take the risk? If you decide to exit, do you care if Bronfman is giving you $200 million less? The answer is no."

Bewkes had already told Sperling that Time Warner wouldn't take them seriously unless the bid was at the high end of the part-ners' tentative valuation of between $2.35 billion and $2.5 billion. Edgar, fearing they'd blow what might be their only opportunity, urged them to pick the higher number.

"The equity guys wanted us to come in at $50 million below that," he recalls, "but I argued that there was no real difference in the two amounts—that all we were saying was, 'We're going to try to screw you every step of the way.' And I knew that corporate guys don't trust equity guys, generally."

Along with Lee, Bain Capital, and a Lexa investment vehicle that Bronfman dubbed Music Partners Ltd., the group included Provi-dence Equity Partners. Bronfman, through Music Partners, con-trolled the second smallest share of the four equity partners with just 12 percent (Lee, which put up approximately $650 million, was the largest with 49 percent). Another partner, Israeli media mogul Haim Saban, dropped out just three days before the investors were to sub-mit their bid, apparently because he couldn't call the shots. "Saban walked because he wanted to be chairman," says one insider. Adds Bronfman: "I think he's used to being a leader. The idea of putting in a lot of money and just winding up with a seat on the board didn't appeal to him."

Replacing Saban's investment—between $100 million and $200 million—wasn't an issue. "Lee was unfazed and said his group would cover," Bronfman says. "What I was worried about was Providence." That firm had come to the table with Saban, and Bronfman fretted they would leave with him. But Providence chairman Jonathan Nel-son telephoned Edgar to say that he had enough faith in him and the deal to stay in. "Things did move very quickly, which was good," adds Bronfman. "When you put a lot of investment groups together it's like herding cats. The fact that it was truncated helped: everyone remained focused on the endgame; there was less time for people to overthink the deal."

On November 18, two days before the Time Warner board meeting, the Bronfman-Lee group submitted a bid of $2.6 billion. "Time Warner was driven to get this done, and I think up until the week before we did the deal the sense was that it would be EMI," says Edgar. But it was clear during a conference call that evening that they'd hit the mark. "They said, 'You heard us on the price,'" recalls Bronfman. "'We're not going to ask you to negotiate.' I think that was the moment it swung our way."

Two days later, Bronfman received the call he'd longed for: the board of directors of Time Warner had selected their bid over EMI's. There was, however, one hitch. In order for Time Warner to preserve the EMI offer as a fail-safe, the Bronfman-Lee deal had to close by Sunday night. The partners had expected to take two or three weeks to complete due diligence and now they had seventy-two hours.

Bronfman had to believe that the absence of a thorough due diligence was ultimately immaterial. "The deal really rested on our belief that we could take costs out of this business," he said. "That was it: Did you believe that *and* that the business is going to get better? And neither of those things is to be found in due diligence."

The deadline was extended until Monday morning. At 8:00 a.m. on Monday, November 24, Bronfman joined Dick Parsons in his office for the conference call from the investors and the attorneys confirming the sale.

Time Warner was finally out of the record business. And Edgar Bronfman Jr., the idiot, the fool, the spoiled rich kid who'd been eaten alive for trying to play with the adults, was back in it.

10

Of Animals and Treason

When Atlantic Records founder Ahmet Ertegun heard the news of Bronfman's successful eleventh-hour bid for the Warner Music Group, he complained to his senior executives. "I can't believe the company is being sold to that snot-nosed kid who used to knock on my door in the Hamptons with bad demos saying, 'I want to be a songwriter.'" Bob Krasnow, the former chairman of Elektra Records, was quick to credit Bronfman with a savvy deal, but saw no reason to believe he could actually run WMG. "This is a financial play," he said, two months after the successful IPO. "Bronfman could never get into [the record business] on his own. I have no lack of respect for his business acumen. But as for building a record company—this is a business about talent and intuition. The guys who are good are good, and they don't need ten years of training. When you know, you know. There are plenty of those guys around, like Jimmy Iovine and [Antonio] "L.A." Reid [CEO of Arista Records]. And then there are the guys who are the last ones picked for the team."

Roger Ames had recommended selling to the Bronfman-Lee

group instead of EMI because he thought it the best deal for Time Warner, but that didn't mean he had much faith in the new owners. He liked Bronfman well enough, but like Krasnow, Ames believed private equity lacked the passion and knowledge to find new talent and opportunities. "They're just in it to make money—which is their business," he told an associate. "That's not *my* business. I'm in the record business. If I could make the same money in the computer hardware business, I wouldn't be in it."

Even more problematic was the tepid public endorsement Bronfman received from his financial partner in the WMG acquisition, Scott Sperling. Sperling oversaw his firm's controlling interest in the music company and was sure to be Warner's most powerful director. In an interview with the *New York Times,* Sperling said Thomas H. Lee Partners had taken a close look at Edgar before joining forces with him and had come to the conclusion that he had been "unfairly knocked." But he also made it clear that as the company's new chairman and CEO, Bronfman would be on a short leash. "The deal with Edgar is, he does a good job or someone else comes in to do a good job."

Edgar was livid, but he couldn't deny his track record.

"I did not like reading it," he said. "But I felt about it a number of ways. First, given what happened at Vivendi, these guys went out on a limb—I was not walking around with the world's greatest rep. So they had to defend that. Second, my equity is my interest, not my salary. Even at Seagram I always felt I had a far greater interest in the company doing well as an investor than as an executive. If I can't do this, it's in my interest that someone else should. And personally, it bothers me when people do bad jobs and there are no consequences."

Bronfman and Sperling's first task was to reduce operating costs and use the savings to recoup the purchase price as quickly as possible, and Bronfman took pains to allay fears that they would accomplish that by flipping the company. Indeed, they passed on a chance to do that in February, before the deal with Time Warner even closed. Eric Nicoli, chairman of EMI—the company that Bronfman-Lee had just outbid—offered to acquire WMG. The two met for five hours at the Cross River, New York, estate of Bronfman's associate Richard

Snyder and a few days later, EMI made an offer of stock and cash worth over $3 billion that would have allowed Edgar to stay on as CEO of EMI Music. It was an intriguing bid: Bronfman-Lee had not yet completed the $2.6-billion purchase from Time Warner, and EMI was offering them more. According to Snyder, Bronfman fretted about having Alain Levy—who'd stymied his initial attempts to buy PolyGram and was now chairman and CEO of EMI Music—as his number two. More pointedly, Edgar and his partners thought they could do better on their own. Months later, when queried about spurning the offer, Bronfman offered a smug smile. "We said, 'Here's what we're going to do—and what we think the company will be worth as a result,'" he said. "So we didn't get very far." Instead, he said, the equity partners were committed to riding their investment for a minimum of three to five years.

Edgar had an equity stake in the company, but along with looking for a profit on his investment, he desperately needed to show that he could run a successful, forward-looking entertainment company. He'd fought with his family over remaking Seagram, insisting that it offered a better future as an entertainment company than in liquor or with DuPont. He viewed his position as chairman and CEO of Warner Music Group as the link between equity and WMG's senior staff. He knew who to hire, and, being sympathetic to the day-to-day struggles, could act as their advocate with the company's backers.

Edgar made a vague offer to Ames to stay as vice chairman, but neither man was particularly hot about the possibility. "It's tough for anyone to go from being CEO to non-CEO," says Bronfman. "And speaking from experience, it's *very* hard to do in the same company." Instead, Time Warner let Ames spend three months helping Bronfman with the transition—an arrangement that meant Ames could accompany the new owners on a bond road show that raised $680 million and immediately repaid half of their $1.25-billion investment.

Particularly helpful were Ames's existing plans for extensive cuts, plans that were shelved when the company was put up for sale. "A lot of the restructuring we did was already in the desk drawer," Bronfman said. "What we did and what they had planned was not that far apart." Along with cutting 20 percent of the company's 5,000 staffers and 30 percent of the artists on its various labels, the restructuring called for international operations to be drastically scaled back. Most dramatically, it would also shutter Elektra, the pop powerhouse that Jac Holzman began in the 1950s. Elektra's most successful artists—including Metallica and Missy Elliott—would be moved to Atlantic Records.

It was similar to General Motors's decision a few years later to eliminate their Pontiac division, and it left WMG with just two primary record companies, Atlantic in New York and Warner Bros. Records in Burbank. Coupled with extensive layoffs and roster cuts at WMG's overseas operations, the plan nearly turned back the clock thirty-five years to the days before the purchase of Elektra, when Warner Music was a strictly American operation.

Bronfman also wanted to rehire Lyor Cohen. At Universal, Edgar had approved the purchase of Def Jam and had been well aware of Cohen's style, track record, and legal problems, but they never had a direct day-to-day relationship and certainly didn't move in the same social circles. Ames, having tried to recruit Lyor to run WMG's record operation, primarily admired his ability to motivate his staff at Def Jam—"He's an extremely driven, fiercely competitive guy"—and he knew that because WMG had been stripped of its rap acts under Time Warner management, it desperately needed Cohen's acumen and experience if it was to expand its market share. In that regard, Cohen was an obvious choice. But the real challenge was reimagining the record operation for a post-Napster world where consumers didn't have to buy recordings. It was a huge leap for Cohen, who wasn't being asked just to make and market hits, but also to figure out how the company was going to stay relevant and survive. Whether he or any record executive possessed those skills was up for grabs. Certainly Doug Morris, the savviest, most successful executive in the business, didn't. Morris insisted that his job was only nurturing hits. "I wouldn't be able to recognize a good technology person," he said, washing his hands of the issue. "Anyone with a good bullshit story would have gotten past me." Morris had been the right man to build MCA Records in the 1990s, but he clearly wasn't up to meeting the industry's current challenges. Bronfman was betting that the ultracompetitive Cohen wasn't wed to anything but succeeding.

The voracious, street-tested Cohen had less in common with Bronfman than he did with Edgar's grandfather, the opportunistic and foulmouthed empire builder, Sam Bronfman. But perhaps that was his appeal to Edgar, who was impressed by Lyor's passion for winning and the loyalty he'd engendered at Def Jam. "In the best way," said Bronfman, "Lyor's an animal."

Running WMG's entire record operation was as big a portfolio as Cohen was ever likely to be offered. Having just recommitted to his marriage, Lyor told Edgar he'd have to discuss it with Amy. The couple ostensibly went off on a snowmobiling trip to Yellowstone National Park to weigh things, but there really wasn't much to discuss.

"There's no one I aspire to be," Lyor told his wife by way of offering to turn down the job. "Why would I do it?"

She knew him better than that. "To redefine the job and make it your own," she told him.

It was all the permission he needed.

"I said, 'Fuck, yeah!'" he later recalled, jubilant at the notion of moving on. "Let me be *me*."

Cohen had to go to Boston and meet Sperling and the representatives for Bain and Providence. "He was so nervous and insecure—he must have changed his shirt five times," says his friend Sean Carasov. "It was the challenge that got him excited, being on the ground floor. And the only guys he'd have to answer to were those money guys."

He need not have been nervous. Sperling admired Cohen's executive skills, particularly his ability to focus and motivate a staff. "Lyor's very good at artist relations, but he's disciplined. And that's not common." Still, Cohen quickly discovered that the investors weren't pushovers. They hammered out a contract that, though potentially lucrative, was pegged to Lyor's ability to institute financial cuts.

At a dinner to celebrate the completion of the sale of Warner Music, the partners were given clocks and engravings, but Lyor received a special commemorative token. It was a mock-up of the bodybuilding magazine *Flex* with Lyor's face on the front cover and a balance scale on the back. The lighter side of the scale was marked "Universal Music Group" while the weighted side had a picture of Lyor's head grafted onto Arnold Schwarzenegger's body. *"The balance is tipped to Warner Music Group!"* it read.

"And Lyor didn't think it was a joke," says Carasov.

Bronfman had not only an admiration for Cohen's work ethic but also an obvious affection for him. And Cohen, with his flair for drama and a lingering enmity for Morris and Universal, swore a personal fealty to Bronfman way beyond the norm. "After TVT I told my wife that I was damaged goods," Cohen says. "How could Edgar Bronfman put himself in such a harmful position with the private equity guys as to suggest me? I don't understand why he's come to me. My sense of obligation is so much more than economic gain. How could I even tell you what it meant to me?"

The month after buying WMG, Edgar had his first chance to hear music and watch videos for the upcoming releases on Warner's British record company, its most important foreign subsidiary. Little of what was played made him think the lagging UK operation was sitting on anything particularly promising. Then he heard singer-songwriter James Blunt. Produced by Linda Perry, an American songwriter responsible for pop hits by Gwen Stefani, Pink, and Christina Aguilera, Blunt had a simple and unabashedly sentimental ballad style and, despite being over thirty, his open-faced good looks made him seem boyish. Blunt's performance struck a chord in Bronfman. Before the presentation ended, he sent a message to Cohen on his BlackBerry. "I'm watching a major star," he wrote.

Bronfman's enthusiasm for the songwriter helped make Blunt a company priority and his mawkish song "You're Beautiful" a global hit. "It was the look, the voice, the quality of the songs that made me kind of pound the table," Bronfman said. Blunt's debut album, *Back to Bedlam,* sold 11 million copies worldwide and gave the new regime its first big seller.

Placing his personal imprimatur on Blunt was a classic mogul moment for Bronfman and precisely the kind of involvement entertainment executives seek out and trumpet when they're crafting a reputation as a star maker or an industry ringmaster. But it's revealing that there aren't any other moments like it. Bronfman's interest in Blunt was a singular case; being a songwriter with a similar sentimental stripe, Edgar admired the talent and became its advocate. But he was not going to play a major role in roster decisions. Along with getting back the money he and his partners had put up to buy WMG, Edgar's primary concern was assembling the senior staff that could recast Warner Music and thrive in a post-Napster world.

First and foremost an investor, Bronfman embraced profit participation as the primary spur for senior executives. "I've spent a lot of time talking with Lyor about people—who we keep and who we hire," Edgar said. "I'm a big believer in entrepreneurship. I think I can create an environment that's supportive with a profit model."

In essence, Bronfman was trying to re-create the management organization with which his idol, Steve Ross, had built the Warner Music Group. But this was a different era. The business wasn't growing by leaps and bounds; it was treading water at best and at risk of drowning. Bronfman's task was to create a team to streamline the Warner Music Group and meet the challenge of the internet. Just as important, he and his partners wanted to take the company public as quickly as possible, and he told senior executives they would be along for the ride. "Obviously, it's a different era than when Steve Ross was here," he said. "But broad brushstroke, he knew to reward great management."

Cohen's first assignment was cutting $225 million, which translated to one thousand layoffs and a 30 percent roster cut. The company needed to be refocused, but the cost savings were also designed to provide a quick financial return for the new owners. Still, they couldn't afford to be seen as profiteers; it was essential to the company's future that the cuts not weaken its ability to deliver hits and attract performers.

There were equally subtle and problematic issues regarding whom to retain among senior management. Many of the key executives who now ran Atlantic and Elektra were people Doug Morris had trained over ten years earlier. Most of them, including Elektra chairwoman Sylvia Rhone, Atlantic copresidents Ron Shapiro and Craig Kallman, and Lava Records head Jason Flom, still felt a personal and professional debt to Morris and remained close. Any Morris loyalists interested in surviving the new regime would have to be reborn as Cohen loyalists.

The bad blood between Cohen and Morris was no secret, and suddenly being known as "one of Doug's guys" wasn't such a great thing. To add to the animosity, Cohen hoped to bring on his own executives from Def Jam, particularly Julie Greenwald and Kevin Liles. But Morris was unwilling to overlook a clause in Cohen's contract barring him from taking Universal executives to another company, despite the fact that if they stayed behind, their close association with Cohen likely meant the end of their careers. Morris eventually relented and released them. And when Doug hired Arista Records executive and producer Antonio "L.A." Reid as Cohen's replacement at Island Def Jam and Reid brought several Arista employees with him, the record business began to look like a game of musical chairs in which longtime WMG execs would be the losers. Recalls one Elektra executive: "The joke going around was that there should have been a memo: 'If you work at Def Jam, please report to 1290 [1290 Avenue of the Americas, the address of Atlantic Records]; if you work at Arista, report to Universal Music Group. And if you work at Elektra, we wish you well.'"

The old East Coast–West Coast animosity between Atlantic and Warner Bros. remained in place. If the record companies were going to achieve cost savings, the most obvious solution was combining backroom functions and standardizing operations. Warner Bros. Records chairman Tom Whalley was in no hurry to surrender anything to Lyor. "Could Tom Whalley have done the job instead of Lyor?" asks a former label executive. "He might be ruthless and standoffish but he has produced cash on the bottom line. He runs the biggest WMG company to great effect. It's got to be a constant irritant to him that Lyor is his boss."

In the weeks following Lyor's arrival, the resistance was immediate and obvious. "We had a meeting about standardizing packaging," one exasperated New York executive recalls. "It was the same bullshit we've been talking about for fourteen years. 'Let's make everything black and white, let's limit the number of pages in the CD booklet to eight,' that kind of stuff. But Warner Bros. says, 'The profit and loss on each project is the way we look at it. So we look at it differently.' It's Warner Bros. running its same shtick and Lyor just punts. I thought, *Not even this gangster can get Warner Bros. to play ball.*"

Indeed, while the West Coast label was going to have to share some of the pain of cutbacks, there was little Cohen could force on Whalley: his label was in far better shape than Atlantic. In the six months following the Bronfman-Lee buyout, Whalley would enjoy the protection of an enormous hit in Green Day's *American Idiot,* which was in the process of selling a reported 22 million recordings worldwide.

Cohen, for all his reputation as a street brawler, opted not to push Whalley. "Lyor made an effort to get them on board—then decided it wasn't worth it," the executive adds. "I think Lyor's strategy was to get the East Coast big enough that he could get on a plane and force Whalley to do what he wanted him to." That meant folding Elektra and rebuilding Atlantic.

"We lived for a long time with the rumor that Elektra and Atlantic were going to be combined and that Sylvia Rhone was going to Motown," says former Elektra marketing vice president Brian Cohen. Under Rhone, Elektra had sputtered. Worse, two years earlier she had made a stupid mistake: she'd tried to muscle Lyor Cohen.

The issue had been competing records. Elektra and Def Jam had important debut albums scheduled to hit the streets the same day. Elektra had a record by Tweet, a young neo-soul singer and the protégée of one of the label's biggest stars, Missy Elliott; Def Jam had Ashanti. Rhone had called Cohen and suggested that Def Jam should give Elektra a clear lane by changing its release date on Ashanti.

Instead, Def Jam offered Ashanti's self-titled album to retailers at a deep discount and promoted the singer heavily on the radio. When the first week's numbers came in, *Ashanti* had sold 504,000 albums to top the *Billboard* Top 200 Albums chart and her single "Foolish" was also at number 1 on the *Billboard* Hot 100 Singles chart. Tweet sold 195,000 CDs and landed at number 3. "She was insecure," one executive said of Rhone. "Lyor *knew* she was weak."

Rhone lamely tried to allay the fears of her staff by telling them that nothing was going to happen, but Elektra soon moved out of its office at 75 Rockefeller Plaza and into Atlantic's at 1290 Avenue of the Americas. Not surprisingly, Elektra's flaws became even more pronounced as staffers grew so worried about their jobs that they couldn't concentrate on making records. Morale was so bad that on one Friday the staff mimicked the Hawaiian shirt day segment of the popular film *Office Space,* with its own "*I'm fuckin' great*" T-shirt day. Lyor was not amused, but label executives encouraged it as a way to rally people even if they were likely to lose their jobs. "I thought, *This is torture—this is wrong,*" recalled Brian Cohen, who'd already decided to leave the company and open a summer camp. "I started counseling people: you need to get your head out of here. Concentrate on the three acts we care about."

The Warner sale closed on March 1. That morning, the chairmen of Elektra and Atlantic, Rhone and Val Azzoli, and Atlantic copresident Ron Shapiro were dismissed. Lyor addressed the Atlantic and Elektra staffs for the first time. Speaking passionately, he talked about being a family man, about how he'd built and loved Def Jam and how hard it had been to leave a company he considered "his" in order to rebuild Warner Music. No matter how the music business changed, he pledged, the company would always be about building careers for great artists and being accountable to that. Says one attendee: "He was talking about doing the job with heart and making it count. He sounded so vulnerable, and I remember thinking, *Gee, I want to work for this guy—how do I get on the list?*"

Cohen had no trouble inspiring people to follow him, but his handling of the layoffs did not inspire continued confidence. He first implied to senior executives that he was going to interview everyone in the company's field offices before making any decisions, but in the end he met only a handful of employees before handing the job off to his protégée, Julie Greenwald, the new president of Atlantic Records.

Greenwald had joined Rush Management, Def Jam's sister company, in 1992 as Lyor's assistant. "I meet this big, tall Israeli guy with either an accent or a speech impediment," she recalled. "He says, 'Why should I hire you?' and I told him that I'm a hard worker. When he asked if I could type, I lied and said fifty words per minute. But we clicked. I sat on the arm of the sofa with a makeshift desk. He'd be screaming, working, doing deals."

True to her word, Greenwald worked as hard as Cohen, and two months later, when he took over Def Jam, he moved Greenwald into the promotion department as his eyes and ears. Ten years later she was a vice president and received a seven-figure bonus from the Def Jam sale before being appointed president of Island Records. Throughout her ascent, Greenwald remained devoted to Cohen and his mission: obliterate the competition. There seemed to be nothing she wouldn't do for him and the company. She risked ruining her credit rating when she covered a Def Jam cash crunch by putting $96,000 of the rap group Public Enemy's tour expenses on her personal American Express card. If possible, she seemed even more driven and abrasive than her mentor. To some in the industry she was Lyor's Frankenstein.

Greenwald moved into her corner office at Atlantic's headquarters when she was seven months pregnant. She hung family photos on one wall, and six business photos on the others—five featuring Lyor, including a shot of Julie wedged between him and rapper Jay-Z in the back of a red Cadillac convertible, a large framed poster of the singer Madonna, inscribed, *"To Julie—the OTHER Madonna. Love, Madonna,"* and a large print from an *Esquire* photo shoot of rapper Ja Rule splayed regally across a chaise longue on a Los Angeles hotel balcony. Behind him, Irv Gotti and Lyor Cohen, in dark suits and looking grim, appear to be dangling someone over the balcony by the ankles.

Craig Kallman, Atlantic's remaining former copresident, and Jason Flom, the head of Lava Records, accepted new positions as the cochairmen of Atlantic. Passionate and knowledgeable music executives, neither was known as an administrator. "Jason has a regular-guy manner and he's trust-driven," says one former associate. "Once he commits to you, he never uncommits. But he's an antimeeting guy." Kallman, also popular with his coworkers, was interested in signing acts, not overseeing budgets. He did his best work at night, visiting clubs in search of new bands and answering emails in the wee hours of the morning. "There's no way a guy like this could run a company," says a former staffer. "But Lyor's girl can run a railroad. It became very clear after Julie got there that she was going to run the company." Indeed, though Kallman and Flom appeared to outrank Greenwald, she didn't report to them. She reported to Lyor.

Greenwald consulted extensively with Kallman on the layoffs, but they were her responsibility. She wasted no time in deciding who would stay. For those let go—most frequently employees who had worked for Elektra or were unfortunate enough to have been hired by a senior executive no longer with Atlantic—it was impossible to discern a plan. "It became a free-for-all," said one.

Greenwald defended her choices. "I had to pick between people at Elektra, Atlantic, and Lava, and I wanted to pick the best people," she said. "I needed people who wanted to sign on—I didn't want the old company, we had a new mantra."

Not surprisingly, that new mantra sounded strikingly similar to Def Jam's. A major record company like Atlantic signed many artists and released hundreds of records, and after radio or MTV responded to a handful of them, concentrated their spending on those few. Def Jam signed just a few artists and marketed and developed them until radio and other media couldn't ignore them.

"Def Jam was the most profitable label at Universal Music Group with just fifteen artists," said Greenwald. "At Island, the story was the same. We slowed down the company, broke Sum 41 and Saliva, and used that to attract better bands. We lived by the 'less is more' philosophy, not by throwing seventeen things out there. We put an X on an act's back. And then we go and get it."

Bronfman had no objection to Lyor re-creating Atlantic in Def Jam's image: Time Warner's decision to sell Interscope and get out

of the hip-hop business had cost the company its leadership position in the American market, and it had never recovered. Nine years
later, hip-hop had generated $1 billion in record sales, and Warner
Music desperately needed to get back in as soon as possible. Still, he
didn't wish to appear disrespectful of the company's history. Ahmet
Ertegun may have been cynical about Bronfman, but when Lyor ini-
tiated a charm offensive on the eighty-one-year-old executive, telling
him that he wanted to sit at his feet and learn everything he could
teach him, Ertegun was smitten. "Lyor is the great thing Edgar did,"
he said. "He's a terrific record man—he has a great sense of what
happens and how to make it happen. And Julie has injected life and
enthusiasm into a dejected company."

The decision to fold Elektra—similar to the way Morris wound
down the Geffen, A&M, and Mercury imprints when Seagram
owned Universal—was not a difficult one. "I think it'd been entirely
adrift for a while, and ten years later there wasn't enough there to
justify a label," Bronfman said. He was spared industry criticism in
no small measure because Elektra founder Jac Holzman agreed with
the decision to shut the label.

Sylvia Rhone had ignored Holzman but he didn't know Bronfman. He was convinced that Edgar had made a good deal and sent
him a congratulatory email. "The way he put the deal together was
very smart," he said later. "The security of having the music publishing company—I would say it covers at least 70 percent of their debt—
that's the big leverage in terms of cleaning this up. I thought it was
the best deal since Sony bought CBS Records. In Time Warner you
had a petrified seller with no understanding of the value of copyright
and catalog that couldn't wait to sell it."

Bronfman surprised Holzman by answering his message in just
twenty minutes and inviting him to lunch, whereupon he asked the
seventy-four-year-old if he was interested in being part of the company again. The offer touched the legendary label head. "Guys my
age don't get asked back. The fact that Edgar doesn't look at the
white hair—that's a point of view that's different. It tells me all that I
need to know."

A lifelong techie—Holzman's post-Elektra career had included stints on the board of directors of Atari, as the chairman of Panavision, as a cable and satellite consultant to Steve Ross, and as a music industry representative to Philips when that company developed the compact disc with Sony—he told Bronfman that he'd like to be involved in Warner's internet initiatives. "Come back with the deal you want on one sheet of paper," Edgar told him. "I want to use you the way Steve Ross did. I want you to create your own job." Pleased and flattered, Holzman soon became chairman of Cordless, WMG's new online label.

At Warner Bros., Seymour Stein, whose Warner-distributed Sire Records had signed Madonna, Talking Heads, and the Ramones, was already on board. But Warner's rift with Mo Ostin had never been repaired. Rejecting a suggestion to offer Ostin a seat on the company's board, a move that would have necessitated making the same offer to Ertegun and Holzman, Bronfman opted to rename the California-based label's Burbank headquarters in Ostin's honor. Like the folding of Elektra, it was the kind of move he'd made before. After purchasing MCA and retiring Lew Wasserman, Bronfman had renamed MCA's famous "Black Tower" for him.

Superficial nods to the company's storied past notwithstanding, Bronfman and Cohen had to convince their artists that they were moving in the right direction. Lyor was a controversial choice to run the record operation. He did not have a strong track record in pop and rock, where WMG did most of its business. While his adversarial style was excellent for motivating a staff, it had not made him popular outside the label. Two top artist managers, Cliff Burnstein and Peter Mensch, who had several important WMG artists, made it clear they didn't trust Cohen with their clients.

Their firm, QPrime, boasted one of rock and pop's premier rosters, ranging from country-pop diva Shania Twain to alternative rockers the Black Keys and Fountains of Wayne. One of QPrime's most successful bands, Metallica, was about to be moved from Elektra to Atlantic as part of WMG's restructuring. Mensch and Burnstein believed that Lyor had reneged on a pledge at Island Def Jam to provide tour support for another QPrime client, the Scorpions. Because they had a good relationship with Tom Whalley at Warner Bros. Records in Burbank–the home of another of QPrime's biggest acts, the Red Hot Chili Peppers–they insisted that Metallica's contract be transferred there.

Bronfman agreed to the move but gave little weight to the underlying complaints. "Artist managers are happy with record companies almost never," he said. "We'll either do the job or we won't."

Dennis Lavinthal, copublisher of the industry trade magazine *Hits,* detested Cohen. Though Lavinthal declined to comment on Cohen, he told associates he had played a role in helping Def Jam make a lucrative deal, but that Lyor had stiffed him. When Cohen took over the day-to-day running of WMG, *Hits* began ridiculing him in virtually every issue and rooting for the company's failure. A video cartoon on the magazine's website regularly portrayed a foul-mouthed version of Cohen, and in one installment gave him a pair of rabbit's ears and obliterated him Bugs Bunny–style with a "Karma Train" emblazoned with the names of supposedly aggrieved former associates.

Most significantly, one of Warner's biggest-selling artists read the change in ownership as an opportunity to extract a payday.

In 1992, at the height of her commercial success, Madonna and her manager, Freddy DeMann, had negotiated a deal with Warner Music for their own label, Maverick Records. Though she would remain on Warner Bros. Records where she'd recorded for twelve years, the new label was a chance for the ambitious singer to prove her mettle as an executive and create equity. Madonna described Maverick as an "artistic think tank," a cross between Andy Warhol's Factory and the Bauhaus of the 1920s that would develop books and films as well as produce records.

Madonna had paid off time and time again for Warner Bros., and the company, which was financing the label in return for a 40 percent stake, doubtless hoped to make a profit on any new acts that Maverick signed. But that was secondary. Madonna had been one of their biggest and most consistent-selling artists for over a decade, and Maverick was a way to compensate her and keep her happy. She had already received Time Warner stock options valued at between $20 million and $25 million, but with the AOL merger the options had lost almost all of their value. And though vanity labels rarely paid off, who knew? Between Madonna and the savvy DeMann—who'd also managed Michael Jackson and Steve Winwood—Maverick might actually make money.

It did make money, and quickly. The Seattle band Candlebox and techno-rockers Prodigy scored hit albums. Then Maverick released *Jagged Little Pill* by the twenty-four-year-old Canadian singer Alanis Morissette, which sold an astounding 23 million copies worldwide.

Neither Madonna nor DeMann was the hot hand behind these hits. That was Guy Oseary, a former classmate of DeMann's daughter at Hollywood High School who had talked his way into the office and a berth as DeMann's protégé. It wasn't long before he was running the label. Two years later Madonna and DeMann ended their management agreement. In 1999, when DeMann wanted to take advantage of a buyout provision to sell Maverick to Warner Music, Madonna decided to double down and buy him out of his stake. The payment—$20 million—was borrowed as an advance against future Maverick earnings when the label signed a new five-year deal with Warner Bros. But despite a pair of million-selling albums from the singer Michelle Branch, Maverick soon took a downward turn. It sold its music publishing company to Warner Music in 1999 and, over the next three years, halved its staff.

In the summer of 2003, Madonna sat down with Time Warner chairman Richard Parsons to negotiate a buyout of her stake in Maverick and was unpleasantly surprised to discover that the price she had in mind—approximately $60 million—was at least twice what Time Warner said it was worth. She hired lawyers Allen Grubman and Bertram Fields, who told reporters that Madonna was considering suing Time Warner for breach of contract. Normally the threat might have prodded the company to move, but that same week the Time Warner board was meeting to determine whether to sell the record company to EMI or the Bronfman-Lee group. Placating Madonna was going to be someone else's headache.

The following spring, on March 23—three weeks after the new

owners closed on the Warner Music Group—Allen Grubman telephoned Bronfman. "Look," he said, "if you don't solve this in twenty-four hours, we'll go to court."

"Allen, this is nuts," said Bronfman. "Give us some time."

"No, she's implacable."

Madonna now proposed that her stake in Maverick was worth $200 million. Bronfman suggested that WMG would be willing to buy her share for $15 million, $5 million less than DeMann had received for his smaller stake five years earlier and half of what Time Warner had valued it at less than a year earlier. Anticipating that the singer might make good on her threat, Warner Music Group attorneys had drawn up a preemptive lawsuit, and the day after Grubman called, they filed it in the Delaware Court of Chancery.

Madonna was outraged—or at least seemed so in the *New York Times*. "I find myself in the ludicrous position of being sued by my own record company, whom I have been loyal, industrious, and reliable to for over twenty years," she said in a prepared statement. "For them to behave this way is nothing short of treason."

Despite Maverick's early hits, Warner's suit alleged that the company had been losing money for the last five years and had $26.5 million in unpaid advances—including the $20 million Madonna and Oseary had used to buy out DeMann—and an additional $66 million in expenses.

Making broad claims for unrecouped costs was a favorite record company tactic for turning back artists' monetary demands, and Madonna responded by filing her own suit in Los Angeles superior court the following day. In it, she charged Warner with "engaging in acts of self-dealing and profit-taking, falsely accounting for receipts and expenses of the partnership . . . and secretly attempting to seize partnership opportunities for their own benefit." She maintained that Maverick was actually profitable but that Warner had employed "artificial and improper accounting methodology to create the false impression of losses." More to the point, her attorney, Bertram Fields, suggested that regardless of how the case turned out, Warner's new owners would live to regret this fight. "It's a very strange way to make your most important artist happy," he said.

Bronfman dispatched his new head of corporate relations, Will Tanous, to speak to the press about the company's "deep respect for Madonna." But Tanous pointedly added that "Warner Music Group is simply seeking to affirm that the claims Maverick Records has been making against the company are baseless, unsubstantiated, and without merit," a remark that, while long on tact, was noticeably short on deep respect.

In the end, Madonna sold her 30 percent interest in Maverick to Bronfman for $17 million—only $2 million more than he'd offered in the first place and a figure that almost certainly could have been reached without any public posturing. Guy Oseary opted to keep his 20 percent of the company, and Warner—which now owned 80 percent of Maverick—gave Oseary a multiyear contract to run it.

As for Madonna, she still owed Warner Bros. two new studio albums and a "hits" collection and wasn't going anywhere for several years. Three months after the Maverick dustup, Cohen and Bronfman invited her in to try to mend fences. Edgar greeted her with a gift-wrapped box. "Look," he said. "You've been incredibly important to this company for twenty years. You are who you are." The gift—a diamond bracelet—wasn't the kind of gesture Bronfman had ever made to one of his artists before, but it seemed to hit the right note. "She was like a little girl," he recalled. "It broke the ice."

Still, Bronfman had the victory he needed: everyone knew who was running Warner Music.

11

The "Try Anything" Company

When the Bronfman-Lee group purchased WMG from Time Warner in 2004, legitimate online sales figures were abysmal: less than
3 percent of the company's $3.4 billion in revenues came from digital
sales. Speaking with potential investors for Warner's stock offering,
Bronfman continued to defend the controversial lawsuits the RIAA
was bringing against individuals for illegal downloading, even when
it was impossible to demonstrate that they were effective. Yet behind
closed doors he was being much more pragmatic in plotting WMG's
internet strategy than he'd been at Vivendi Universal. In the five
years since Napster's debut he had seen firsthand how the record
industry's efforts to master or make money on the internet had failed
at every turn, and he recognized that single-mindedly asserting the
record industry's legal rights and trying to limit how music was used
with services like Pressplay had proven a dud. Music was as readily
available on the internet for free as ever. More ominous, CD sales
had been slipping steadily since 2000, decreasing at an average annual rate of 5 percent to 8 percent. Mall chains like Sam Goody and

Musicland were closing stores, and Tower Records, the superstore chain that pioneered full-catalog record retailing, declared bankruptcy in early 2004. (Tower went out of business in 2006.)

The retailers' woes didn't bother Bronfman. He viewed the shakeout as part of an evolution away from physical product toward online and mobile delivery of music, and his chief concern was how to make money from that. Armed with a United Nations study predicting that half of the world's population would have cell phones by 2008, Bronfman came into WMG expecting a huge cellular market for music—one in which he planned to sidestep the piracy issues plaguing the music business online by being more willing to make deals with the service providers than Universal had been with internet music startups. While predicting that things would get worse before they got better—"There are no hockey sticks in our financial projections," he said, adding that he bought the company expecting WMG's revenues to be lower in 2008 than they had been in 2003—he assured his partners that there was ultimately a rosy future for music in a world built on direct contact with billions of potential buyers. "In the old business, we were selling through ten thousand to twelve thousand retailers," he said. "Now we're going to be selling on tens or hundreds of millions of phones and computers. We have the opportunity to significantly increase the number of clients."

Also fueling Edgar's optimism was the news that one company had finally figured out how to sell music online: Apple.

Steve Jobs, the cofounder of Apple, had revolutionized personal computers with the Macintosh in 1982. Forced out of his own company by the board of directors three years later, Jobs didn't miss a beat. He purchased the computer graphics operation of Lucasfilms Ltd. to create Pixar Animation Studios and produced blockbusters such as *Toy Story* and *Finding Nemo*. After selling Pixar to Disney for $7.4 billion, he became that company's biggest stockholder. He also founded NeXT, a designer of specialty computers for universities and businesses, which provided Jobs with a road back to his old firm. Though NeXT's computers were only a moderate success, Apple purchased the firm in 1996 for $429 million in order to acquire NeXTSTEP software as the basis for the Mac OS operating system. The following year Jobs returned to Apple when he was named interim CEO, and he immediately refocused and simplified its products. "There was a mission to switch from selling very few of expensive products to selling very many of inexpensive products," said David Sobotta, then a sales director for Apple. One of those products was the iPod, a portable music player, introduced in October 2001.

Mac-compatible, the first iPods could hold one thousand songs. Though a good deal cheaper than a computer, the sleekly designed device was expensive at $399 and comparatively late to the market; MP3 players had been widely available for three years. It was incompatible with Windows-based PCs, but it had a major advantage for Mac users because it could play files from iTunes, an Apple program that let them rip CDs to the computer. With iTunes, an iPod made a Mac's music files portable. "The beauty of the iPod is not the iPod itself, but the integration with iTunes. iPod without iTunes would be just another MP3 player," said Guy Kawasaki, an Apple employee hired to promote the iPod to Mac users.

When Napster lost its case in 2001 and had to close its initial service, Jobs saw an opening. In early 2002, he met with Paul Vidich and Kevin Gage, a pair of new-media executives at Warner Music, and pitched the iTunes Music Store as an online service that would use iTunes. Taking the proposal back to Roger Ames, Vidich and Gage proposed a price of 99 cents per DRM-controlled song, which Jobs quickly accepted. Warner became the first major record company to license its music for sale on Apple's site. When Universal signed on a few weeks later, BMG, Sony, and EMI Records followed.

When it opened the last week of April 2003 with a catalog of 200,000 songs, the iTunes Music Store was the kind of clean, easy-to-use site that music fans had said they were willing to pay for. One million songs were sold the first week. But it didn't take the music industry long to find a reason to complain.

Out of the 99 cents per song, Apple took a 22-cent cut as the retailer, leaving just 77 cents to be divvied between the labels, music publishers, songwriters, and performers. After decades of selling LPs and CDs—with list prices that ranged up to $18.98—that was a very unattractive number. iTunes would have to sell *a lot* of songs just to replicate the old business: approximately fifteen downloads to equal one CD. "Roger and I did the Apple deal and found the parameters," said Vidich ruefully. "Which did more for them than us." Indeed, Jobs didn't seem to care that the iTunes Music Store price provided Apple with a limited margin: he made his money on the player, and the downloads were simply another reason to own one. Before long, the record labels were carping that iPods were only valuable because of music, and that they should receive a royalty on the hardware.

Record executives were also unhappy about something else that they hadn't anticipated. Prior to iTunes, they had turned down licensing requests for online music sale sites. Part of the reason was greed and poor management, but the industry had long viewed radio and MTV as businesses they empowered and, instead of owning, wound up having to provide product to and spending a lot of money on. They dreaded making the same mistake in cyberspace. But they had been unsuccessful with their own startups and forced to contend with a host of unfriendly and unlicensed sites. iTunes seemed worth a flyer because it was both a good system and limited to Apple users. Virtually everything Apple did set it apart as smarter, hipper, and better than PCs. The result was a schism in personal computing culture and products that looked as permanent as the one between Rome and the Eastern Orthodox Church. So in October 2003, the record companies were shocked when Jobs threw away his own playbook and introduced iTunes for Windows. More than 1 million songs were sold in the first three days. Suddenly, iTunes wasn't a specialty retailer—it was the only mass-market music site on the internet. That would give it a tremendous advantage over any other startups.

Bronfman didn't think the iTunes Music Store was a very good deal for the record companies. But he acknowledged that it proved music could be sold online, and he believed that Warner and the rest of the industry should be encouraging other sites and models that paid better. To reinvent and supervise Warner's digital initiatives, Edgar hired his brother-in-law and investment partner, Alejandro Zubillaga, as executive vice president of business development and digital strategy. It was as large a job as any in the company. Zubillaga didn't have the visibility and staff that Lyor Cohen commanded as chairman and CEO of the US recorded music operation, but he was going to be equally key to WMG's efforts to survive in the digital age.

"I'm a huge believer that the value of content is going to increase," he said not long after taking the job. "People really buy content—the bits and bytes fall away. What's been fascinating for me is that this industry has had it so good for twenty years. But right now, the only question analysts are asking is, 'Is digital going to make up for physical decline?' and answering that it won't. It can't be that our most ambitious goal is staying even."

Indeed. If online music followed the pricing structure of the iTunes Music Store, "staying even" didn't look possible. The single-song MP3 file, which allowed listeners to hone in on the one or two tracks they really wanted, exposed the serious weakness of most albums. Even a legitimate and healthy online music retail environment that sold individual songs was an unappealing replacement for albums. "How are we going to make money selling things for ninety-nine cents?" interim CFO Michael Ward asked Zubillaga. As Bronfman had suggested, part of the answer would come from expanding services to reach more customers. "I'm happy about Apple, but ideally we'd like to have three or four other online players plus wireless offering something similar," Alex said. But they also wanted those sites to reverse the online world's dismantling of the album.

Zubillaga soon believed that he knew how to do that. If albums conceived as CDs didn't work online, then the album should be reinvented as a unique multimedia package that *did* work online. The collections would include exclusive material not available anywhere else, giving consumers a reason to buy rather than take music and WMG a chance to make more money than it would on a single song. Music, video, artwork, lyrics—anything could be grist for the new digital mill. At one point he suggested to Mike Shinoda, a member of the band Linkin Park and a painter, that he might want to include his art as part of an online package. "We don't believe like Jobs that it's just a ninety-nine-cent business," Zubillaga said. "Consumers are willing to pay for real compelling stuff. What's the end product? I think it's going to keep evolving."

The collections, referred to as "bundles" rather than "albums," could be as elaborate or simple as buyers wanted. But they would require a corporate restructuring and financial investment in the recording, production, and assembling of additional material. More than 95 percent of the recorded music division's income still came from CDs, so artists and company employees would obviously continue to concentrate on making traditional albums—and Atlantic and Warner Bros. would still have to focus on signing and developing artists whose music they believed in. But Zubillaga suggested to Cohen that WMG would have to alter what it did and also develop exclusive material appropriate to the internet in order to grow online sales. "There's no reason this shouldn't be fifty percent of our business five years from now," he said.

In March 2005, the week after the Lee-Bronfman group completed its purchase of the Warner Music Group, Alex and Lyor made a trip to the West Coast to meet with internet executives at Microsoft and RealNetworks in Seattle and eBay CEO Meg Whitman in San Jose. The online auction giant had started its own 200,000-song music site, PassAlong, the previous September, and Zubillaga wanted to launch a joint-venture eBay site. Throughout the trip Alex, who barely knew Lyor, harped on the need to produce more material for the internet if the company was to develop a digital business, but he wasn't sure Cohen was listening. Alex got his answer when the duo's trip concluded in Los Angeles with a visit to Warner Bros. Records. The first night there, Cohen took him to Universal Studios to watch Atlantic artist Rob Thomas make a video for his song "Lonely No More." To Alex's surprise, Lyor commandeered the shoot and turned the cameras on the crew, cast, and manager, interviewing anyone who might prove interesting enough to be included in a behind-the-scenes video.

"Lyor grabbed a camera guy and said, 'Shoot this, shoot that,'" said Zubillaga. "Up until that moment I hadn't been sure he agreed with me. All of a sudden we had all this extra material and content we could use." The next day, Tom Whalley, the chairman of Warner Bros. Records, greeted Cohen by wryly asking if he could come to all of the label's shoots.

Additional material and online exclusives became a central piece of Cohen's efforts as he started refocusing all the record division's departments from A&R through marketing and sales on their new digital reality: the company had to create new and unique items beyond the CD. Lyor soon turned Alex's need for online material into programming his labels could exploit on their own. He particularly liked the idea that Warner could sell things like video that they had previously given away to MTV and online music sites. "I view us as an independent producer of content," he declared. He thought that whatever he created for Alex to bundle with songs for online sale could also be packaged as shows to be sold to websites and broadcasters. The new initiative made for vintage Cohen. In meetings, he tended to spew a stream of ideas—many of them awful—but he came up with more good ideas than anyone else.

At one point he suggested that Atlantic Records create a show about how groups got their names. "You stick a camera in your artist's face and produce a four-minute segment on how they created themselves. It's interesting to consumers. You create something with an MTV-type intro and outro and once you've got forty of them, you go to Yahoo!, you go to AOL and Google, and you say, 'How much?'" He also wanted to rebuild the back half of a tour bus on a soundstage for an interview show. "How about a segment called *Smokin' on the Bus*?" Whether anyone was interested in paying for half-baked, on-the-cheap promotional clips masquerading as programming was up for grabs (though it had certainly been done before), and the only series that came to fruition was *The Biz,* a record industry spin on the Donald Trump show *The Apprentice.* Shown on AOL, with Lyor standing in for Trump and putting young would-be executives through their paces with help from WMG executives and artists, the embarrassingly threadbare show bombed. But Cohen was earnest about reinventing the company to survive in the digital world and pushing employees to think about how that affected products, artists, and marketing.

He had fewer distractions once TVT's contentious suit against him evaporated. On June 14 the US Court of Appeals for the Second Circuit reversed the lower court's ruling and erased the remaining $3-million judgment Cohen had to pay TVT and its owner Steve

Gottlieb. Ironically, the three-judge panel ruled that there were no grounds for tortious interference in any deal between TVT and Murder Inc. because Def Jam coowned Murder Inc. and so couldn't be held to have interfered with its own contract. After the ruling, Bronfman claimed not to have been worried. "I always believed the TVT case was bogus. I've been very fortunate. I've had great success in believing in people even when it appeared not to make sense. I hired Doug Morris three days after Time Warner fired him for cause."

Cohen's marital problems, however, were not resolved so neatly. Despite initially pledging to Amy to recommit to their marriage, running Warner Music Group proved all-consuming. He moved out of the couple's Upper East Side town house and the couple soon divorced.

Cohen concentrated on redirecting and motivating the record operation, fighting his temptation to micromanage. Like Bronfman, he shied away from taking a direct role in guiding talent. In an industry where CEOs, chairmen, and division heads often commandeered A&R budgets for pet projects and ego trips, Cohen said he wanted Whalley, Kallman, and Greenwald to run the labels as they saw fit. An autodidact, Cohen found the model for his new job in a surprising place. A basketball fan with floor seats for the Knicks, he made a special point of getting to Madison Square Garden when the Dallas Mavericks were in town. He didn't go to watch the players. He wanted to see how the team's opinionated and outsized owner, the internet entrepreneur and billionaire Mark Cuban, interacted with his coach. "The coach never looked at him once during the whole game," Cohen said. "So clearly, game plays were the coach's decision. I don't want to embarrass myself. I'm not running a record company. That's the most seductive job in the world—I know, because I did it. I will not buckle to that desire. I'm a fucking administrator, and to think anything else is dangerous to this organization."

Cohen embraced the role of guru. At his staff meetings, integrating internet-marketable material into every level of product development became the mantra and the industry's digital troubles were to be viewed as a personal and professional test. "True trust comes from surviving bad things," he said, urging his staffers to push artists to deal with the economic challenges ahead and come up with additional material. "If you weed the roster, you have to sell more records and monetize more from these."

In May, WMG tested its new online philosophy with the first bundles on the iTunes Music Store. Apple wasn't particularly enthusiastic, but Cohen, Zubillaga, and Bronfman were insistent. Like his lieutenants, Edgar frequently portrayed the company's problems as a blessing in disguise and their solutions a matter of experimentation and patience. "The disaggregation of the album is a fantastic opportunity," he said. "If it turns out [bundles] only produce two-thirds of our traditional margin, then guess what? We have to figure out how to sell more and make more money. Any time you can create a win for the consumer, you should."

He was also willing to try unorthodox business plans. Cordless, Warner's experimental internet-only label run by Jac Holzman, didn't release physical product, but it gave WMG a means of seeing what kinds of packages and promotions worked online. Most striking, Bronfman was willing to play by the new rules set by the online sites that posted music for up-and-coming performers: Cordless artists retained ownership of their masters. "We're continually trying to broaden our thinking, and sometimes we might run against our own ten commandments," he said.

The labels experimented with different bundle configurations, looking to see what buyers really wanted. In October, when Reprise released *Playing the Angel* by the British synthesizer band Depeche Mode, the iTunes bundle included the complete album, a digital booklet, and a code enabling early purchase of tickets for their US concert tour. The company was even more ambitious with the following month's big release, Madonna's *Confessions on a Dance Floor*.

The singer had called Cohen and Bronfman that spring. "I want to come in and play my record," she said. Bronfman cringed. It was just the kind of situation he hated. "I don't want to sit in a room with the artist and have to come up with something supportive when it's . . ." he said. Edgar need not have worried. At the conclusion of the record he told Madonna she was the company's queen. "She gave us a great record." *Confessions on a Dance Floor* reached number 1 in more than forty countries and sold 8 million copies, making it the singer's biggest album in seven years.

Madonna's album also provided Zubillaga and WMG with their first real chance to see how willing online and mobile buyers would be to spend money on music and packages created specifically for them. At the iTunes Music Store, Warner offered two different bundles—a digital copy of the *Confessions* album for $9.99 and a deluxe version including a video, photos, and information for $12.99—as well as the usual single tracks for 99 cents each. The results bolstered Alex's strategy: the expensive package sold better. "The beauty of the internet is that you can have as much depth of product as you want," he said. "There are rabid fans that will spend a *lot* for limited offers."

Just as encouraging, the company found they could make money and promote the album with cell phone items like ringtones. Since its inception in 2003, the growing market for ringtones and other musical add-ons for cell phones had been one of the music industry's most encouraging indications that mobile and cybertechnology could produce new applications and markets. Created and marketed independent of the record companies, the first ringtones were synthesized samples of popular songs. When those proved a hit, Warner and the other record companies jumped into the market with thirty-second samples of the original hits. Termed "master tones" to differentiate them from the generally cheesy-sounding cover versions, they sold for $3—triple the price of a complete recording at iTunes. By the time of *Confessions'* release, ringtones, ring backs—the music someone hears when they call your phone—and other musical items were a $500-million market in just the United States, which lagged behind Western Europe and parts of the Far East in cell phone penetration. Soon there were million-selling ringtone versions of hip-hop and pop hits, essentially re-creating the singles market that the record industry had killed a decade earlier when it opted to sell only complete albums on CDs. Warner aggressively used ringtones as both a promotional and a moneymaking vehicle for *Confessions.* The album's first single, "Hung Up," was released a month early exclusively as a ringtone in several countries and sold strongly. It also helped push the song to number 1 on pop charts around the world.

Driven largely by teenaged cell phone users, worldwide sales of ringtones leapt 40 percent in 2005 to $3.5 billion, and master tones alone were predicted to top $6 billion by 2010. The popularity of hip-hop ringtones was particularly good news for Atlantic Records which, while still offering a broad range of artists, was looking and sounding more like Lyor Cohen's old label, Def Jam.

The marketing of *Confessions on a Dance Floor* was savvy, and by early 2006, WMG had assembled and sold forty premium online bundles—more than the rest of the major record companies combined. Despite that success, Zubillaga was frustrated in his attempts to convince more online music sites to add bundles along with single songs. Few wanted to buck the single-file format of MP3s—or iTunes's success with a simple low-price formula.

"Every time Rob Glaser [of RealNetworks] or Napster [though the original Napster had been sued out of business, its name was valuable enough to be sold and used by another company employing a different online technology] came to me for a better deal, I said I wouldn't do it without bundles—even offering them exclusives," Alex said.

Still the sites were loath to add the bundles and that, along with the admission that the record industry wasn't going to be able to create its own music sites or even dictate systems and formats to the companies that could create them, spurred WMG to create an online and mobile licensing policy that was virtually the opposite of the one the industry had initially followed. Instead of blocking legitimate music services and applications, Zubillaga signaled that the company was willing to take a flyer on interesting startups.

The decision came at a moment when Warner and the other major labels had reason to be optimistic. On June 27, the United States Supreme Court found in favor of the record companies and movie studios in the Grokster case, ruling that services employing peer-to-peer (P2P) sharing could be held liable for copyright infringement. Though much of their legal costs had been borne by Mark Cuban, who offered himself as a financial angel to counterbalance the deep pockets of the RIAA and the studios, Morpheus and Grokster were soon out of business, and Grokster settled its battle with the plaintiffs

by agreeing to pay $50 million in damages. The decision extended the industry's win in Napster, and its message was clear: anyone looking to start a legitimate online music business sidestepped the copyright holders at their own peril.

But Grokster was a very limited victory. P2P users didn't need a commercial service to find each other, and six years after Napster's debut virtually everything the record industry had ever offered for sale could be found squirreled away for free online. Search engines made finding blogs and music boards with links to download music through file-hosting sites like RapidShare as easy as finding a weather report or the latest headlines. Another P2P protocol, BitTorrent, made it easier to share large media files like albums and films. And although the RIAA did sometimes target individual blogs for removal, the labels did not go after fan-run sites the way they had commercial services. "There'll always be piracy," said Bronfman. "I don't like recreational piracy, but over the long term it's easier to live with than commercial piracy."

The Grokster decision did appear to deal a severe blow to the business prospects of unlicensed music sites, "Venture capital migrates away from risky, litigation-prone areas," Gary Shapiro, the president and CEO of the computer and tech firm lobby group the Consumer Electronics Association, said after the court's ruling. "Before developing a product in the post-Grokster environment, an innovator or entrepreneur will have to persuade everyone—from outside bankers to inside counsel—that it can be sold without risk of a lawsuit." The ruling gave record companies greater control over their destinies, yet cyberspace still presented a life-or-death challenge to them. It was clear that, like everyone else in the music business, Bronfman—despite bundles, ringtones, and repackaged music—had no idea *what* better product consumers would pay for.

Hoping to encourage the development of this yet-unknown breakthrough, Zubillaga made licensing deals with more than three hundred cell phone and online companies around the world. Some were three-year deals with incentives to encourage the use and promotion of bundles, though most were simple and shorter and could be easily terminated if they weren't panning out. Zubillaga saw them all as a

low-risk way to seed the marketplace and to get a better idea of what did and didn't work. "I'm most focused on production innovations, not replicating records on P2P. It's really about creating an affordable, cool experience."

Changing WMG's online philosophy had another strategic advantage that was more subtle but no less important. As the music business shifted from physical sales to digital, artists obviously had to shift with it. In the past, managers and lawyers frequently counseled artists to avoid all-inclusive worldwide deals with record companies. That way, an act had money coming in from more than one source—say, a different music publisher or overseas record company—and wasn't beholden to the US label for everything. That independence could also help artists resist label demands they disagreed with. But new configurations were morphing and outlets emerging so rapidly that any artist operating on his own risked missing opportunities. A single artist—particularly a talented unknown—couldn't negotiate the dozens of deals required to make his work available to mobile phone and internet users around the world. But those markets were there if you could get to them, as Zubillaga's efforts with Madonna's album had shown. If labels had the reach and catalogs to make online deals wherever they were needed, it was likely to make signing a worldwide agreement more, not less, attractive to performers with commercial ambitions. "I think it's going to be difficult to have all your eggs in different baskets if you've got seventy-two hours to negotiate a deal with Vodafone," Bronfman said.

Warner Music was the smallest of the four major record companies, so its market share was very much on Edgar's mind. One way to increase it was to take it away from rival Sony BMG Music Entertainment, which was stumbling badly. Second in size to Universal Music, it had been created when Japan's Sony and Germany's Bertelsmann merged their music divisions as a fifty-fifty joint venture in March 2004, approximately nine months before the Bronfman-Lee group made its bid for WMG. With a sprawling catalog that ran the gamut from Yo-Yo Ma to Britney Spears, the new company started with 33 percent of the US market. But merging the two distinct corporate cultures proved more difficult than combining and

culling the roster, and it hadn't been managed anywhere near as well as Morris had managed the earlier MCA-PolyGram merger for Seagram. In the first year, Sony BMG's market share dropped sharply to 26 percent. In February 2006, CEO Andrew Lack—who had been widely criticized for giving Bruce Springsteen a new contract rumored to be worth between $50 million and $100 million just when the industry was contracting and older artists were finding hits more elusive—was replaced by Bertelsmann's Rolf Schmidt-Holtz. Simultaneously, WMG's US market share rose. But if Bronfman saw an advantage for Warner Music in Sony BMG's internal clashes, he didn't say. "I think Sony BMG is more a problem for us than an opportunity," he said. "Sure, it's easy to gain market share when a competitor stumbles. But the problem is that we have not figured out how to re-create a dynamic industry. It's better for the industry if Sony BMG is healthy."

He focused instead on the independent label market and made three separate moves toward pulling a greater share of it. He let Cohen proceed with his idea of an "incubator system" to make deals with small, independent labels with the aim of expanding their acts' followings and then transferring the artists to Atlantic and Warner Bros. for mass marketing; he bought the independent record company and distributor Rykodisk; and he placed an increased emphasis on Alternative Distribution Alliance (ADA), an existing WMG company that sold records for smaller rock labels.

Cohen revived two dormant Elektra imprints, Asylum and East West, as incubator labels to handle hip-hop and rock respectively. Explained Todd Moscowitz, the Cohen protégé and former Def Jam executive selected to run it, "He told me he wanted to set up a system for entrepreneurs to plug into." Cohen envisioned it as a low-budget, two-man operation that simply cut deals, but Moscowitz quickly talked his way into a more realistic staff of ten who would work on records. His pitch was that the incubator should offer more than the promise of a major label hookup if the artist could get himself to the next sales level. "Why don't we meet them at the fifty instead of the goal line?" he asked Cohen. Asylum and East West provided marketing, sales, A&R, and promotion—the primary tools a major record company uses to bring along an artist—but with an unusual cost-control incentive to the artists and original labels: the less money WMG spent, the less ownership they received. "It's really just a risk allocation model," said Moscowitz. "You put up the money and own the masters; if you put up the bulk of the risk, you get most of the money. Rather than give a big advance, we put in sweat equity. We'll take a distribution fee and give you these other services for free—in return for upstream rights. And I'll take a little less on the upside to have them incentivized and taking all the risk." It proved an attractive model, one that required independent artists and label entrepreneurs to sell a little bit less of their souls to the major label devil for national distribution and marketing while encouraging them to control budgets. He knew the labels were buying into the plan when one of his bestselling artists, rapper Paul Wall, called to complain that the company wasted money when it booked him into a four-star hotel.

Asylum got off to a fast start. It picked up local rap hits by Wall and Mike Jones in Houston and with the group D4L in Atlanta and turned them into national Top 10 hits. The labels had the pulse of the street. Said Joie Manda, a former Def Jam employee who became the head of A&R and promotion for Asylum, "Sometimes I go to the strip clubs and ask the strippers, and they tell me what's hot." Perhaps not surprisingly, one of Asylum's biggest hits proved to be D4L's "Laffy Taffy," a licentious pun on a Nestlé candy. The record sold over 500,000 digital singles, was the bestselling ringtone for a month, and reached number 1 on the *Billboard* Hot 100 Singles chart. Most encouraging, Asylum's customers were young and technologically savvy, and overall digital sales were unusually high. "We're fashion-forward in terms of new technology," Moscowitz said. "We had five of the top twenty ringtones in our first summer."

WMG was more than happy to take the hits wherever they could find them. "We're not in first place," Moscowitz said. "We don't have the luxury of *not* trying. We're the 'try anything' company, and that's no accident. It's the only way we're going to grow."

Bronfman's $67.5-million acquisition of Rykodisk in March 2006 was a more tried-and-true method of holding on to market share.

Founded as a CD-only label in 1983—when vinyl LPs were still dominant—Ryko was self-distributed. It acquired and represented other independent labels, but it was built by making deals to rerelease older albums by established artists like David Bowie, Frank Zappa, Elvis Costello, the Meat Puppets, the Residents, and Yoko Ono as well as release original recordings. In 2000 it was sold to veteran record executive Chris Blackwell for a reported $35 million. Blackwell, who'd unloaded his renowned Island Records to PolyGram two years earlier, hoped to use Ryko as the backbone of a new multimedia company, Palm Pictures, with financing from JPMorgan Partners and former Viacom chief Frank Biondi. Ryko made a five-year deal with Warner Music's sales and distribution company, WEA, but in 2001, Palm Pictures overextended itself and JP Morgan took ownership of Ryko. The company generated approximately $75 million a year in billing for WEA, but the relationship was rocky. "They had agreed to lower manufacturing costs and then didn't deliver," said a former Ryko executive. "Eventually we had to sue them." Though WMG was part of AOL Time Warner when the suit was filed, Bronfman took control just before the case reached arbitration in 2005. He saw immediately that if he didn't cut a deal with Ryko, they would go somewhere else when the distribution agreement expired in April 2006. That meant a 1 percent market share loss—and a swing of 2 percent when it went to a competitor. "Edgar got it in about ten minutes," says the executive. "His response was, 'We're a totally new company, we see the value, and we're going to get in and do our work.' He was very professional—he was going at it from an experienced, broader perspective and was enthused about the indie sector, believing a major needed to be there."

The other opportunity for growing WMG's share of independent label sales was through Alternative Distribution Alliance. Begun in 1993, a time when the web of older independent regional distributors that handled recordings for labels too small to distribute themselves was disappearing, ADA became one of the most successful distributors of alternative and independent rock recordings. Among its dozens of labels were Sub Pop (which had cofounded ADA and was now partially owned by WMG), the Beggars Group, Epitaph, and Matador, with hundreds of artists of every stripe from England's Arctic Monkeys to the American singers Cat Power and Neko Case.

In June 2006, ADA sponsored a three-day conference for its labels in Philadelphia, a city once known for a vibrant local recording business. Part pep rally, part sales pitch, the meetings were largely designed to give ADA a forum for encouraging labels to expand and extend their deals. The most optimistic message came from guest speaker Chris Anderson. The editor of *Wired,* Anderson had created a minor sensation a few months earlier when his article "The Long Tail" predicted that the internet would radically alter and improve retailing. It would allow the smallest and most specialized markets to be served as cheaply and profitably as mass markets, creating a potentially infinite "long tail" of product to be sold to individuals. His new book of the same title, given to attendees, would spend fourteen weeks on the *New York Times* nonfiction bestseller list. The Power-Point presentation to the ADA audience was a small record label's dream. The internet, Anderson predicted, would prove an inexpensive and ubiquitous vehicle for reaching virtually everyone interested in whatever the labels sold.

The person who seemed least swayed by Anderson was Bronfman. He didn't see how the effect Anderson was proposing would translate into a scalable business for him—or how producing an endless array of products for very limited audiences could replace a business predicated on mass hits. WMG's strategy in each endeavor associated with the independent and specialty markets was to identify and expand the most commercially viable segments, not spread itself out infinitely. (Some of Bronfman's reservations were echoed two years later when the *Harvard Business Review* published Anita Elberse's article "Should You Invest in the Long Tail?" Elberse, an associate professor of marketing, looked at book publishing and concluded that blockbusters had and would continue to fuel the business even as internet retailing became prominent.)

WMG's biggest message to the independent labels at the Philadelphia meeting was that they should expand their product partnerships to include digital exploitation. And in that context, Zubillaga's web of music sites, aggregators, and mobile phone companies wasn't a difficult sell. "It becomes more and more attractive to have that pipeline to go through for making digital deals," said one independent executive who dealt with WMG. "You've got fifty labels in ADA being provided with digital distribution. How is a little label going to contract with 350 providers? There's no way."

After a year under Bronfman WMG was transformed into something far more energetic, although it was still too soon to say whether it was the company it needed to be. But Bronfman could be surprisingly tone-deaf when it came to the public's perception of the company and its new owners. The board gave $23.2 million in bonuses to Warner's top five executives, including $5 million each to Edgar and Lyor, for the first year, after instituting a corporate bloodbath in which 20 percent of employees and 30 percent of the acts were dropped. Those executive compensation figures weren't high for senior management in the entertainment industry—Doug Morris, still chairman and CEO at Universal Music Group, received $18 million in salary and bonuses that year, not counting stock options, about six times what his boss, Vivendi chairman Jean-Bernard Lévy, received—but they were still an easy target for criticism. Indeed, Cohen's bonus was contractually keyed to the cuts, which meant his $5-million payday was predicated on making sure 1,000 people lost their livelihoods. If no one had yet to compare Cohen to "Chainsaw Al" Dunlap, the highly compensated, waste-cutting chairman of Sunbeam, the priorities in the executive suite were getting noticed, particularly when Bronfman and his partners opted to use virtually all of the $750 million raised in the company's public offering to pay back their initial investments. Just $7 million was allocated for use by the company—an insignificant and apparently random figure that drew a big red circle around where the rest of the money was going. "The guys who are running this thing are looking at it pretty cynically," music business attorney Peter Paterno complained to the *New York Times*. "It's not about the music or the employees; it's about a return for private equity investors. It's kind of astounding when you sit back and look at the audacity."

Paterno was at least partly wrong: it was about the music and building a company to survive into the future because that was the only way Bronfman could prove himself and make real money. And while he needed a $5-million bonus less than almost anyone, it was hard to argue that Bronfman the investor wasn't entitled to get his money back. But there was still a cultural disconnect between Bronfman's and Cohen's Rockefeller Center offices and the new realities of the business. Both men were engaged and approachable at the ADA conference, asking questions of their customers and answering ones from their own employees, showing that they were rolling up their sleeves and building a future in cyberspace. But there was something absurd and insincere about executives who could go to a meeting to argue that the old business was dead and that massive layoffs and rethinking were required—and arrive and depart by helicopter.

The ongoing policy of suing consumers for illegal downloading had made Warner and the other major record companies extraordinarily unpopular with a large segment of the people they wanted as customers. They would be quick to believe the worst of its executives, and anything that fed the perception that the record companies were out of step or cynical was unnecessary static. That was a shame, because in all other ways Bronfman was determined to deal with the industry's new economic reality, and Warner Music Group had quickly become the most forward-looking company in the business. "These guys are superprogressive," gushed Paul Reddick who, as vice president of business development at Sprint Nextel, negotiated deals with each of the major record companies. And John Stratton, the chief marketing officer for Verizon, characterized the record companies as operating at "different speeds," while calling Bronfman "the guy that's really sort of lighting the path for the music industry." But Warner Music was still the kind of record company you could hate.

12

Ruling the Wasteland

In the last week of April 2006, British business reporters heard rumors that EMI Music was about to make an offer to take over Warner Music Group. They called Bronfman's senior vice president of public relations, Will Tanous. Privy to the discussions at board and senior management meetings, Tanous had heard nothing, but instead of dismissing the possibility out of hand, he wondered if he was out of the loop. After all, there were cost and size advantages in a merger of the two companies. But after calling Bronfman and satisfying himself that there had been no approach from EMI, Tanous issued a flat denial. The whole thing struck him as weird and unlikely. WMG was now a public company, but the four initial equity partners still controlled 75 percent of the stock. If EMI was going to make a bid, there wasn't much pressure to be exerted by a public approach.

The following Monday, May 1, Bronfman came out of a meeting to find an urgent message from Eric Nicoli, the executive chairman of EMI Music. Nicoli arrived at Bronfman's office around lunchtime and presented Edgar with an offer letter. "I've long thought these companies belong together," he said. "Our board thinks it's a good time because we're both in a position of strength." Nicoli outlined the proposal, which was $28.50 a share in cash and EMI stock for WMG's stock, and Bronfman promised to call his board immediately. Before the day was over, rumors of the bid with a higher estimated value of $30 to $31 had leaked to CNBC.

Bronfman didn't like the offer. WMG was trading at $27, which made the price feel low, even if the CNBC story was a signal from EMI that they would improve the bid. On top of that, WMG was carrying less debt than EMI, making a stock swap unattractive. But it wasn't his call. The opinion of Scott Sperling, the board member who controlled Thomas H. Lee's 37 percent of WMG, was likely to be definitive. When the board met informally on a conference call that night to consider the offer, they immediately turned it down, a decision formalized the next morning after conferring with legal and financial advisors. "There was not a fraction of hesitation on anyone's part," says one participant.

It wasn't that a merger didn't make sense. A combination could produce $350 million in cost savings by creating a company with both greater market clout and a stronger presence in the world's two most important recorded music markets, the US and the UK. The problem was that each company wanted to be the buyer.

It was largely ego: each company's executives and directors thought they were better and smarter than the other's. But there was also a distinct advantage to being the acquiring company. If the deal fell through, the company to be bought became a bride abandoned at the altar; the only certainty would be a lingering stigma. Moreover, management's willingness to cede decision making to someone else would then look like a poor decision and would make regaining momentum extremely difficult.

There were also real regulatory hurdles. No one expected the US Department of Justice to object to an EMI-WMG merger, but once again the European Commission's approval was far from guaranteed. The EU had cleared the Sony BMG merger in 2004, but that decision went under review in the European Court of First Instance after Impala, an organization of independent record companies, issued a challenge.

Convinced that it only made sense to be the buyer, Bronfman and his board decided to double down and make a counteroffer. "There's so much more in us buying them than in us being acquired by them," said Bronfman. "When you get the synergies, it's terrific for us. If Eric accomplished anything with this ploy, it was the board saying, 'Look, there's no interest in selling as long as there's a way to get more value.'"

Bronfman wanted to do more than turn Nicoli down—he wanted to prevent EMI from coming back with another bid. He called Nicoli, who was jetting back to London. "Eric, don't pursue this," he said. "It's not that the company isn't for sale—it's just not for sale at a price you can pay. And I'm not saying that to negotiate."

That didn't faze Nicoli or stop the steady stream of news stories suggesting that EMI's acquisition of WMG was an eventuality. Looking to slow EMI's spin, Tanous retained Hugh Morrison, a London-based PR consultant with a track record in mergers and acquisitions. "In everyone's mind they were buying us and it was a done deal. Several times reporters asked me, 'Will, what'll you do next?'"

On June 14, WMG offered to buy EMI Music for 315 pence per share, valuing the company at $4.6 billion—a lower premium than EMI was offering but one WMG characterized as equivalent to EMI's deal based on comparative earnings. Terming the offer "wholly unacceptable," EMI offered the same amount for WMG, this time as an all-cash offer of $31 per share. Warner rejected that, noting that EMI didn't actually have the money in hand, and claimed that the offer was too encumbered by conditions such as the sale of the publishing company, Warner/Chappell. They upped their own bid slightly, to 320 pence. EMI again dismissed the offer as "unacceptable."

The standoff ended abruptly on July 13 when the European Court, after reviewing the Sony BMG merger, instructed the European Commission to revise the way it approved mergers. The regulatory uncertainties made a WMG-EMI merger unattractive, at least until the commission revised its standards. Whoever became the buyer would have to pay a premium to cover the other company's exposure if the regulators rejected the deal. After six years and three separate merger attempts, WMG-EMI was back on the shelf. "There'll be a merger between Warner and EMI and that's going to be the last of the shell game moves—then it's over," said former Warner Music executive Tom Silverman. "The business model doesn't work: companies are writing things off, firing people, selling assets. And it's not coming back. The list price is slipping in a marketplace where the price of everything else is going up."

Cost savings and investor paydays had made the deal attractive, but the fact remained that they were all a merger would provide. Putting together EMI and WMG wouldn't have taken the resulting company one step closer to solving the real issue facing the industry: the digital revolution and the labels' crumbling fortunes. But without a transforming deal, market interest in Warner's stock would have to be based solely on the company's prospects for growth. And those prospects weren't very good for the foreseeable future. Trading at over $27 during the merger talks, WMG's stock began a steady decline and by the beginning of 2008 it had plummeted to $4.65. Bronfman wouldn't second-guess himself, but with the stock hitting the skids he again became a figure of easy ridicule. To many observers, the fact that WMG was constantly retooling and steadily gaining market share in a shrinking, volatile music business didn't seem as salient as the fact that he'd turned down an offer from EMI that was five times the current price of the stock.

Alex Zubillaga and Edgar believed they could reverse WMG's fortunes and sidestep their biggest internet problem—the ready availability of free music—by encouraging mobile phone companies to create attractive, easy-to-use music services and put them in place as soon as possible. When questioned about his mobile strategy, Edgar was succint: "More, more, more."

In January 2006, Alex went to the annual World Economic Forum in Davos, Switzerland, expressly to find partners. Buttonholing CEOs from Vodafone, Advanced Micro Devices, and other mobile media firms, he laid out WMG's plans, preaching the gospel of bundles and pointedly telling them that with the exceptions of iTunes and the Japanese mobile phone company KDDI, virtually no one was ready to deliver what WMG could offer. "We're reengineering our business and technology, but the platforms aren't there," he said. "I want to understand your road map and manage our plans."

Assured by virtually every carrier that they were eager to add multimedia services and that the necessary platforms would soon be in place, Zubillaga blanketed the world with mobile phone agreements. Bronfman bragged that Warner Music had the largest mobile distribution network of any media company. "We made wireless deals everywhere," Zubillaga says. "China, Russia, *everywhere.*" And then they sat back and waited for the platforms to come online.

And waited.

In their dream scenario, Warner and other record companies wanted a handset big and flashy enough to make someone leave their MP3 player at home and an exciting service that made him want to load the phone up with music, screen savers, ringtones, ticket-buying plans, and other goodies purchased from the carrier. But it was hard to tell what was more disappointing about the mobile music market, the services or the phones the companies were selling. The first cell phones sold with music packages by US carriers Sprint and Verizon came with just enough memory to hold about 250 songs–at a time when the 30-gigabyte iPod could hold 7,500. The plans were limited in selection and with a price range of $1.99 to $2.50 per track, they were noticeably more expensive than iTunes. Not surprisingly, most users didn't buy any music for their phones; they just transferred songs that were already on their computers.

The cell phone market's failure to launch was made doubly frustrating by the continuing, steady erosion of the CD market. In 2006, Atlantic had a big debut hit in the Gnarls Barkley album *St. Elsewhere* and its huge single "Crazy." Tellingly, the album sold fewer than 4 million copies worldwide, though "Crazy" achieved a notable first when it topped the British singles chart solely on digital downloads. A year after Blunt's *Back to Bedlam* sold 11 million copies, this was the new market reality. A bracing double album by the Red Hot

Chili Peppers on Warner Bros., *Stadium Arcadium,* which provided a springboard for the band's successful worldwide tour, sold just 2 million copies—a fraction of what the sales would have been ten or even five years earlier. In October, a week before all albums in stock at the bankrupt Tower Records chain were auctioned off to a liquidator, Bronfman said he didn't expect the company to have much of a Christmas.

He was right. Christmas sales for the industry fell 20 percent, not good news for a business where the fourth quarter usually generated 40 percent of revenues. For Warner, that translated into a knee-buckling 74 percent drop in profits for the quarter. CD sales were falling at a faster rate than digital sales were growing. If 2006 was any indication, the record industry was no longer shrinking 5 percent a year—it was shrinking 10 percent a year. Bronfman tried to sound stoic. "Any business that fails to innovate for twenty-five years gets what it deserves," he said. "There's always a way to create value. I have to make lemonade."

Toward that end, Bronfman squeezed the mobile industry a little harder. Customers had been given no compelling reason to leave their MP3 players at home, and he chastised the carriers for making buying music on a cell phone a tedious experience. "To be frank, we often get very frustrated," he told a gathering of mobile executives. "So many of the world's platforms are still not capable of handling even the most basic content configurations: a ringtone and an audio track, for example, or a track bundled with a video." He added that while the number of cell phone subscribers with access to music services was increasing rapidly, less than 9 percent of them ever bought anything because the services were completely unappealing. "It's expensive, it's complicated, and it's slow . . . Our essential challenge is to make it affordable, easy, and quick to download tones and songs as well as new music experiences—including video—to mobile phones. Until we achieve that, we're not just falling far short of our potential, but we're also leaving billions of dollars in profits unrealized."

To WMG's further chagrin, Apple appeared likely to extend its hegemony over paid music downloads into the mobile world when it finally brought a sophisticated, relevant turn to cell phones in January 2007. The iPhone—a combination mobile phone, iPod, and web browser—was in a design and technology class all its own. Though a handful of European mobile companies including Nokia and Omnifone hustled to create music products and services intended to slow the iPhone's introduction there, Omnifone's subscription model, MusicStation, never attracted a significant number of users, while Nokia's highly anticipated Comes With Music, a cell phone sold preloaded with music, stumbled repeatedly with licensing issues and launch dates and never found its footing.

The biggest problem remained the sluggishness of mobile carriers. They liked the idea of selling all kinds of information—they didn't care if it was music, video, news, sports events, television programming, or internet access—but still focused their attention on signing customers for basic service. WMG was champing at the bit. "In wireless, they *know* their future is in data revenues and that voice is going to be a commodity, but it's still the cash cow today," a weary Zubillaga admitted. "The companies are public and concerned with their results and profits and don't have the support to be aggressive."

By the end of 2007, as CD sales fell off a cliff, a desperate Bronfman was literally begging the mobile carriers to provide better music services. Speaking at a conference in Macau, he cited the record industry's own mistakes and urged the carriers not to cede the market to Apple or someone else. "Ladies and gentlemen, take it from an industry that learned its lesson painfully. *Very* painfully. Our world was rocked. Now it's your world that is being rocked. And it's not just by Apple or a single great device. How long do you think it will take Google to develop the killer mobile app on an internet-based platform? Or two kids in a dorm room for that matter? Don't let 2008 be for your industry what 1999 was for the music industry."

It was a bitter public admission that the mobile companies weren't going to solve Warner's problems by providing a quick and easy second bite at the cyberspace apple. The scenario Bronfman had used to lure investors—billions of mobile customers buying music on portable phones and devices—might still come true, but not today.

It was hard to watch WMG without a feeling of déjà vu. As he had at Seagram, Edgar was making moves with a strong and informed sense of where a media and entertainment business should go to thrive in the internet age.

But an investment was also a bet on how and when it was going to get there. For all his optimism and insight, Bronfman was finding again and again that he couldn't control or even predict either. No matter how much the business changed, he still believed that the company's future ultimately hinged on the strength of its most important asset, its artists. He and his partners continued to spend on finding and developing acts even when they weren't sure how they were going to sell them, and the result had been the resurgence of Atlantic Records under Cohen, Kallman, and Greenwald and the continuing strength of Warner Bros. Records under Whalley. Both labels were annually in one of the top two market positions in the US. But working smarter wasn't smart enough. Edgar had been right to foresee music growing in popularity as technology gave people new ways to use and enjoy it, but too optimistic regarding how and when Warner would benefit—even when he told initial and secondary investors not to expect a turnaround for four or five years. The way things were going, the music industry was going to be a good deal smaller, even as its music reached more people. Bronfman and his partners hadn't bought Warner Music just to see if they could acquire a dominant position in a dying business. They'd never cash out at a premium unless they could demonstrate that the business had a vibrant future. Who wants to rule a wasteland?

Liberalized internet and mobile licensing policies weren't getting WMG where it needed to go. Bronfman began to look for a different map.

According to the legend, YouTube started because of a dinner party. Two Silicon Valley twentysomethings working for the internet payment company PayPal, engineer Steve Chen and web designer Chad Hurley, were having dinner with friends at Chen's San Francisco apartment in February 2005. As they later told the story, they wanted to share pictures and videos of the dinner online and were surprised to discover that, while it was easy to post pictures, it was difficult to find a good video posting site. Jawed Karim, another young PayPal engineer who became the third partner in YouTube, later said that the dinner never happened and that the idea to make YouTube a video-sharing site was actually his, but everyone agrees on one thing: eleven months after opening their website from a San Francisco garage with an eighteen-second clip of Karim at the zoo, YouTube was one of the world's most popular websites, showing 30 million videos a day.

YouTube's young founders, while appealing in a geeky, gee-whiz kind of way, were also savvy. Hurley's father-in-law, James Clarke, was the technology entrepreneur and billionaire behind several successful firms including Netscape and Silicon Graphics, and Hurley, Chen, and Karim had benefited from PayPal's 2002 IPO and subsequent sale to eBay for $1.5 billion in stock. The connection proved useful again when YouTube received $11.5 million in financing from Sequoia Capital, where PayPal's former CFO, Roelof Botha, was a partner.

The site's success was more than a matter of finding and filling a niche. YouTube's real brilliance was its simplicity: whether you were posting a video or just wanted to find and watch a clip, it was easy to use, completely self-explanatory, and free. But critics saw an emperor with no clothes—and a business with no plan for making a profit. Mark Cuban, who founded the web radio company Broadcast.com and sold it to Yahoo! for $5.9 billion, described YouTube as an economically unsustainable sinkhole for bandwidth and compared the service to Napster because it ignored copyright law. "Considering the RIAA will sue your grandma or a twelve-year-old at the drop of a hat, the fact that YouTube is building a traffic juggernaut around copyrighted audio and video without being sued is like . . . well, Napster at the beginning as the labels were trying to figure out what it meant to them," he said. "With the Grokster ruling, it's just a question of when YouTube will be hit with a charge of inducing millions of people to break copyright laws, not if."

Realizing copyright would be a delicate dance, YouTube limited clip length to ten minutes, which made posting and watching feature films and television programs less attractive. But Cuban had one thing right: if anyone was likely to sue YouTube it was the record companies because the vast majority of their video clips were under ten minutes and easy to post. Before long, YouTube's music video selection was so broad that the site could be used as an on-demand music player. Along with clips made for MTV, it was packed with a never-ending supply of homemade videos employing popular songs as the soundtracks—a mix one wag termed "a lot of junk and stuff that's stolen." Some postings were video interpretations of favorite songs, others simply home movies of everything from cavorting cats to drunken revelers at bar mitzvahs. If a copyright owner wanted to complain or sue, he certainly could. As a remedy, YouTube offered a broad takedown policy to copyright holders and removed anything when asked. Among the companies that did complain were NBC Universal and Viacom, and popular clips from *Saturday Night Live* and *The Daily Show* were removed and subsequently blocked.

At Universal Music Group, Doug Morris was itching to sue YouTube. "We believe these new businesses are copyright infringers and owe us tens of millions of dollars," Morris told a Merrill Lynch conference. "How we deal with these companies will be revealed shortly."

Bronfman saw things differently. The record companies had been lambasted for suing Napster rather than capitalizing on its visibility and turning it into a legitimate service. Much of that criticism, from bloggers and journalists covering the media, overlooked the obvious question of whether consumers would have stuck with Napster once they had to pay for it. But there was no denying that the road of litigation that the record companies had followed with Napster hadn't taken them where they needed to go. YouTube, like Napster, was a new and wildly popular internet application employing music. Perhaps a different approach would produce a different outcome, one that actually made money for labels and artists.

Instead of suing YouTube, WMG cut a deal with them. The September 2006 agreement gave YouTube permission to post both Warner-owned videos and user-generated videos that employed their recordings. The terms, though undisclosed, gave WMG a share in money generated by ads placed alongside songs and videos it owned as well as warrants to buy shares in YouTube. The other record companies, including Universal, soon followed suit. When YouTube was sold the following month to Google for $1.65 billion, the labels exercised their options, reportedly valued at a combined $50 million. Though Bronfman said WMG would split any income from YouTube ads with the artists, he saw no reason to set aside any stock income for them. "We've invested billions to aggregate, and that's what creates the opportunity for us to get stock," he said.

Not surprisingly, that didn't please some artists and their representatives. The head of the International Music Managers' Forum, Peter Jenner, who has represented Pink Floyd, the Clash, and Billy Bragg, denounced the majors. "No one has mentioned payment to the artists or the writers or the publishers, either for past usage of their material or for future use," he complained. "What has happened with YouTube is that rampant copyright infringement has been allowed to flourish, then the community of users, creators, and editors and all their infringement has been sold to the highest bidder, and the majors have put their noses eagerly into the trough and turned themselves into manifest hypocrites. The people in the middle—the majors—seem so desperate to protect their terra that they are willing to drag the rest of us down with them."

At the other end of the spectrum, a group of marketing and public policy professors at the Wharton School saw it as a breakthrough deal for copyright owners. "This changes everything, and people will look back at it as a turning point," said Peter Fader, who went on to call the agreement "the single biggest business development deal in the history of digital media."

WMG and the other labels may have finally made a proactive decision regarding the online world, but they didn't look nearly as smart as the people who'd backed YouTube. For its one-year investment of $11.5 million, Sequoia Capital received $450 million—or about nine times the amount paid to the owners and creators of the clips people were watching and listening to on the site. If that irked Bronfman, he chose not to say. But a massive return on a short-term investment in a related business wasn't the kind of thing that would escape his—or his private equity partners'—attention.

YouTube wasn't the only internet play involving music made by Sequoia Capital. With Morgenthaler Ventures, the firm also backed imeem. Initially a social network site focusing on instant messaging, imeem had been a startup in search of a niche until it let users post and share music. By the start of 2007, it was growing rapidly and claiming 16 million users, and had an enormous online library of songs. "They were getting a pretty big audience," says a WMG executive. "We talked with them about a deal, but they didn't seem serious. So we sued them."

WMG filed a copyright infringement suit in May. In the wake of Grokster, there was little doubt that imeem would lose, and the suit was settled just two months later. WMG agreed to license its music catalogs to imeem for streaming, meaning users could listen to songs and use them online but couldn't download or store them on computers or iPods. Imeem would pay WMG every time one of its songs was streamed and try to earn money from ads; though neither company said what the rate was, it was widely assumed to be four-tenths of a cent per play. As with YouTube, the other labels soon followed suit and by December there were 5 million songs licensed for on-demand listening at imeem. Its search function made imeem akin to a free online jukebox, capable of playing nearly any popular song on demand. Additionally, it added buttons and links to encourage users to buy downloads of whatever they were hearing from iTunes or Amazon.

Imeem was a progressive model, addressing the ready availability of free online music. Instead of competing with free, it embraced it and hoped to make money selling ads. That record companies were willing to make deals with imeem and YouTube instead of trying to shut them down signaled a willingness to try something new and less controlled—and a tacit admission that they'd had very little success selling music in cyberspace anywhere other than iTunes.

It was also evidence of how much more complicated it had become for a record company and its artists to make and collect money from recordings. Before MP3s, record companies made almost all of their money from selling CDs, and it was a straightforward proposition. A disc that retailed for $17.98 wholesaled for approximately $10—about as simple a retail model as any manufacturer ever enjoyed. Now, with internet music retailers offering online stores, monthly subscription services, and ad-driven streaming sites, the record companies were getting paid based on all kinds of new formulas ranging from a per-song basis to a monthly fee to a fraction of a cent for each time a song was played. Aside from being an accounting nightmare—some mobile phone companies lacked systems to track which songs they were selling and simply sent the record companies a lump check, leaving it to them to determine how much money specific artists were due—it was clearly less profitable than selling one configuration. For one of Atlantic's most popular 2006 albums, *King* by rapper T.I., the label offered more than one hundred different variants for sale, ranging from ringtones to single tracks to custom album packages for different online sites.

The next dramatic steps were Bronfman's decisions to invest $15 million in imeem and $20 million in Lala, a website for trading used CDs founded by Bill Nguyen. A college dropout, Nguyen had made a huge score when he sold his first online company, the email technology firm Onebox, for $800 million. By 2007, Lala had an expanded plan to take on iTunes by letting users listen to whatever they wanted online for free but charging them to download songs and albums to their iPods.

Placing financial bets on internet entrepreneurs was a new twist, and it was clearly spurred by YouTube. It still wasn't clear how Google, YouTube's new owner, was going to make money from the site, but its creators and first-round investors had already pocketed a bundle. Investing in and managing businesses was what Bronfman and his partners did—so why not give WMG another way to participate in the online music world by purchasing equity in startups? Bronfman and Zubillaga's initial strategy of seeding the online and mobile marketplace with a lot of short-term deals hadn't borne fruit, and investing in a few select sites looked at least as lucrative as actually trying to sell music. Why not back those that looked particularly promising?

It was a defining moment—or, more accurately, a redefining moment. Three years earlier, Bronfman acquired Warner Music with an abiding belief in the continuing value of record companies, assuring his partners and investors that it was just a matter of time before order and ownership rights were restored and the instant availability of recordings became an asset rather than a liability. But by mid-2007, CD sales had plummeted by 19 percent, any meaningful mobile phone market was still years away, and the internet, with the exception of iTunes, was resistant to commercial music ventures. But consumers hadn't lost their interest in music. The concert business looked stronger than ever, and free music was inarguably one of the internet's greatest drivers. "The overall music business including management, touring, sponsorship, merchandising, is growing," admitted Bronfman. "The recording business at present is not."

Edgar didn't have to look far for lessons in the costs of ignoring new technology. He noted that in the late 1980s, digital photography eliminated the need for film stock, and neither of the mighty commercial giants, Polaroid and Kodak, proved nimble enough to respond. By 2001, Polaroid, which had virtually invented instant photography in the 1960s, was bankrupt, its product a relic. And Kodak, despite becoming the leading American manufacturer of digital cameras, couldn't earn the same margins it enjoyed as the king of film and developing. By 2007, Kodak's stock was trading at the same price it had in 1965 and had lost money every quarter for two years. Edgar used the example as a rallying cry, and told employees that WMG wasn't going down that road.

After the investment plunge with imeem and Lala, Bronfman expanded the strategy beyond online startups, tentatively repositioning WMG not just as a recording company, but a broader music business firm. With music strong and recordings weak, Warner Music began looking at segments of the industry that were more likely to grow. He tried to buy Front Line, the artist management firm headed by industry veteran Irving Azoff. Its wide-ranging list of over two hundred clients included the Eagles, Christina Aguilera, Miley Cyrus, Jimmy Buffett, and Neil Diamond. But WMG stepped back when concert promotion giant Live Nation offered to pay Azoff more. Instead, IAC, the far-ranging media and internet firm controlled by

Barry Diller—on whose board Bronfman sits—topped Live Nation's offer and then sold a 30 percent stake in Front Line to WMG for $110 million.

"That was sort of a consolation prize," says a WMG executive involved in the negotiations. But WMG couldn't consolidate Front Line's financial results into their own, and their stake wasn't large enough to block anything the famously irascible Azoff might want to do. In October 2008, WMG sold out to IAC's Ticketmaster for $146 million. That was $36 million for a year's investment—not exactly YouTube money, but more than they were making from online music subscription services like Rhapsody and Napster. But in February 2009, just four months after Bronfman sold out WMG's position, Front Line and Ticketmaster announced a merger with Live Nation to create an entertainment behemoth boasting the largest concert promoter, pop and rock management firm, and ticketing agency. With one deal, it would create precisely the kind of entertainment conglomerate poised to take advantage of where consumers still spent money on music. And WMG didn't own any of it.

Unable to purchase a meaningful stake in the management or concert industries, Bronfman thought WMG could move into concerts as a niche player. In early 2007, he steered WMG to an investment in Bulldog, a New York concert promoter specializing in high-priced private shows. The brainchild of Joe Meli, a thirty-two-year-old banker-turned-impresario, Bulldog was to debut that summer with a five-concert subscription series in the Hamptons featuring Prince, Billy Joel, Tom Petty, Dave Matthews, and James Taylor. The price tag was even heftier than the talent: $3,000 per show—and you had to buy all five concerts. After that, the plan was to expand the luxury show concept to Aspen, London, Geneva, Paris, and Dubai.

Lyor Cohen, who had cut his teeth in the concert business, didn't think Bulldog was a smart bet. At the company's Monday morning senior management meeting, he argued against the deal, suggesting that Meli, whose résumé consisted of producing a handful of shows in the Carolinas, didn't have the experience to warrant an investment. Bronfman disagreed, and in the spring of 2007 bought the company outright for $6 million. "I think the premium concert business is a real business," he said. "Does Bulldog have it right? I don't know. But it's a small investment."

Bulldog was an almost immediate bust. "The rich people they are targeting all have connections to get tickets for free, so no one was buying," one insider said. By the following March, WMG had written off $18 million on Bulldog, and one financial analyst, Rich Greenfield of Pali Research, thought the actual losses closer to $30 million.

The risks in diversifying were obvious—especially for a public company like WMG. As much as the major record companies knew about selling records and building careers, they had no track record or special expertise when it came to any other area of the music business. And in the case of Bulldog, Bronfman's guess—which ignored the more informed opinion of Cohen—proved as bad as anyone else's. "Just because you buy a business doesn't mean you understand that business," said Ed Bicknell, who managed Dire Straits and ran the William Morris Agency's international music operation. "Record companies going in that direction may be surprised by how tight promoter margins are, and that just occasionally they lose money."

Taken together, Bronfman's decisions painted a confounding picture. On the whole, his executive performance was the best in the record business, shepherding the company through a major restructuring and an IPO in his first year on the job. The record industry was shrinking, but WMG's share was growing each year, owing to a combination of careful signings, streamlining and closely managing its labels, and aggressively experimenting with online product. And if Bronfman still hadn't figured out how to stay on the internet bronco, it was clear that he and WMG were willing to take their lumps and keep getting in the saddle. Still, Bulldog was one of several plays that cast doubt on Edgar's judgment. It wasn't a question of sometimes making the wrong call; no one is right all the time. It was a question of values and perspective.

In 2006, Warner ended a nine-year licensing arrangement with Ha-Tav ha-Shmini, an independent Israeli record company focusing on alternative rock, and turned their distribution in that country over to the Lev Group. The firm is coowned by Edgar's sister Holly, and her husband, Yoav Lev. Bronfman insisted that there was nothing out of the ordinary in the arrangement: John Reid, who oversaw WMG's operations in the Middle East, wanted to change licensees and Edgar's sister and brother-in-law said they could do it. "It went before the independent directors—as I told them it would—and I was studious about not being involved," Edgar said, adding that there were other bidders. After agreeing to pay $2.8 million to license the catalog for three years, the Levs, who live in Boulder, Colorado, and spend much of their time overseeing an organic tea company in Lucknow, India, turned around and subcontracted WMG's recordings to an experienced Israeli music company, High Fidelity. That same year, WMG approved at least $240,000 in funding for Green Owl, a label coowned by Edgar's eldest son, Ben Brewer, a critically lauded musician.

The intersection of Edgar's personal and professional interests was also illustrated in his and WMG's dealings with one of the company's directors, billionaire Len Blavatnik. On the business side, Bronfman said he met the American-educated Russian oligarch— whose US-based Access Industries has extensive interests in Russia's oil, coal, plastics, and chemical industries—when he was looking for investors to join Music Partners Ltd., his Warner investment vehicle. "My father knew him from the Jewish world, and when I said I was looking for money, he said, 'You should talk to Len.'" Blavatnik was willing to invest $25 million in return for a seat on the WMG board; Edgar was happy to oblige.

Blavatnik remained on the board until January 2008, and during his tenure a joint venture among Blavatnik's Access Industries, WMG, Sony-BMG Music, and two Russian record labels was launched to exploit digital rights in Russia. The company reportedly achieved annual mobile sales of $120 million before being sold in 2009.

On the personal side, in the fall of 2007, Blavatnik purchased Bronfman's East Sixty-fourth Street town house for $50 million in cash. He already owned two other Manhattan properties that he'd paid nearly $60 million for as well as a London estate costing $100 million. It was a wonderful deal for Edgar, being the second-highest price ever paid for a single-occupancy Manhattan home and more than eleven times what he paid for it twelve years earlier. In the interim, his wife, Clarissa, had spent millions gutting the interior and rebuilding it around waxed steel walls, internal balconies, and a modern, two-and-a-half-story atrium described in a feature-length story in the *New York Times* as "something like a minimalist opera set for 'Cavalleria Rusticana.'"

When a reporter reached Blavatnik by telephone and inquired about the sale, the tycoon hung up on him. Questioned about the sale, Bronfman says that as with Blavatnik's agreement to invest in Music Partners, the Russian was simply being obliging. "He came to the house and liked it. When he heard I wanted to move, he said, 'I'd like to buy it.'"

One industry watchdog who doesn't take such a glib view is Nell Minow. Minow is the editor and cofounder of the Corporate Library, which provides independent corporate governance research and analysis, and coauthor of *Corporate Governance*, an MBA textbook now in its fourth edition. She says the personal transaction with a WMG director, particularly one who had business before the company, could be construed as a conflict of interest. "A shareholder could suggest that it might impair the objectivity of the chairman."

Told of Minow's assessment, Bronfman, who didn't consult WMG's corporate counsel regarding a possible conflict of interest before selling the house, was unmoved. "To me there's zero conflict and we've had zero inquiries," he said. "You can get sued for anything—and you do."

Whether he was or wasn't guilty of a conflict, Bronfman was the chairman and CEO of a public company, and his judgment and image needed to be sound in both fact and perception. In most cases, the financial scope of the decisions wasn't as dire as what they suggested, which was that Edgar was running a public company with an air of imperious entitlement. That hadn't been questioned at Seagram, where the Bronfman family's continuing control was part of the corporate cocktail. No such argument could be made at Warner Music when Edgar—while laying off employees and cutting the roster—made deals as if he were Mr. Sam, running a family business. Even more troubling than any business decision he made at Warner was his personal investment as one of three general partners in Accretive. One of its deals looked downright slimy.

Accretive invested mostly in firms providing a range of outsourcing services to companies. One was the National Arbitration Forum (NAF), a private company arbitrating credit card debt and other disputes, in which it has a 40 percent stake and governance rights. At the time of the purchase, Bronfman had been an Accretive general partner for five years.

In 2006, Minnesota's attorney general filed a lawsuit against NAF, accusing it of consumer fraud, deceptive practices, and false advertising, charging that it had held itself out to consumers as independent while hiding financial ties to credit card companies and collection agencies, some of which Accretive owned.

Minnesota's case against NAF presented an extraordinarily unflattering portrait of Accretive and its founder, J. Michael Cline, alleging that the firm and NAF's senior management created a series of wholly owned intermediary companies and funds with different names to mask a relationship intended to exploit credit card arbitrations in order to improve the fortunes of both NAF and the collection agencies. Indeed, the suit included correspondence from NAF's top executive fretting that the financial relationship with Accretive would have to be "unwound" if it became public knowledge, and showed that 60 percent of the debt arbitration claims handled by NAF in 2006 were filed by collection firms owned by Accretive. Who ultimately won those claims? A separate, yet-to-be-heard action filed by San Francisco's city attorney paints NAF as in the tank for creditors, claiming that out of 18,075 credit card cases arbitrated over four years, NAF found for the card holders just thirty times. And according to *BusinessWeek,* those results were no accident: NAF arbitrators—lawyers and judges hired on a freelance basis—told the magazine that the company stopped using them if they repeatedly found for consumers.

Less than a week after the Minnesota suit was filed, NAF settled with the state by agreeing to get out of the credit card arbitration business. For the record, the company denied the accusations and cited mounting legal costs as its reason for quitting the market.

Brokering and financing a hand-in-glove relationship between credit card companies, debt collection agencies, and a private arbitrator might not have earned Accretive a lawsuit of its own, but the suggestion that they had clandestinely cultivated an uneven playing field on which to bludgeon debt-hobbled consumers looked like a hell of a way to make a buck. Particularly if, like Edgar Bronfman Jr., you were already a billionaire.

By 2007, the record business had been shrinking for seven straight years. Yet to Bronfman's credit, WMG had not. In the three years since he had acquired WMG, the value of the rest of the recorded music business had declined more than 15 percent, but revenues for WMG had held steady at around $3.5 billion per year and were even slightly higher than they'd been in 2004. Even more impressive, the margin on overall income was rising. Much of the success was due to Bronfman reducing fixed costs through staff cuts and trimming back to a smaller, more profitable roster. He'd also been able to take advantage of management troubles among his competitors: WMG's 5 percent rise in US market share coincided with drops at EMI and Sony BMG Music. And while WMG hadn't mastered the internet, they were more aggressive than anyone else. The percentage of WMG's recorded music revenue from digital had risen from under 3 percent to over 20 percent; at Atlantic, which had undergone the more sweeping roster change, it was approaching 50 percent. WMG was the most profitable company at iTunes.

Warner management's continued faith in the ultimate worth of music and their own ability to manage and wring value from it made them eager for another shot at EMI.

Things at EMI were not going well. The company began 2007 with two warnings to investors that earnings would not be as high as expected. Recorded-music profits tumbled 61 percent and its two top executives, Alain Levy and David Munns, were let go. The executive chairman of the company, Eric Nicoli, assumed Levy's duties as chairman and CEO, but EMI's worldwide market share continued to drop through the year, from 12.8 percent to 10.9 percent. The company's board was shuffled to include members who could facilitate a sale.

Looking to avoid the regulatory pitfalls that tripped up the Sony-BMG merger, Bronfman worked out an anticipatory agreement with Impala, the consortium of independent European record companies whose objections to the Sony BMG merger had led to that merger's dismissal in the European Court. In the event of a merger with EMI, WMG would sell several labels to European independents and provide funding for Merlin, a digital rights platform for Impala's members. In return, Impala said it had no objections.

In March, WMG offered to buy EMI for 260 pence per share—significantly less than the 320 pence they'd offered a year earlier. Said Scott Sperling of the old offer, "Clearly, that's not anywhere near what you'd want to pay today," adding that EMI's recent results were disappointing "and we don't see it turning around." EMI immediately rejected what they considered a lowball bid.

Several other suitors, including JP Morgan's One Equity Partners, the Fortress Group, and Cerberus Capital Management, were reportedly also interested, but executives and directors at WMG liked their chances. They would have to pay a premium as a set-aside against the possibility that the EU could still derail a merger, but they stood to gain the most in cost savings and believed their previously rejected bid of 260 pence was 25 pence more than any private equity bidder would offer. They expected their own next bid to be closer to 230 pence.

In May, after signing a nondisclosure agreement, WMG executives were given a look at EMI's financial data and a meeting with management. The early morning telephone conference at 6:00 a.m. East Coast time between EMI executives in London and the WMG staff in New York lasted about half as long as the Warner people expected. "We have to leave," EMI finance director Martin Stewart said as he cut the meeting short, "and you'll know why soon."

Within the hour a reporter from London's *Financial Times* called WMG spokesman Will Tanous for a reaction to the news that Terra Firma, a British equity fund, had bid 265 pence—and that EMI management was recommending it be accepted. It was a stunning offer, worth £3.2 billion including debt—and more than double the price Bronfman-Lee had paid for Warner Music three years earlier when the global market for recorded music was 15 percent larger.

The sharp-elbowed jockeying between Bronfman and Nicoli over who would be the buyer the last time around suggested that the timing of the Terra Firma bid was no accident. Frustrated, the Warner executives involved in the talks with EMI suspected they had been held at bay and given just enough access to comply with the law. And any WMG bid would now have to be over £3 a share to cover the risk of not getting regulatory approval.

"The pressure was to say, 'Three hundred,'" said a WMG executive involved in the purchase talks. "And we're wondering if that makes sense with a declining record business, internal EMI data that didn't show a healthy company, and what appears to be a different credit market on the horizon. Were we to make a bid close to our initial one, we'd have to go through selling the publishing company and the regulatory hurdles. And at that price, what would we have to get when we resold EMI publishing? Five billion dollars?" In the end, Bronfman and his board decided to punt and didn't match Terra Firma's bid.

EMI's directors strenuously objected to the suggestion that they had avoided a sale to WMG, claiming they got a better deal for their shareholders from Terra Firma than they would have from Bronfman. "If management was in control, EMI would not have been sold to Terra Firma," says an EMI executive knowledgeable about the sale. "We were sold to Terra Firma to deliver the greatest value to the shareholder. So all this stuff about a war between Nicoli and Bronfman—Eric may not have wanted to lose his job, no one does, but that wasn't on the table. Three other private equity companies were in and not far off Terra Firma's bid. What that tells me is that Bronfman and his bankers don't believe in the business, even with £200 million of synergy. He didn't bid anything. Terra Firma saw a way to make a business that was more flexible, more productive than Edgar did."

That remained to be seen. In the interim, EMI had a new owner and the record industry had another player who was going to cure its ills. Guy Hands, forty-eight, was an Oxford-educated financier with a personal worth pegged at £200 million and an unusual business approach. Reportedly dyslexic, Hands was said to eschew in-depth financial reports for his own system of looking at key components to evaluate a business. He made his mark in the mid-1990s at Nomura, the Japanese bank, by packaging cash flow as a tradable security and investing the proceeds in such wide-ranging assets as pubs, trains, and housing, reportedly netting the bank £1.4 billion. In 2001 he bought the securities and investment business from Nomura, changed the name to Terra Firma, and developed a portfolio that included the Odeon cinema chain and a string of betting parlors. Britain's financial press portrayed the EMI deal as one Hands made on the rebound after losing several others including an £11-billion bid for Alliance Boots, Britain's largest drugstore chain.

Hands prided himself on being a practical manager who had employed common sense solutions to shake up and improve businesses such as the German gas station chain Tank & Rast and British waste recycler WRG. After his son told him that the limited graphic capabilities of CDs made them less desirable than LPs for many music fans, he suggested EMI explore packaging CDs in album-sized sleeves. The observation wasn't without merit, but the idea died when someone explained to Hands that music retailers had scrapped LP-sized display bins when the CD came in and weren't likely to repurchase them in order to stock the titles of one company.

Characterizing former management as wasteful, Hands intimated that EMI's acts had been pampered and would have to work harder for their money. The suggestion angered and alienated some important talent managers, whom the British press dubbed the Black Hands Gang and counted on for a negative quote about the new chief whenever EMI made news. When expected staff cutbacks became a certainty, Robbie Williams's manager, Tim Clark, said the British pop star was going to hold back his album. "We won't deliver an album to a company where we don't know what their structure will be or how they will handle things," Clark said. When the Rolling Stones's EMI contract lapsed, they departed for Universal.

Even more damaging to EMI was the popular rock band

Radiohead's decision to spurn a £3-million advance for their next album, *In Rainbows*. The band was not shy about its reasons for leaving. "EMI is in a state of flux," Radiohead guitarist Ed O'Brien said. "It's been taken over by someone who's never owned a record company before, Guy Hands and Terra Firma, and they don't realize what they're dealing with. It was really sad to leave. But he wouldn't give us what we wanted. He didn't know what to offer us. Terra Firma doesn't understand the music industry." The band revealed plans to post *In Rainbows* online and ask listeners to pay whatever they thought it worth.

O'Brien's words were truer than he knew. To buy EMI, Terra Firma had borrowed £2.7 billion from Citibank. By the end of the year, the worldwide credit market was on the verge of collapse. Neither Citibank nor Terra Firma was able to repackage and sell the debt as planned. And though Hands mimicked Bronfman-Lee by cutting staff and paring back the roster, he was not able to lay off his initial investment the way they had. EMI couldn't earn enough to pay its loans, and the equity firm was forced to repeatedly pump more money into the music company just to pay the debt to Citibank.

EMI's old board had gotten a good deal for its shareholders, but now that the music company was privately owned, the price was proving wildly optimistic and its future was in doubt. EMI's prior suggestion that Bronfman hadn't matched Hands's bid because he "didn't believe in the business" had proven to be an empty insult. WMG knew enough about the business to run the numbers, and they couldn't make them work. And neither, apparently, could Hands, at least not in this extraordinary credit market. Within two years Terra Firma wrote off half of EMI's value and forced Hands to relinquish the CEO slot at Terra Firma to placate investors. "EMI Music has not done very well and he was instrumental in investing in EMI," said one of those investors, Andrew Alleyne. Hands remained Terra Firma's chairman and chief investment officer, but it couldn't have been easy for the self-made mogul to be demoted at his own company. Bronfman, who'd made his own disastrous entertainment industry deal with Vivendi, could certainly commiserate, but WMG was now more interested in keeping its powder dry, constantly monitoring EMI's credit for a chance to buy up its debt on the cheap. Said a senior WMG executive, "I just don't think this dance will end until the two companies are combined."

Guy Hands's unhappy experience with the uncertainties of the music industry underscored just how well Bronfman-Lee had done with WMG, but it didn't disguise the fact that CD sales were approaching free-fall and the future of the recording business looked bleaker than ever. In November 2008, Atlantic Records reported it had reached a milestone with over 50 percent of its US sales derived from digital products like song downloads and ringstones. That was significantly higher than WMG's overall worldwide sales, where digital accounted for 27 percent, and Atlantic's numbers were widely promoted to portray the label as forward-looking and technologically advanced. But because WMG didn't break out the sales figures for its labels, it was impossible to tell what the information really meant. Was Atlantic growing or shrinking? The digital market wasn't coming close to replacing evaporating CD sales—total US record revenues had been $14.6 billion in 1999 without digital sales but were just $10.1 billion including digital sales by 2008. Atlantic was clearly a smaller record company than it had been under Time Warner.

The most deeply troubling development, however, was the growing realization that YouTube and the streaming and free-to-consumer music websites that WMG and the other labels had been willing to try were generating very little in the way of additional sales and royalties and no meaningful advertising income. The biggest problem with YouTube was its microscopic payments. According to Tube Mogul, which measured internet traffic, music and videos featuring music had been played 8 billion times on YouTube by the end of 2008. Yet of the $639 million in digital revenues that WMG reported for the fiscal year, YouTube accounted for less than 1 percent.

British songwriter and producer Pete Waterman wrote an essay for the English tabloid the *Sun* detailing his YouTube earnings as cowriter of the song "Never Gonna Give You Up." Recorded by Rick Astley in 1987, the song's video had an unusual second life twenty years later as a bona fide internet phenomenon when the practice of "Rickrolling"—a practical joke in which the victim is either emailed or pointed to what is purported to be an important link that, when opened, proves to be the Astley video—became an enormously popular meme. According to Waterman, the clip was played over 150 million times on YouTube; the site itself placed the number at 40 million. Either way, Waterman's YouTube payday was a bit of a shock: £11. After pointing out that the site's corporate parent, Google, had made over $3 billion that year, Waterman rolled his eyes at the company's justification that the exposure was generating other income for the song. "Everybody says YouTube has promoted your work to new audiences who have then gone out and bought it. That's BS. Nobody buys music they can get for free on sites like YouTube."

WMG was coming to the same conclusion. Unable to negotiate better licensing terms with YouTube, Bronfman terminated the agreement at the end of 2008, forcing the site to take down all clips and recordings featuring WMG artists and music. Neil Young was among the company's artists who spoke up for the move. But less well-known artists who relied on the site were frustrated and even furious. Amanda Palmer, who was signed to Warner's Roadrunner label as half of the Brechtian glam-rock duo Dresden Dolls, had no inkling of WMG's split with YouTube until her videos suddenly disappeared from the site. Palmer had little contact or promotional support from the larger company and was in the middle of a shoestring worldwide tour and campaign for a solo album, *Who Killed Amanda Palmer?*. An active blogger, she used the internet to maintain almost daily contact with her fans, and the keystone of the promotional campaign was a series of episodic homemade videos posted on YouTube. Although the clips soon resurfaced on a different video site, Palmer was upset to see her work yanked because of WMG. "It's absurd," she blogged. "They are looking for money in a totally backwards way. Money that, I should point out, I would *never* see as an artist. If they got their way and YouTube decided to give them a larger revenue share of the videos, it's very unlikely it would ever make its way into the artists' bank accounts."

Palmer's frustrations were seconded by thousands of YouTube's users. "My video got 30,000 views/listens of a pretty obscure song," commented a YouTube poster in one of the few profanity-free responses to the news about WMG's withdrawal. "How can that be bad for the artist? Bad for him now 'cos in [the] future I'll be sure I never buy a WMG product again." WMG's decision was just one more move by the same greedy bastards who had closed Napster and sued thousands of downloaders.

The financial failure of the new models was a bigger and more immediate problem for Bronfman than Warner's image problem. The bottom line was that the streaming and ad-supported music sites that WMG had taken a flyer on just didn't make money. Payment rates for services like imeem were reportedly so low that a user would have to listen to 1,400 songs—which took over ninety hours—to generate the same revenues as someone who purchased one album. Perhaps worse, while advertisers were willing to spend billions with Google or Yahoo!, they weren't particularly interested in much else on the web, including music sites. Subsequently, even when the labels accepted modest, fraction-of-a-cent rates, the ad-supported streaming sites couldn't pay. Their futures looked shaky. Less than two years after investing in Lala and imeem, WMG would write off both investments, a $33-million loss. "We do not intend to make more digital venture capital investments," Bronfman said flatly.

Most troubling was the industry's inability to capitalize on the popularity of music on the social networking site MySpace. Purchased by News Corp. in 2005, MySpace was a top-five web destination that let users create personal pages with profiles and a wide variety of postings including blogs, email, photos, chats, and music. By 2007 literally millions of songs had been posted to its pages, and the following year MySpace Music was formed as a joint venture between the major record companies and News Corp.

Built around a search engine to find and play any song posted to MySpace, the site used free music streams as bait: the idea was to sell other music products to the millions of MySpace users—a track, an album, a T-shirt, concert tickets, *anything.* "It's such an obvious idea," Eric Garland, chief executive of a leading internet market research firm, BigChampagne Media Measurement, said. "MySpace is already a destination for music and music fans. You could argue that MySpace is one of the top distributors of music in the world." But a year later, the site still hadn't developed the tools to sell anything. "We continue to hold out a good deal of hope for its potential," Bronfman told financial analysts. "But, without putting too fine a point on it, it has disappointed us so far."

What did work at MySpace Music was the search engine–in fact, it worked spectacularly well, and the music of the most obscure cult figures and many of the biggest stars was available on demand. "Cloud computing," the idea that information and programs stored on personal computers would move onto the internet and become more accessible, was just being discussed by the general public, but it was already reality in the music world. Any computer terminal or smartphone with internet access now provided instant access to any song you could think of. So why would anyone actually pay for recordings? For the rapidly decreasing number of moments in life when you couldn't connect to the internet?

The first rounds of poststreaming consumer research appeared to suggest precisely that. The heaviest users of on-demand music sites like imeem and MySpace Music–young adults and teenagers, traditionally the most avid music buyers–said they were buying fewer downloads than they had in the past. A new generation, unaccustomed to getting music as a physical product, was perfectly content with that arrangement. The music, the performance, the artists still held the same power and cachet for them, but they were also perfectly content not to pay anybody to produce it, frequently suggesting that their support of the artists through the purchase of concert tickets and other merchandise that they couldn't get their hands on for free was a fair trade. Unfortunately for WMG and the other labels, they weren't in those industries. Unless things changed drastically and quickly, there wasn't going to be a record business for much longer.

Almost incredibly, Bronfman and his partners continued to believe they should invest in music even as their most important customers showed less interest in buying it. An internal WMG study by Bain Media Partners showed that money spent on frontline music yielded a 30 percent internal rate of return in the United States during the first three years under Bronfman-Lee. That was an excellent return, and the report credited a combination of consumer interest and tight financial management. But with CDs continuing their inexorable slide and free streaming growing in popularity but unable to produce advertising income, WMG appeared trapped. Recordings still fueled careers; the problem was that there was no longer any reason to buy them. For performers, the answer was obvious: focus on other income opportunities like touring, merchandising, licensing, or endorsements until things changed again. But for the record companies, there was no obvious solution. They'd have to effect the change. If WMG wished to avoid Kodak's fate as a casualty of a technological revolution, Bronfman would have to find a way to redefine the business instead of settling for what he could get. After the miscues with Bulldog and the internet investments, he'd have to play his way to a better hand with the few good cards he still had. Edgar's ace in the hole was that even when fans weren't buying records, those recordings were still the most important factor in building careers and making stars—and he recognized that artists could be convinced to pay for that with a share of their touring and other nonrecording income. Bronfman was going to leverage WMG's services to radically alter the relationship between record companies and artists, abandoning traditional recording contracts to demand wide-ranging partnerships that could encompass every phase—and revenue stream—of a career. It was a sweeping redefinition, born of desperation. But reshuffling the deck hadn't been Edgar's idea. It came from John Janick, a young executive with a keen eye for the way record companies could improve their hand.

13

The Circle Game

In 2005, when Lyor Cohen bought a stake in Fueled by Ramen Records, an up-and-coming rock label with a knack for finding and developing pop punk bands, he didn't imagine that the label's twenty-five-year-old founder John Janick would help WMG's entire record operation redefine the business it was in. Janick's insistence on participating in other segments of his recording acts' young careers would prove a revelation to Cohen and Bronfman and give the company a lifeline.

Janick was a born record business hustler. As a high school student in Port Charlotte, Florida, he was the punk devotee who would dig up the latest releases on the small, hard-to-find labels—and then resell them to his classmates. By the time he entered the University of Florida in 1998 John had struck up a partnership with Vinnie Fiorello, the drummer with the popular pop punk band Less Than Jake, and started Fueled by Ramen. An homage to the three-for-$1 instant noodle that was the cornerstone of his college diet, the label operated out of Janick's dorm room in Gainesville. And like its namesake,

Janick built his new company to be fast and cheap: one of his first investments was a T-shirt press. "I had no money," he recalled with a shrug. "So I knew I couldn't get radio or video play for my artists."

Janick's do-it-yourself ethos was par for the course on the independent punk scene, where a sense of community, student-friendly prices for CDs and tickets, and a one-to-one rapport with fans were the norm, even for a band with a successful recording career and national following like Less Than Jake. But along with preaching extensive touring and a hand-to-mouth existence to his young bands, most of whom fell within the teen-oriented pop punk genre, Janick was quick to see that the internet was an inexpensive and easy way to keep in constant touch with fans and drum up excitement. Fueled by Ramen was soon selling its bands' souvenirs and merchandise—as well as their CDs—at concerts and online.

By the time he entered the MBA program at the University of South Florida in 2003, Janick had his first bona fide hit act, the Chicago band Fall Out Boy. Fall Out Boy's management used Ramen as an incubator to nurture the band's following and after one album took them to the better-heeled and more sophisticated Island Records. Janick kept the band's merchandising and their first Ramen album, *Take This to Your Grave,* went gold. He also made a deal with one of the band members, Pete Wentz, to release records he produced.

Janick—who had shed his partnership with Fiorello—wanted to find his own Island deal for Ramen and the rest of his roster. His CDs were already being sold by WMG through their Alternative Distribution Alliance (ADA), and he pitched his label to Tom Whalley, the chairman of Warner Bros. Records. Whalley passed, but Lyor, who was overseeing Island when Fall Out Boy was signed, bought a stake in the label and made Fueled by Ramen a joint venture with Atlantic.

Cohen and Atlantic president Julie Greenwald believed that Ramen could get the ball rolling on other acts for Atlantic. They also liked the fact that Janick still budgeted as if he were working out of his dorm room: Panic! at the Disco's 2005 debut album, *A Fever You Can't Sweat Out,* was recorded for $18,000; it has reportedly sold over 2 million copies.

"John thrived on not having any money," said Cohen. "He's a

true independent-spirited entrepreneur." Comparing Janick to Chris Blackwell, who'd fed such stars as U2, Bob Marley, Traffic, and Robert Palmer to Atlantic, another senior executive at WMG confessed, "If we had five executives like Janick, we'd be in great shape."

It wasn't just that he was frugal. Janick had built a broader business relationship with his artists and shared in the profits from more than their songs and recordings.

It was hardly a new idea. When T-shirts and other concert souvenirs became a big business in the 1980s, making millions for arena acts like Journey and Bruce Springsteen, record companies tried to get on board, arguing that labels helped create and popularize both the music and the graphic images, particularly album covers, that frequently showed up on T-shirts and that they deserved a piece of the income. CBS Records even bolstered their argument by purchasing part ownership in Winterland, a leading tour merchandiser founded by San Francisco promoter Bill Graham. But artists and their managers weren't swayed. The labels had no leverage to demand that kind of concession from a star unless they wanted to pay an enormous advance, and even new artists found it easy to refuse a recording contract that included merchandising rights, arguing that it was a business the record companies knew nothing about. CBS soon saw it the same way and sold the business to MCA.

Janick found a way to succeed where they had failed. First, he was small and nimble and worked only with young, unknown artists who were willing to sign all-encompassing deals in order to make records and launch their careers. Second, unlike CBS, he actually understood the merchandising business, particularly as it applied to the high school–aged music fans Ramen catered to. He knew what they wanted to buy, what it should look like, how much to charge, and how to get it to them online, at concerts, and through mall retailers like Hot Topic. Most significantly, he thought more like an artist's manager than a record executive. He hadn't failed to notice that successful recording careers frequently became springboards for other commercial opportunities: Mariah Carey and Britney Spears were being paid millions of dollars to endorse perfumes, and rappers like 50 Cent and Jay-Z were getting similar money for clothing lines and other endorsements. Janick defined the mission of Fueled by Ramen as something more than selling records and even more than helping to create a pop star. "I view our business as building a brand," he said. Arguing that the record made everything else possible, Janick wanted to use it as leverage to tie Ramen to the artist's entire career and income including merchandising, concerts, licensing, and endorsements.

Shortly after the label teamed with Atlantic in 2005, Ramen signed a traditional recording deal for Paramore, a high school–aged quartet from Tennessee featuring singer Hayley Williams, a sixteen-year-old Kewpie doll with Creamsicle-colored hair. A little later, company executives came back to the band's representatives. "We said, 'We think Hayley is something special,'" recalled Craig Kallman, Atlantic's chairman. "We'd like this to be the first of our new, expanded deals."

The contract hammered out over the next six months was surprisingly comprehensive, giving Atlantic and Ramen a piece of the band's merchandising, licensing, and touring income. Since it would likely be years—if ever—before those rights became valuable, the arrangement made sense only if the company was making a long-term commitment to Paramore. That wasn't the way record companies usually worked. In general, contracts for unknown bands guaranteed only one or two records, with any subsequent albums at the discretion of the label. But building Paramore's following from the ground up followed the plan used by Fall Out Boy: let the band play clubs and expose its songs on new music websites like PureVolume and find a solid fan base before looking for hits at radio and big tours. The gradual approach had some benefits for the young musicians, with the label paying not just for their van but the cost of tutors while they toured. Not surprisingly, the band's first album, *All We Know Is Falling*, wasn't a hit, but Atlantic liked the upside of the deal enough to make a similar arrangement without Ramen for another band, the Los Angeles hard-rock group Operator.

When Bronfman took over WMG he was not a fan of expanded rights arrangements, which had been on the fringes of the record industry for some time. In 2002, EMI had created a stir when it signed Robbie Williams to a reported $120-million, five-album contract that gave the record company a cut of his publishing, merchandising, and touring income. A one-of-a-kind deal, Williams's contract didn't signal a move into any of those businesses by EMI and appeared largely a way to justify giving an unusually lucrative contract to a coveted act. Conversely, the management company Sanctuary had started a record company for its clients. But Edgar preferred the cards he held: a big hit record generated more free cash than any other segment of the music business. "I'm not convinced it's in my best interests," he said of deals like Williams's. "I'm presuming I have to give up something to get something."

Indeed, Bronfman didn't like paying a premium for talent. He was leery of signing established stars and thought record companies were better served financially by developing new talent. Although there were obvious exceptions, most stars recorded their signature work earlier rather than later in their career—at a time when the record companies could buy their services for less. When he purchased PolyGram in 1998, he'd had no choice but to re-sign U2 or lose the company's biggest rock act. Swallowing hard, he agreed to a hefty advance and top-of-the-market royalty rate. When the band's first album under the new contract, the unexpectedly mainstream *All That You Can't Leave Behind*, proved a worldwide hit that reinvigorated their career, Bronfman counted himself lucky rather than smart. Even the Rolling Stones hadn't enjoyed a significant hit in decades, and record companies signed them and other veteran rockers through an equation based largely on what their back catalog could sell and the less tangible but still valuable goodwill their presence created.

By 2007, the multiplatinum blockbuster albums that produced the best profit margins for labels had taken the brunt of the internet assault. Since 2000, prerecorded music sales had shrunk by 36 percent, but total sales for the Top 10 were off by 57 percent—which meant not only that record companies were making less money, but that it was costing them more on average to do so. Warner Bros. had the bestselling album of the year, Josh Groban's Christmas album, *Noël*, but the 3.7 million copies it sold wouldn't have put it in the Top 10 in 2000. That was WMG's story in a nutshell: they were doing better than anyone else in a bad business. In the deepening gloom, Bronfman had a change of heart. He decided he was more than willing to give up some of what he had to get a piece of something else.

Atlantic had not yet seen a return on its investment in Paramore's career, but they liked where it was going. In 2007, the band's second album, *Riot!,* sold more than 1 million copies. "Most of the revenues and profits at the outset are from recorded music," said a senior WMG executive intimate with Paramore's contract. "It's only as the band's reputation and touring grows that the other income streams grow." Looking at the increase in Paramore's popularity and sales over the first two albums, the company was confident that with the release of the next album touring and merchandising profits would kick in.

Cohen, with Bronfman's approval, made it company policy that 20 percent of Atlantic and Warner Bros. A&R budgets would be spent on "360 deals," expanded recording contracts that might include income from any part of an act's career.

The details varied from act to act, but a 360 had two primary features. The record company might pay a substantially better record royalty rate on a shorter contract—e.g., 30 percent instead of 15 percent for a term with three album options instead of seven. Additionally, the artist would receive payment in return for a similar interest in a number of areas including merchandising and ticket sales.

Atlantic and Warner Bros. Records weren't in those businesses, and the labels wouldn't be doing many of those things. Nevertheless, they were arguing that even as sales fell, records drove a career and made all other opportunities possible, and that in order to continue to underwrite career development, the company would have to participate in nonrecording income.

As they explained the new policy to artists and their representatives, the company's executives were frank: with record revenues shrinking, they needed to find new ways to get a return on the investment the company was making. As Atlantic's Kallman saw it, "If they're going to steal our music, then we've got to do something else."

At first, Kallman found it difficult to get more than recording rights when an act he wanted was being wooed by a competitor. But after Atlantic got a few artists to grant the additional rights the problem disappeared as the other labels began to ask for them as well. By the end of the year, the company's policy was to sign all new artists to 360 deals, and its strategy was to keep pushing the parameters of participatory rights. "We kept expanding what we were asking for," said one WMG executive, "in part because we were generally getting things within a year of asking."

Artist representatives resisted the rights grab, but they also saw the logic. "The record companies were circling the drain and their ability to make someone famous has diminished," said Ken Abdo, an industry attorney. "But the fact remains that if you want to sell a million 'things'—whether CDs or downloads or ringtones or whatever—the probabilities are in being with a global record company."

For once, the record companies recognized that the internet had handed them a cudgel. On one hand, the web had decimated CD sales, but it had also made it possible for anyone to post music online—and the result had been a flood of new and undifferentiated releases. In 2008, 105,575 albums—the vast majority by internet-empowered hobbyists—were released. Of those, just 110 sold more than 250,000 copies. Clearly, making a record and releasing it through the internet wasn't difficult. But standing out from an army of competitors and turning your record into a hit and a successful career was harder than ever. That was the business WMG now declared it was in.

"They were saying to the new artists, 'Nobody has ever heard of you or really cared about buying what you made before we spent the risk capital to make you a star,'" said attorney Kendall Minter. "But we don't want to be limited anymore to just getting revenue from sales of records. You're going out as a result of our risk, our investment, and you are having a career that can bring you great financial rewards from touring, publishing, merchandising, film, and book deals. What the record companies did slowly but surely was say, 'Now we want a piece of the pie that you're enjoying from our risk capital.'"

With the move to 360, the rosters got younger, in part because established acts had no incentive to sign over more of their rights—

people already knew who they were. But the established artists were also getting more attractive offers, and not from other record companies. The American coffee chain Starbucks was making inroads in the territory. In addition to selling CDs through its stores and opening several Hear Music shops, a combination coffee bar and record store, it formed a Hear Music label with the established independent record company Concord Music Group. Testing the waters, Hear Music released a Ray Charles duets album, an acoustic version of Alanis Morissette's *Jagged Little Pill,* and arranged with Sony and Bob Dylan to sell the artist's historic early-'60s recordings from New York's Gaslight Cafe as well as the soundtrack to Martin Scorsese's documentary *No Direction Home.* When the Charles album sold over 2 million copies, Starbucks jumped into the record business with both feet, making deals in 2007 to release albums by Joni Mitchell, James Taylor, Carly Simon, and, most significantly, Paul McCartney.

The notion that one of the Beatles was more valuable to a chain of coffee bars than to a record company was jarring, even if McCartney hadn't enjoyed a significant hit in twenty years. Just how valuable was closely guarded, but the lion's share of the reportedly $5-million budget for McCartney's *Memory Almost Full* went directly to the artist. More valuable to McCartney than the money was the publicity: the unique arrangement generated far more interest in him than he could have achieved by just switching record companies. Apparently, it wasn't such a great deal for Starbucks. *Memory Almost Full* sold just over 500,000 copies—less than McCartney's last album for EMI—and by the spring of 2008 Starbucks had sold its interest in Hear Music to Concord. Angered by its quick exit from the record business, Carly Simon later sued Starbucks for $10 million, claiming they deceived her.

Still, other enterprises were getting valuable publicity by releasing recordings by established stars. In the summer of 2007, Prince struck a deal with the British newspaper the *Mail on Sunday* to tuck 3 million copies of his album *Planet Earth* into the paper. If the internet meant he couldn't sell an album as he had in the past, at least Prince had found a way to get paid for giving it away. The arrangement also created a huge buzz for the rocker and the series of twenty-one concerts he was slated to play at London's O$_2$ Arena—a series expected to gross over $26 million if it sold out. "It's direct marketing," Prince said at the time. "And I don't have to be in the speculation business of the record industry, which is going through a lot of tumultuous times right now."

It was further proof of how the internet had stood the music business on its head. Every label's CD sales were off, but established artists had a cushion. Even if their new albums rarely sold as robustly as their early work, they could still make a lot of money on the road catering to older fans who were less interested in buying new music than hearing the hits they'd grown up with. As a result, artists who rarely had hits anymore, like the Rolling Stones and Bruce Springsteen, or the reunited Police, were the biggest earners on the concert circuit. Several veteran rock acts including the Eagles, Journey, Kiss, and AC/DC opted to forego a record company altogether and made exclusive deals to manufacture and deliver their next albums to the retailing behemoth Walmart. The arrangements bypassed many of the bands' fans—the chain didn't even have a store in New York City—but that didn't bother longtime Eagles manager Irving Azoff. As far as he was concerned, the band's *Long Road Out of Eden* was only an advertisement for its world tour, and the 2.6 million copies that Walmart sold were an added bonus. "The business is going to have to wake up and realize that recorded music sales are an ancillary business," he said.

Given this landscape, it was hardly surprising when Madonna, a savvy and hard-nosed performer, struck a deal that capitalized on the new reality. Bronfman had been more than pleased with the success of *Confessions on a Dance Floor*, but when she began shopping for a new deal in 2007, his biggest competition wasn't another record label but the world's largest concert promoter, Live Nation.

The company had already struck lucrative, worldwide touring deals with U2, the Rolling Stones, and the Police that included merchandising, and proposed its own spin on the 360 deal. It offered Madonna a massive contract reportedly worth $120 million over ten years. Along with a $17.5-million signing bonus, it not only included the rights to present the singer's tours and handle her merchandise and licensing, but was also structured to pay her between $50 million and $60 million for three albums, at least double what any record company was likely to offer her. Whether that figure was cross-collateralized—whereby the individual record advances could be recouped out of her concert earnings—wasn't revealed. One thing was clear: Madonna was so valuable as a touring artist that Live Nation could afford to pay her far more to make a record than any record company could.

Attempting to stay in the race, Bronfman turned to Barry Diller's IAC, which owned Ticketmaster, as a possible partner in Madonna. (Ticketmaster had not yet proposed its merger with Live Nation.) In the end, even they couldn't assemble a counteroffer as compelling or as rich, and Madonna's breakthrough Live Nation contract was widely heralded as one more example that the record industry was dying. Though Live Nation had no expertise or mechanism for releasing and marketing the records Madonna would deliver, the company could easily strike a deal with any of the majors to distribute her physical and digital recordings for a percentage. No one said at the time that that deal was mostly to be struck with WMG, since they owned the rest of Madonna's catalog and could market them together.

Compared to WMG or the other labels, Live Nation's version of the 360 deal made more financial sense because the promoter was better prepared to bring value to the partnership. They were precisely the reverse of the deals made by the labels, which had the expertise and structure to sell records, but little else. Live Nation had been acquiring a wide variety of services over the preceding years including companies that made and sold merchandise, and their savviest move had been to buy a majority stake in Musictoday, a company begun by Coran Capshaw, an alternative marketing maven and as close to an oracle of underground business models as the music industry had produced.

Capshaw, through his first company, Red Light Management, had managed the Dave Matthews Band and expanded to handle dozens of bands including Phish, Drive-By Truckers, Ben Harper, the North Mississippi Allstars, Tim McGraw, and the Decemberists. He also bankrolled Tennessee's popular annual music festival, Bonnaroo, and cofounded ATO Records, a label boasting My Morning Jacket, David Gray, and Liz Phair. Musictoday, which is run out of a former frozen foods factory in Crozet, Virginia, employs two hundred people who create and manage internet fan and merchandise sites for artists and process and ship orders—everything from shower sandals to concert tickets—for over five hundred acts including Bob Dylan, Metallica, and Eminem. When Live Nation bought its stake, Musictoday was generating $100 million in revenues.

Considering where Bronfman wanted to take WMG, his investments in Lala, imeem, and Bulldog didn't look near as savvy as Live Nation CEO Michael Rapino's decision to buy a piece of Musictoday, which bought infrastructure. Even better, Rapino now had the insightful Capshaw on his team.

Without real services to offer, Bronfman could only argue that WMG deserved a greater share in an artist's career because they were "providing the seed money" and that a recording career created the notoriety upon which all other success depended. As a business proposition, that sounded more like a strong-arm tactic than a partnership. To fill the breach, Bronfman made a significant tweak in his strategy of investing in music companies: WMG would continue to diversify but would invest only in companies that could contribute value to a 360 deal. Each potential acquisition that came before the Monday morning senior staff meeting that Edgar chaired now had to have two benefits: give the company the tools it needed to be a meaningful partner in a 360 deal and provide WMG with a new opportunity to make money off those deals.

One of the first acquisitions was Artist Arena, a builder and administrator for fan club sites. Though experienced at online ticket sales for artists and adept at creating sites, Artist Arena was hardly Musictoday—they didn't handle any merchandise themselves. To help the labels move into that area, WMG hired Peter Scherr, who'd developed and managed the website for budget airline JetBlue, which sold 80 percent of its tickets online.

Next, WMG started a joint venture with Chris Lighty, a leading hip-hop manager, to pursue endorsement deals for artists called the Brand Asset Group. A former protégé of Lyor Cohen at Rush Management and Def Jam, Lighty had formed Violator Management and oversaw the careers of 50 Cent, P Diddy, and Missy Elliott. Lighty proved particularly adept at finding new opportunities for his clients. The rapper 50 Cent had an impressive array of deals including a book, a video game, his own clothing line, and endorsements.

With the rudiments of a structure in place, Kallman and other executives began to draw a distinction in artist negotiations between what they termed passive and active investments. "Active" meant WMG was going to provide the service, such as a fan site or merchandising. A "passive" investment was an advance against a share in income from an area WMG had no involvement in, such as concert earnings.

Inside the company, the discussion turned to which part of their artists' careers WMG should be active in. "It's been a little by design and a little by chance," admitted a senior executive. "We want to play a bigger role at the center of our artists' careers. We're never going to be Live Nation in terms of concerts, but the tip of the spear is that we're going to be the marketing engine, so why can't we widen that?"

Bronfman shied away from the touring and concert business in general, but he was eager to get a piece of ticket sales. Most deals with concert promoters allow bands to reserve a percentage of tickets, usually around 10 percent, to sell directly to their fans. Among bands with a dedicated following, this had evolved into a web-based business—and a very good one, since the hard-core fans who subscribe to a band's fan club or website are most likely to buy concert tickets anyway. Bands could give those fans something extra—early access to tickets—while pocketing a bit of the gate. By taking an active role in building fan sites, either on their own or with Artist Arena, Bronfman wanted the labels to get control of this and other online merchandising. To that end, Atlantic hired BandMerch executive Matt Young and made him their in-house guru.

By mid-2007 WMG's record companies were insisting that every 360 deal include active rights in recorded music, merchandising, and fan clubs. Everything else was on the table as well—endorsements, touring, even income from acting careers—as passive rights.

"We do have a form, but we're constantly working on it, and it's just a starting place," said Kallman. "We usually start every deal with the last one we did with the act's lawyer."

Virtually every one of WMG's 360 deals was with a young or up-and-coming performer. After Madonna, Live Nation had made a similarly lucrative deal with the rapper Jay-Z before signaling that it was turning off the spigot—at least until an appropriately exciting deal for a superstar came along. The promoter never indicated interest in making 360 deals with young or midlevel acts.

For many young artists, the business of making music was as harsh as ever, and 360s were a steep price to pay for help. Nonetheless, it was even harder to get on the public's radar without a record company. Since Napster, music had continued to be a major part of the internet's appeal, yet a repeatable, scalable way for younger musicians to turn that interest into a career had yet to emerge. Very few bands had been able to build a reputation by themselves on the internet and cross over to radio and concerts. The Brooklyn band Clap Your Hands Say Yeah was one of the few exceptions: their self-titled, self-released 2005 album received a lot of attention from bloggers and the influential music website Pitchfork, leading rock radio to play the record and jump-start their career. But after opting not to sign with an established label, the group was unable to replicate the success with its subsequent albums.

Another band, Vampire Weekend, made a more promising start. Formed in early 2006 by four Columbia University students, the group soon recorded a no-budget, three-song EP. Guitarist Ezra Koenig sent a track, "Cape Cod Kwassa Kwassa," to one of his favorite music blogs, Benn loxo du taccu, which focuses on African pop music. Blogger Matt Yanchyshyn posted it in October 2006 along with a nice notice. Whether it was the record itself or the notion that a New York band was being touted on an African music board, bloggers at bigger alternative rock sites like Stereogum and Music for Robots jumped, and the buzz landed the band on *Late Show with David Letterman* and *Saturday Night Live*. Unlike Clap Your Hands Say Yeah,

Vampire Weekend then turned to the established record business, signing with manager Ian Montone, whose other clients include the White Stripes, the Shins, and M.I.A. The group's self-titled album on XL Recordings, an independent distributed by WMG, sold over 300,000 copies. It remained to be seen whether the band had the creative firepower to continue to produce engaging records or if their route to notoriety would prove a smart model or idiosyncratic. Unlike the underground rock press and radio that sprang up in the late 1960s to help usher in the era of album rock, the internet hadn't produced influential gatekeepers like *Rolling Stone* or San Francisco disk jockey Tom Donahue, whose thumbs-up for a new band could translate into a career.

The availability of free music cut deeply into record sales for young and independent bands, forcing them to try to make a living on the road—and not just from performing. It became standard operating procedure for a band to come out after the show and man their own merchandising table, selling and signing T-shirts, CDs, posters, and other souvenirs. It was a grind.

"It's hard to tour these days," said attorney Chris Castle, who has been a record executive and also represented Napster. "Getting a per-show guarantee that's over $700 is a major accomplishment for an independent artist, and it's hard to cover gas, hotels, and food with low guarantees. You have to sell merchandise and CDs at the shows in order to survive, and you have to be good at it."

"A lot of people don't understand the gigantic difference between indie bands and successful major label bands," said Kevin Barnes, songwriter for the long-running and popular underground group Of Montreal. "If someone is in a supersuccessful indie band, then they're middle class. Even if a band has a T-shirt at Hot Topic, that doesn't mean they're even paying their rent."

The search for money led to endless fan-building: home pages—on Facebook, MySpace, and the web—had to be updated and maintained. Aside from samples of songs, that frequently required musicians to write blogs and answer email from fans, often on a daily basis. That meant a longer day for artists—or having to hire it out. "The bass player is probably not going to do it," said record executive Tom Silverman. If free music on the internet was liberation from the tyranny of an unjust record industry model, the only people it seemed to be liberating were the ones who weren't paying for music. It was at least as hard as it had ever been to make a living as a musician, and likely harder. And as 360s took hold, it was difficult to argue that young bands seeking broad commercial success weren't being driven into less favorable deals with the people who could help them achieve that goal—particularly record companies—by the culture of free.

"It hurts, it sucks," attorney Kendall Minter said of the emerging economics. "When you look at the numbers, the artist is getting squeezed and squeezed and squeezed. Yeah, the record company is investing risk capital. But they always have. Traditionally the artist has been the one who has to be in the studio, go out and work the record, promote, stay up late, get up early, get on the bus, stay in hotels, eat bad food, work to bring value to the record and the song. Now you have the record company saying, 'Pay me 20 or even 25 percent of your net from touring,' you have a manager who says, 'I want 15 to 20 percent of your gross,' you have a booking agent who may take 10 percent. If you're an established artist, you have a business manager who is probably getting 3 to 5 percent of the gross of all your income. Your attorney may have the same deal as the business manager. So by the time you're finished on a typical live date, an artist may only take home 30 percent—which is not a significant amount of money if you're not making $60,000 a night. The 360 relationship will last for the time of the deal. So if it's a four-record deal, all of the provisions are going to last for the length of the deal. Now, if you're successful, you're going to have the leverage to renegotiate for an improved deal. That will probably give you a little better participation, but I doubt very seriously it will completely eliminate it because once the foot is in the door you'll only remove it one toe at a time. But absent the leverage and success, you're kind of stuck for the ride."

In March 2007, every division at WMG was told to prepare for a series of meetings with senior management dubbed "the Baker's Dozen." They had to bring twelve proposals plus an overview of how they would work together and create a company that could weather a shrinking record business.

Atlantic's Baker's Dozen presentation, on March 21 in the thirtieth-floor conference room at WMG's New York headquarters, included several suggestions for ways to use the internet to identify and sign artists. The label had recently done well with a ringtone-oriented act, Cupid, so there was a good deal of talk about signing others and about trying to attract some of the independent artists whose music was being licensed for use in television shows. The shows didn't pay the artists much, but they were an excellent starting point for building a following. Most suggestions, however, were regarding how to redeploy the company to make the most of 360 deals.

"The idea is to enter into every business where music plays a key role," Kallman said. Atlantic had plans to sell T-shirts online and on tours and wanted to make corporate licensing deals for their artists and start a new "digital product innovation" department to create items that took advantage of new technologies as they came online. Kallman, who had to approve all of Atlantic's artist signings and was personally involved in many contract negotiations, was also concerned about making their new financial agreements transparent.

Historically, record companies had been a good deal less than forthcoming when it came to record royalties. The traditional recording contract paid an advance against a royalty rate that was usually 15 percent to 18 percent of a recording's wholesale price. Along the way, artists were also charged for a broad array of services from money advanced as tour support to promotional expenses. The upshot was that even artists who had considerable hits were likely to be presented with an accounting showing them to still owe the record company money. If an artist disagreed, he could conduct an audit of his account—at his own expense and without any cooperation from the label. Instead, artists and managers often tried to get as much money upfront as possible, believing the advance was likely all they'd ever see and that they could renegotiate another, better advance if they were successful.

Now WMG's labels were asking for a share in tour earnings—and the artists and their advisors would be doing the accounting. When asked about labels offering to pay tour support in return for a piece of an artist's tour income, attorney Peter Paterno said, "We'll agree," but made a point of noting that the record industry wasn't the only outfit capable of creative accounting. "We just won't give the labels money. Payback is a bitch, as they're about to discover."

Kallman's need for financial transparency had found an advocate in Lyor Cohen, who was confident that WMG would prove savvy enough to not get fleeced by artists and their managers. He proposed that WMG create a secure website where artists could view their financial stats in real time, but the company's accounting initiatives had so far failed. Along with accounting reforms, Kallman used the "Baker's Dozen" meetings to caution against any wide-ranging corporate makeover being done at the expense of the company's primary business—which continued to be finding and developing artists. "How do we not take our eye off our core business?" he asked.

In the coming months, Atlantic would prove quite adept at juggling both those balls, developing artists while trying to figure out how to make money off their careers even as recording sales continued to diminish. "This is the music business now," remarked one WMG senior executive. "Somebody is going to figure it out. It should be us."

If that sounded like a rallying call, it also signaled an historic retreat from the company's real business of finding a way to sell recorded music. Particularly telling was the departure of a frustrated Alex Zubillaga as head of digital strategy in early 2008. Demoralized by WMG's inability to create meaningful businesses either on the internet or with the phone companies, he believed it would take many more years before music became a viable moneymaker in cyberspace. And with no foreseeable prospects for a personal payoff on his remaining WMG stock—he had been an original partner in Lexa with Edgar—he returned to the financial world by joining Rhône, a new equity firm. Before he left, Zubillaga counseled Bronfman to try to get the other labels to work toward industrywide digital solutions. But that, too, continued to be an elusive goal. The following year, WMG started a new company, Choruss, with the aim of providing blanket copyright licenses to universities. Under the plan, schools would pay a fee to the record companies and their students could use the university's system legally to download music. The cost would ultimately be billed to individuals just as student organizations, copying, internet access, and other service fees are. Choruss was also viewed as a way to establish a precedent for payment elsewhere, such as through commercial internet service providers. Though several universities expressed interest, the plan stalled when other record companies declined to participate.

At Atlantic, the day-to-day business of "figuring it out" fell largely to label president Julie Greenwald and her lieutenant, Livia Tortella, Atlantic's general manager and executive vice president of marketing and creative media, who had followed Greenwald and Cohen from Def Jam. All business but far from humorless, Tortella had ultimate responsibility over marketing, which made her more important to an Atlantic artist's career than virtually anyone else. Supervising a team of product managers who designed and implemented marketing plans for each artist, Tortella was discovering that there were no one-size-fits-all programs anymore. "You have to be innovative *and* traditional and ready for anything at any time," she said. When rapper T.I.'s fans wanted ringtones and downloads more than they wanted albums, Atlantic implemented a program to maximize that, offering over one hundred different combinations of tracks, bundles, and other products. Conversely, the Detroit singer and rapper Kid Rock saw himself as an album artist and wouldn't let Atlantic license individual tracks to iTunes, forcing Tortella and the label to go out and find those places where album sales and Kid Rock converged. "I'm going to truck stops," Tortella said. She must have hit a lot of them: Kid Rock's last album, *Rock n Roll Jesus,* sold 3 million copies.

The business had changed so much in five years that as far as she was concerned, MTV was the only surviving power broker from that era. "There was no iTunes five years ago, and it was all traditional CD marketing," Tortella said. "Now we're looking to measure success all over. We measure how often a song is streamed on MySpace, how many downloads are sold, tickets, merchandise. Each artist becomes a brand that is successful or not. We're not just selling a Rob Thomas record anymore—our eye is on the Rob Thomas ball and we're selling twenty things. I'm in a brand situation with an artist. I think the model is P&L—profit and loss—for each artist. There will be various mixes of income for each one, and the connection with the fan will result in a sale of some kind. You've got to be able to do it all and not blow your brains out. The product changes, but the service the label delivers doesn't. We develop and market artists and fine-tune that in whatever medium comes along."

Despite the company's uncertain future, Bronfman had managed it well enough to have an optimistic story to tell the financial world. In his five years at the helm, WMG went through major shifts in philosophy, adopting and discarding strategies in a fight for survival. They resisted the internet, then embraced it. They sued their own customers and then tried to sell them anything they wanted. They pushed mobile phone companies and others to develop services and ultimately despaired of their ability to move the needle. They rolled the dice as investors in startups. They broadened their definition of the business they were in and reached out for new revenues and businesses. They completely altered their relationships with their artists.

The benefit of 360 deals was obvious: it offered WMG entrée to other revenue streams and could lessen its dependence on recordings. But it was also a self-serving sleight of hand that didn't produce a solution to its most basic problem: what recorded music product—if any—would consumers buy and how would they sell it to them? The encouraging news was that the relentless search for answers had produced a more thoughtful, inventive company. Even as CD sales continued to slide faster than other areas grew, digital revenues for the industry were going to top $4 billion in 2009. The record industry had been the canary in the coal mine for all media in the digital age—the first to gasp for breath and still not sure of its fate but far ahead of other industries like newspapers and book publishing in digital revenues and models. What the future held was anyone's guess.

In May 2009, Bronfman started his fifth year as chairman and CEO of the Warner Music Group by announcing he was moving to London for the next two years and would spend only two of every four weeks at the company's headquarters in New York. Describing the move as purely personal, Bronfman said he and his wife believed their children would benefit from living outside the US for a year or two. The news produced a myriad of reactions, both in the press and the industry. Some viewed it as the kind of cavalier attitude to business that only a rich man could afford, and others wondered if it wasn't a smokescreen for yet another attempted merger with the London-based EMI.

That same month, Edgar hosted a leadership conference for eighty of his most senior executives from around the globe. The two-day meeting, held across the street from Ground Zero in Lower Manhattan, was a mix of presentations, brainstorming, and pep rally, and its reports highlighted the fact that under the ownership of Bronfman-Lee, WMG had managed one particularly impressive feat: in the four years between 2004 and 2008, industry revenues had shrunk by 23 percent. Yet WMG's revenues had actually risen slightly, from $3.4 billion to $3.5 billion, with 27 percent of its revenues now earned digitally—a mark that was also better than the industry at large. By its own estimation, if WMG had performed like the overall industry, it would have earned $1.5 billion less in revenues during that period.

After opening the conference, Bronfman was a sporadic presence, ducking out for phone calls and meetings. At the end of the second day, he was the last scheduled speaker. What he had to say was a surprise.

His absences from the conference, Bronfman explained, were due to a bond float. When Edgar and his partners had acquired WMG from Time Warner, they had raised $680 million of the financing through a bond road show. Those notes were due in 2014, and the company had loans due in 2011. In recent weeks, the partners had noticed an opening in the financial markets, and had parlayed it into a chance to refinance. They hoped to raise $500 million in new bonds and use the money to pay off some of its debts and extend others, since no one knew what the credit market would be like when the bonds came due. "We're not sure we could have gotten credit then," Bronfman explained. Not knowing how the financial community would react to a record company, WMG had laid its numbers down and held its breath. Now, Bronfman said, he had just learned the results. He paused a moment before revealing that the offering had proven so popular that WMG had been offered $1.1 billion in financing. The company's flabbergasted executives looked at one another in disbelief before breaking into applause.

The bond's overwhelming success showed that Wall Street, unlike the record business, hadn't changed at all. Financial institutions that didn't understand the nuances of the music business back in the days when it cranked out money were no wiser now that record companies were in dire straits. They weren't backing Bronfman because he'd found a new way to sell music, but because he'd shown he could tread water when others were sinking and prudently manage the finances of a downsized and continually shrinking company. In truth, WMG was still a company in search of a business. It had signed or converted 327 artists—half its roster—to 360 deals, while still waiting for the first one, Paramore, to pay off. Pressed about when the company will know if it has gone down the right road, the normally cocksure Lyor Cohen suggests it might be "ten or twenty years," fobbing off serious analysis in the name of the Big Picture. No one knows if 360 deals are good for artists, music, or record companies.

Thanking everyone, Bronfman reminded them that Green Day, whose new album, *21st Century Breakdown,* had been released that week, was playing at a private party for them that evening. No one expected the album to sell the 17 million copies of its predecessor, 2004's *American Idiot,* but they still had high hopes.

"We're all getting paid," Edgar Bronfman Jr. said in closing. "We're going to keep getting paid, and we're going to have fun."

That sounded like the record business.

Epilogue

In October 2006 Ahmet Ertegun fell backstage at the Beacon The-
atre in New York before the Rolling Stones show celebrating Bill
Clinton's sixtieth birthday. After six weeks in a coma, he died on
December 14 and was buried in his native Turkey.

At his memorial service the following April at Jazz at Lincoln Center's Rose Theater, the speakers included former secretary of state
Henry Kissinger, Mick Jagger, designer Oscar de la Renta, Bette
Midler, New York mayor Michael Bloomberg, and two of Ertegun's
most notable protégés, David Geffen and *Rolling Stone* publisher Jann
Wenner. Lyor Cohen, who had arranged Ertegun's final transit to
Turkey and accompanied the body from New York to its burial, sat
in the second row with Craig Kallman and Julie Greenwald. No one
from the Warner Music Group spoke, and Edgar Bronfman Jr. did
not attend.

Ertegun was remembered as a man of many worlds: at a state
dinner in China; bargaining for Olympic tickets with a street scalper;
in a Bangkok brothel. But it was with musicians that Ertegun was

often most comfortable and on whose lives and work he had had the greatest impact. Among the performers paying tribute to him were Solomon Burke, Phil Collins and Genesis, Ben E. King, Stevie Nicks, Kid Rock, Sam Moore (of Sam & Dave), Crosby, Stills, Nash and Young, and Eric Clapton.

It was difficult to discern what was most revealing. Was it that Kid Rock and Michael Bloomberg adored and sought counsel from the same man? That Clapton's fondest memories weren't of their shared triumphs with Cream, Blind Faith, or Derek and the Dominos, but the late-night drinking sessions when he and Ahmet would sing and play old Atlantic R&B and blues songs? Ertegun the businessman also necessitated the creation of the Rhythm & Blues Foundation, a musicians' charity Time Warner had to endow in 1988 to stem a class-action suit by former Atlantic artists charging they'd been systematically deprived of royalties. Yet the record man's passing and the end of his era left a huge hole, one that looked unlikely to be filled in a world where recorded music wasn't deemed worth paying for. As Neil Young and Stephen Stills prepared to play "Mr. Soul," a song they'd recorded for Atlantic forty years earlier as members of Buffalo Springfield, Neil said, "I just hope today's musicians have someone like Ahmet, because we were really lucky."

It was more than luck. In the new universe of online music, no Ahmet Ertegun has emerged. The reason is plain. With paid downloads accounting for just 5 percent of online music, the vast majority of users don't see anything to buy that's significantly better than the MP3 files already free for the taking. Bronfman and Alex Zubillaga had it right when they formulated WMG's online strategy as creating an enhanced product that people would value. "Unless the industry finds a way to provide something that the consumer is willing to pay for, there is not going to be any music," said EMI's Guy Hands. "If the industry doesn't want to move, it will die." Enhancing the value of music and then marketing it remains the record industry's real task regardless of the enormous frustrations posed by new technology. U2 manager Paul McGuinness, who has credited record companies as key financial and marketing partners in the band's success, has rightly termed 360 deals "dreadful" and suggested that record companies should offer to cancel those terms if the recording business recovers. But do consumers want it to recover now that they have free music? If they believe recordings are important, yes.

As shortsighted as the record companies' rights grab is, internet users who don't pay for music are creating an economy more stultifying and unfair to artists than the old record industry model. Consumers always want to pay as little as possible, and it is hard to reject free anything—especially something as fulfilling as music. But far too many downloaders flatter themselves with the self-serving canard that they are facilitating a new anticorporate Robin Hood music culture, which one *New York Times* editor celebrated as "the guerrilla savvy of kids who have computers and a bottomless thirst for music." That outlook refuses to consider what is likely to happen when unpaid creators are forced to find another way to make a living. It is also difficult to see what is progressive about devaluing someone's livelihood while reaping the benefits. Why advocate fair-trade coffee but not fair-trade music? Proponents of free-for-the-taking music are voting with their wallets as much as record companies while pretending to be taking a moral stance that liberates artists from a corrupt industry.

Indeed, if you accept most of what's been written over the last ten years, it's hard to imagine the major labels were anything more than criminal enterprises. The consumer anger at the record companies—and sense of online entitlement—can be palpable. When a hip-hop blog, Blunt Rapps, didn't respond to an August 2009 takedown notice from Warner Bros. Records regarding the posting of an unreleased song by the rapper Gucci Mane, the blog was taken offline by the internet service provider until the song was removed. That period lasted approximately two hours, and the blog's owner and author, Noz, was livid. Charging Warner Bros. with "sending in the internet storm troopers," he characterized the company as "the same dudes who deleted 'Cop Killer,' shelved *Black Bastards* and *Live and Let Die,* and had Prince writing 'slave' on his cheek," references to recordings by Ice-T, the group KMD, and the duo Kool G Rap and DJ Polo, and a tactic used by Prince during a 1995 contract dispute. The takedown was noted on other music blogs as one more instance of the record industry being blind to the realities of the internet, and Noz's own post received approximately sixty responses, virtually all of them a variant on "fuck Warner Bros." No one remarked that, while the three recordings had indeed been pulled and Prince's relationship with the label ended on a sour note, Warner Bros. had financed the start of Prince's recording career, let him produce his own album at seventeen, and helped him become a star. Nor did anyone comment on how many of the recordings in their collection had been released by WMG. They preferred to view record companies solely as parasites that perform no functions for artists, and the act of posting and giving away someone's work—complete or not, with or without their permission, with or without payment—as a supportive, progressive act.

Characterizing the record industry as the evilest of empires isn't the sole province of fans and hobbyists. The antipathy for record companies and other big media is felt particularly keenly in segments of academia, where it is rooted in frustration over the power that large, deep-pocketed companies have had to extend the length and parameters of copyright. Those extensions are viewed by some legal scholars and economists as a perversion of copyright's intent, which is to encourage the creation of works that can benefit the public. The internet and Napster were hailed as potential game changers for reversing the corporatization of copyright, and law and technology centers at Harvard, Stanford, and Berkeley have subsequently proven very unsympathetic to copyright holders. Harvard law professor Charles Nesson attempted to turn an RIAA downloading case against a college student into a show trial and public referendum on the legal remedies available for copyright infringement; his client, Joel Tenenbaum, was found guilty and a jury ordered him to pay $675,000 in damages. The most influential voice is law professor Lawrence Lessig, who has criticized media and entertainment corporations for being in the business of preserving economic and commercial models rather than encouraging creativity.

"The publishers, such as the recording industry or the movie industry, aren't so much defending the rights of creators; they're defending a certain business model," Lessig said. "The music industry, for example, is going to make money by selling copies of pieces of plastic. They're going to control distribution as much as they can." Record executives respond that selling pieces of plastic is just a method to monetize their real business of developing and marketing creative ideas and careers—and that's precisely what they are arguing to artists with 360 deals. But the historic friction between performers and record companies suggests that Lessig is right that labels are commercial ventures and concerned with their own success and survival. Where he gets it wrong is denying any overlap in the interests of the artists and the record companies or suggesting that significant benefit doesn't accrue to artists who make those deals. To Lessig, it's one-sided: "Creators have all sold their rights to these people. They don't have any more they're going to get from it."

That's simply not true, as any act that ever had an old song resurrected on a hit soundtrack or sampled on a rap hit can attest, to take just two examples. Artists also enjoy obvious financial leverage when there is a marketplace—i.e., when their records are being purchased or their services sought by competitors. Lessig and others, like Michele Boldrin and David K. Levine, economics professors at Washington University in St. Louis, who have argued that copyrights, patents, and trademarks are more detriment than goad to the public good, are throwing the creative baby out with the commercial bathwater, as copyright advocates frequently highlight.

"The desire to attack the 'cartel' is fine, but don't pretend you're doing it to benefit artists and creators," said Patrick Ross, executive director of the Copyright Alliance, an organization funded by media and communications companies. "Indulge hostility against distributors if you wish—buy an author a drink and you'll never hear the end of the evils of publishers—but don't buy into the notion that artists don't willingly enter into business relationships with distributors, that there isn't a symbiotic relationship between them."

The antagonistic relationship between rock star Don Henley and his record companies—particularly Asylum, which recorded the Eagles—was the classic example. Henley has long complained that the relationship with record companies is tipped against the artist. He has sued them, cofounded an artists' rights organization, and bypassed a record deal to make an album exclusively for Walmart. No one deserves to be gamed, and any step Henley takes to improve his financial and creative leverage is admirable. Yet the inequity of record deals notwithstanding, the record business is just that—a business. So far, the internet hasn't made any artist's work as ubiquitous as major record companies have made Henley's—or bought him as nice a house. Artists and the people who facilitate their work are still entitled to a fairer economic model than the one favored by free internet music advocates, which has been accurately derided as the give-it-away-and-pray model. And a "fairer economic model" simply means one with enough of a financial reward to encourage artists to continue to create recordings.

Proponents of free online music such as Mike Masnick, a blogger and business consultant who advertises himself as a cyberspace visionary, want artists to take it as a matter of faith that they'll be better off not protecting copyright online. They say peer-to-peer distribution on the internet is too porous to be policed and suggest that the broad exposure offered by the internet provides musicians with access to a wide audience which, if it likes what it hears, will then support them by attending concerts or buying T-shirts and other hard goods. Similar arguments are advanced for other media easily converted to free files: it's been suggested that authors should view books as a spur for speaking engagements rather than as a viable economic product themselves.

It may be impossible to police distribution on the internet, yet there are a lot of problems with this approach, both economic and ethical. Aside from wondering why the fact that the internet is too porous to be policed means content shouldn't be paid for, the most obvious is that something that doesn't pay its own way will fall to the wayside.

Setting aside that some of the most influential and popular recording artists such as the post-1966 Beatles, Steely Dan, and Brian Wilson at his most interesting didn't play concerts, not paying for recordings begs artists to stop making them. The British rock manager Peter Jenner has pointed out that Wells Fargo began as an overland express service that, obviated by railroads and telegraphs, became a bank; American Express is a similar example. Jenner was suggesting that record companies need to make a transition in a technologically shifting landscape, but the analogy doesn't hold for artists: you're either creating or you're not. Newspapers are another medium wrestling with the internet. Several large newspapers in major cities including the *Seattle Post-Intelligencer* and the *Rocky Mountain News* in Denver have ceased printing, and others are in dire financial straits that have been exacerbated by the internet's impact on advertising, sales revenues, and readers' habits. This has left print news searching for a new business model. Even the *New York Times* is facing serious financial problems. So far, it has managed to maintain its standard of coverage. But when the newspaper recently started hawking a *New York Times* wine club, one immediately thought of Wells Fargo. What will happen if being a wine club is profitable and being in the news business isn't?

Not making money on recordings and creating them solely as drivers for other forms of income—think of T-shirts as the musicians' wine club—is economically inefficient. Recordings are unlikely to survive without their own financial reward. How long will it take someone to discover a more financially rewarding system for selling concert tickets and T-shirts than producing recordings that don't pay for themselves? Financial pressure will push musicians away from recordings, as it is already pushing record companies away from them and toward something that produces the same opportunities and fame as a record but isn't a financial drain—perhaps television talent shows like *American Idol* or composing for film and television or corporate sponsorship deals.

That doesn't sound like a better way to encourage the creation of music, and Chris Castle, a former record executive and attorney for Napster, has suggested that anyone who thinks record companies are crass and exploitive is going to hate what music sounds like when it's financed by major brands. "What I'm really worried about is the influx of dependency on advertising and sponsorship," he said. "The corporatizing of music is starting to happen. I can't see this new music business producing another Bob Dylan—or anyone like that who openly defies corporatization. When I talk to artists who are young—seventeen or eighteen—many of them seem to have given up the idea of making money off recorded music."

Ultimately, if recordings have no financial value other than to create a notoriety that must then be capitalized some other way, artists will be forced to put less effort into them and eventually skip the recording part of the equation altogether. Clearly, that will not be good for the public—and that's exactly why there is copyright.

Critics of commercial copyright companies sometimes appear eager for artists to embrace any other model. As a lyricist for the Grateful Dead, Electronic Frontier Foundation cofounder John Perry Barlow witnessed how allowing fans to record shows and trade those tapes increased the band's live following and income. He has complete faith in the economic wisdom of free music. "Fame is fortune," says Barlow. "And nothing makes you famous faster than an audience willing to distribute your work for free." However, should this not work as well for other artists as it did for the Grateful Dead—a group that had made and sold albums for a decade before it encouraged fans to tape shows—Barlow suggests that rather than sign with a record company they find a patron, "the economic model that supported most of the ancient masters." By patrons, Barlow means not just rich individuals, but also wealthy corporations and foundations, and he gives a shout-out to the Samaritans at IBM for sponsoring research into fractal geometry. Barlow doesn't like commercial publishers because they're self-perpetuating and only pursuing the public good when that happens to make money—something he apparently doesn't believe of IBM. How vesting the power to decide what we hear in the rich is more democratic than an open market dictated by consumer tastes—or how it widens rather than narrows creative opportunities for either artists or the public—is a mystery.

More than economically inefficient, not paying for recordings is counterintuitive and probably dishonest: we value recordings enough to want them. It may be human nature that we don't want to pay for them, but it's not in our ultimate interest if we want people to continue to make quality recordings for us. We don't expect people to produce other things we like—say, ice cream—in return for a vague indication that if we enjoy it we may pay for something else some other time. What would that even look like? And how long would it be before we had to make our own ice cream?

In fact, we don't expect people to give us ice cream because no situation exists for us to simply take it as it does with music, films, news, and other content on the internet. It's hard to shake the impression that the anger expressed toward the record industry is driven largely by the opportunity to breach its commercial wall—the industry *deserves* rough justice. Tickets to concerts and sporting events can be expensive, yet no one is suggesting those businesses shouldn't exist or that athletes would be better served by patrons than agents. Based on what has happened to music since Napster, one can expect that attitude to change the day someone demonstrates how to get into an NFL game without a ticket and not get arrested. Likewise, the music lovers agitating for free music who say they are buying T-shirts will certainly stop doing so as soon as they figure out how to get them for free.

The financial impact of free downloads isn't borne solely by companies: artists are being driven into worse business models. Now, with 360 deals, record companies get nonrecording income that used to go to the artists. That artists are willing to make those deals demonstrates that recordings are indeed a career driver, that artists still want the financial, editorial, and marketing services of a label, and that those things have to be paid for somehow. Yet considering the antipathy for record companies, surprisingly little is said against 360 deals by free music advocates, cementing the impression that free music is about getting something for nothing, not creating a fairer market. Instead, Masnick and others suggest it just isn't necessary to sign a deal with a record company. They repeatedly point to Trent Reznor, Radiohead, and Jill Sobule as artists who have financed and released recordings without them. Several nonlabel startups such as Polyphonic, a kind of venture capital model providing financing for recording, publicity, merchandise, and touring services, are experimenting with alternative models as well.

More than anyone, Reznor has accepted the challenge of free music and demonstrated a viable business model. For the album *Ghosts I–IV,* released in March 2008, he used free downloads of nine songs as a come-on to sell a variety of expanded premium products topped by a deluxe, limited-edition, $300 box set. The program reportedly grossed $1.6 million in its first week.

When Radiohead passed on extending its contract with EMI, the group instead offered its album *In Rainbows* as a download in October 2007 and let fans name their own price. The strategy proved a financial success and publicity coup. The average voluntary payment was $2.26 with total online sales estimated at between $2 million and $3 million while generating far more press coverage than the band's recent albums. Still, the majority of downloaders didn't pay anything or even bother to visit Radiohead's site. According to internet research firm Big Champagne, most users got the album from free trading sites like the Pirate Bay—400,000 the first day and 2.3 million within the first three weeks.

The singer Jill Sobule funded her 2009 album *California Years* by launching a website, jillsnextrecord.com, and raising $85,000 from fans. A clever mix of support levels started at $10 for a prepaid download of the album and ranged up: $500 got you listed on the album; $1,000 a personal theme song; $5,000 a concert in your home; and $10,000 an appearance on the album as a backup singer. Sobule, who was able to hire the well-known producer Don Was and several top-flight studio musicians for a week of recording sessions, was pleased. "People can use this model whether they have one hundred fans or one hundred thousand fans. You don't have to have a gold- or platinum-selling album to be successful, because you don't have to worry about the record company selling so much. The first record I sell, that first $10 I sell at a show or online, it's mine." As with *In Rainbows,* the clearest upside was the publicity. The trade-offs in spending time and energy on fund-raising and marketing—not to mention having to sell vocal slots on a record—were just as obvious.

Clever and creative as each strategy is, it is also worth noting that each of these artists already had an established following earned in conjunction with a record company. That remains the trump card in selling artists on 360 deals: CD sales continue to fall, but the record company, with its ability to promote an act to radio and provide marketing and financial support, is still the best vehicle for launching a career, especially in pop and rap. Free music isn't freeing musicians—it's forcing the most ambitious to pay more for the chance to be heard.

We don't protect businesses against changes in technology; if we did, there'd still be stables in every town. The record industry's attempt to control and forestall legitimate music services on the internet was wrong, and they got rightly creamed for it. But copyright provides a public good and courts have repeatedly upheld it online. If the online world is to truly be a commons, it doesn't so much need to be free as fair, acknowledging value when it is put in and offering an equitable system that encourages continued creativity. Alas, that includes paying the producers even when they are large media companies.

The charged rhetoric around this issue hasn't done the internet or artists any good. After the RIAA sought legislative protection and characterized individual downloaders as thieves, Lawrence Lessig charged record labels and movie studios with launching "a holy war" against new technologies. The heated words divert attention from the fact that labels and studios were doing what any corporation— and, very likely, any small business owner—might reasonably do: defending against a commercial raid. Shawn Fanning was an amateur hacker when he started working on the program that became Napster, and there's no indication he was up to anything more nefarious than being a precocious nineteen-year-old trying to solve a problem. But the next step was that Napster became a commercial enterprise, introducing itself to the world as an application for giving users access to the work of others without recompense. Its popularity spawned imitators with venture capital backing who definitely were not of the wouldn't-it-be-nice-if-we-all-shared ilk. In the years it took record companies to defeat unlicensed commercial internet music ventures and make them unpalatable to investors, P2P technology gained a foothold and file swappers no longer needed a Napster.

Saying that the internet can't be policed, as some free music advocates do, also ignores that content has become a driving economic force on the internet—perhaps the most important one. Obviously, the internet has intrinsic value, but it is no longer an academic/

military research and communication system; it is a growing *commercial* creature. It has been variously estimated that 50 percent to 80 percent of internet bandwidth is used to stream and download music and films.

"I've met a lot of today's heroes of Silicon Valley," U2's McGuinness said. "Most of them don't really think of themselves as makers of burglary kits. They say: 'You can use this stuff to email your friends and store and share your photos.' But we all know that there's more to it than that, don't we? Kids don't pay twenty-five dollars a month for broadband just to share their photos, do their homework, and email their pals. These tech guys think of themselves as political liberals and socially aware. They search constantly for the next 'killer app.' They conveniently forget that the real 'killer app' that many of their businesses are founded on is our clients' recorded music."

It's a model that for-profit internet companies are trying to extend. In 2009, Google solicited original art by professional graphic artists, and used the same pitch as free music advocates: that providing "a unique and exciting opportunity for artists to display their work in front of millions of people" was payment enough. Though print opportunities are shrinking, it was an easy offer to refuse. And artists were correct to ask why the company benefiting most from that shift—Google earned income of over $4 billion in 2008 by helping people find content—wasn't making a fairer offer.

Fair payment has to become part of the cyberspace equation, for the sake of both its creators and the internet. Agreeing on a collection method or payment formula won't be easy, but it is necessary. Some in the record industry have suggested that service providers charge users by the amount of bandwidth they consume, using it as an indicator of downloading. Others want a blanket licensing system in which a certain percentage of the service bill or an additional flat fee is divided among creators and copyright holders.

In Europe, the debate over blanket licensing is further along, and proposals to suspend connections for downloading have been offered in France and Great Britain. Notably, recording artists working through Britain's Featured Artists Coalition have been sensitive to civil liberties and consumer rights—far more sensitive than consumers have been to artists' rights—and rejected the idea of disconnecting users. At the same time, they've pointed the way to a fair future by urging record companies to improve their dealings with artists and asking fans to take a realistic approach to copyright. "We have made a stand over suspension because we want to have this debate out in the open. . . . It is our belief that all of us need to work together in order to convince consumers that music makes a great contribution to quality of life and as such should be paid for. This cannot be achieved by a few retrograde slogans that recall the 'home taping is killing music' campaign of the eighties. If we hope to educate the public to pay the artists that make the music they love, then we, as an industry, will have to make some changes in the way that we remunerate artists."

Creating and equitably dividing a huge pot from which a wide variety of content creators—including musicians, writers, filmmakers, and newspapers—receive payment is going to be a nightmare. It's also essential, with one key caveat: payment should be high enough to recognize and encourage work but not so high as to discourage the development of new and better services. If the last decade has demonstrated anything, it is that copyright is not a firewall against technology. Record labels and other media companies are entitled to payment on their properties, but if they want to grow, they should be forced to devise new products in accordance with evolving technologies. There are many ways this might work. Based on my own use of music on the internet, I'll suggest one.

While listening to a free streaming broadcast at a British music site, folkradio.co.uk, I heard a song by an artist I was unfamiliar with, Jolie Holland, of the Canadian band the Be Good Tanyas. I liked the tune enough to go to imeem.com, the American website that record companies have licensed to aggregate and stream songs, and listen to more of Holland's solo recordings, and I liked them as well. But though imeem offered an option for purchasing MP3 versions of songs from Amazon and iTunes, I didn't pull the trigger. (Imeem, which couldn't attract enough advertising, has subsequently gone out of business.) Why should I? The experience of listening to Holland's songs as an on-demand musical stream and having them stored on my computer isn't different enough to warrant a purchase. I am, however, more than happy to pay a monthly royalty surcharge to support streaming and downloading.

One reason the record industry has been hit so hard by the internet is that the CD was not a beloved product. Audio arguments aside, its only selling point was convenience. Its appearance marked the end of great album graphics, and it never inspired the passion that the vinyl LP did. CDs just weren't as much fun to own, and when MP3s appeared, CDs were easy to abandon. Today, as nice as it is to be able to go online and hear virtually whatever I want whenever I want, I miss the experience of buying a music product worth owning; filling a terabit storage device with ten thousand music files isn't anywhere near as engaging as wandering through a great record store or even a good used bookstore. That–and not 360s–is the business record companies should be in: creating products and online services that add value to recordings and excite people rather than writing off a generation that never had anything worth buying. Until then, media companies–even with some measure of online rights protection–won't have any real spur to growth. And there'll never be another Ahmet Ertegun.

Notes

Prologue: The Opening Bell

Page

2 *"Wall Street's favorite whipping boy"*: in Andrew Ross Sorkin and Geraldine Fabrikant, "Edgar Bronfman Jr.'s Backup Band," *New York Times,* November 30, 2003.

2 *"The story that's told is that I squandered the family money"*: Edgar Bronfman Jr. to Stephen Adler, *BusinessWeek*'s Captains of Industry Series at the 92nd Street Y, May 4, 2006.

3 *"Why do people buy this"*: author interview with Edgar Bronfman Jr., September 14, 2005.

3 *"I wrote my check because"*: Bronfman made his remark as part of WMG IPO presentation, Hotel W, New York, May 3, 2005.

5 Details of Scott Sperling's education and career are taken from the bio posted on the Thomas H. Lee website. His Hollywood investments were detailed in Stephen E. Frank's "Aeneas Portfolio Attracts Scrutiny," *Harvard Crimson,* April 29, 1992.

6 *"The deal with Edgar"*: in Sorkin and Fabrikant, op cit.

7   *"The days of the record industry dictating formats":* author interview with Edgar Bronfman Jr., March 22, 2005.

7   *"I think it's finished":* in Greg Kot, "Exclusive: Eric Clapton Talks About His Passion for Chicago and Its Guitarists," *Chicago Tribune,* June 27, 2007.

8   Linkin Park's criticisms of the Warner Music Group public offering were detailed in a press release from their management company, the Firm, of May 2, 2005. The release was entitled "Linkin Park Opposes Fleecing of Warner Music, Demands Immediate Release."

8   *"The joy of this business":* from WMG IPO presentation, May 3, 2005.

8   *"They immediately fired all their bullets":* confidential source.

Chapter 1: Family Business, or the Tale of Two Edgars

Page

11   *"I'm not sure what he brings to the table":* confidential source.

12   *"It's terrific":* in Colin Leinster, "The Second Son Is Heir at Seagram," *Fortune,* March 17, 1986.

12   Details of the early Canadian years of the Bronfman family and the founding of the company that would become Seagram are chronicled in depth in Michael R. Marrus, *Mr. Sam: The Life and Times of Samuel Bronfman* (Toronto, Ont.: Viking by Penguin Books Canada, 1991), and Peter C. Newman, *King of the Castle: The Making of a Dynasty; Seagram's and the Bronfman Empire* (New York: Atheneum, 1979).

12   *"If they were, then they were the best in the West!":* in Newman, op cit, p. 63.

14   *"The business is mine":* in Marrus, op cit, p. 398.

16   *"Cocksucker. Isn't that a charming word?":* in Leo Kolber and L. Ian MacDonald, *Leo: A Life* (Montreal, QC: McGill-Queen's University Press, 2003), p. 32.

16   *"a two-bit lawyer":* in Newman, op cit, p. 48.

16   *"Next to my father, Queen Victoria looked like a swinger":* in Edgar M. Bronfman Sr., *Good Spirits: The Making of a Businessman* (New York: G. P. Putnam's Sons, 1998), p. 30. All quotes from Edgar M. Bronfman Sr. are from this source unless otherwise noted.

17   *"You're an old man":* in Saidye Rosner Bronfman, *My Sam: A Memoir by His Wife* (privately printed, 1982), p. 72.

18   *"Now I know what it feels like to be the poor relation":* in Stephen Birmingham, *Our Crowd: The Great Jewish Families of New York* (New York: Harper & Row, 1967), p. 378.

20   Information on the Bronfmans' sidestepping taxes on the family trust can be found in Randall Morck and Bernard Yeung's "Some Obstacles to Good Corporate Governance in Canada and How to Overcome Them," a study commissioned by the Task Force to Modernize Securities Legislation in Canada, published August 18, 2006, p. 307. Write the authors: "There is no allegation

that the Bronfman family broke any law, only a concern that their influence affected public policy in a way few others could match."

20 *"I don't want you in the goddamned movie business":* in Kolber, op cit, p. 179.

20 *"It doesn't cost $40 million to get laid":* in Newman, op cit, p. 184.

22 *"I had been unhappy for some time":* in Bronfman, op cit, p. 145.

22 For a fuller discussion of Sam Bronfman II's kidnapping, see Stephen Birmingham's *The Rest of Us: The Rise of America's Eastern European Jews* (New York: Little Brown & Co., 1984), pp. 366–67.

24 *"would have had your father dancing in the streets":* in Kolber, op cit, p. 69.

24 *"My clearest memory is of him cheating on the tennis court":* confidential source.

25 *"From the time I was ten, I always knew":* in Ken Auletta, *The Highwaymen: Warriors on the Information Superhighway* (New York: Random House, 1997), p. 140.

25 *"avoid what he didn't want and get what he did":* in Leinster, op cit.

25 *"He was the one who first decided":* Edgar Bronfman Jr. to Stephen Adler, *BusinessWeek*'s Captains of Industry Series at the 92nd Street Y, May 4, 2006.

26 *"I wish the sons of our very rich families were like him":* in Leinster, op cit.

27 *"As a teenager I always acted older than I was":* in Auletta, op cit.

27 *"They put us together and we disliked each other instantly":* author interview with Bruce Roberts, March 28, 2006.

27 *"I didn't have much money":* author interview with Edgar Bronfman Jr., July 18, 2006.

27 *"From his standpoint, it wasn't a 'business'":* in Bronfman Sr., op cit, p. 188.

Chapter 2: The World's Most Expensive Education

Page
30 *"I was very reluctant to take him":* in Auletta, op cit.

30 *"nobody comes to work here thinking they're in line to be chief executive":* in Leinster, op cit.

31 *"You're good":* ibid.

31 *"Edgar was mesmerized by his son":* in Kolber, op cit, p. 78.

31 *"What I should have done":* in Bronfman Sr., op cit, p. 194.

32 *"It bothers me when people do a bad job and there are no consequences":* author interview with Edgar Bronfman Jr., March 22, 2005.

34 *"I'd already sat on the board of DuPont for a number of years":* interview with Charlie Rose, aired March 14, 2001.

34 *"We became convinced that the communications-media-entertainment area was one in which a lot of money would get made":* in Auletta, op cit.

36 *"We were part of CBS":* author interview with Al Teller, June 2, 2006.

37 *"If my dad can't work, he'll die":* author interview with Edgar Bronfman Jr., July 18, 2006.

38 *"I think he, more than anybody, knew how to manage an entertainment company":* Edgar

Bronfman Jr. to Stephen Adler, *BusinessWeek*'s Captains of Industry Series at the 92nd Street Y, May 4, 2006.

38 *"I'm a very different person than my father":* in Zena Olijnyk, "Charles Bronfman," *Canadian Business,* May 26, 2003.

39 *"Unless you're growing a company, you're losing ground":* in Bronfman Sr., op cit, pp. 204, 208.

39 *"just a commodity play":* in Kolber, op cit, p. 198.

39 *"DuPont is a great name":* in Bronfman Sr., op cit, p. 201.

39 *"DuPont is a great company, but you're one accident away from conflagration":* author interview with Edgar Bronfman Jr., September 14, 2005.

39 *"This is a benign investment":* in Auletta, op cit.

40 *"Jerry never believed me when I said we wanted to stop at twenty-five percent or thirty percent":* author interview with Edgar Bronfman Jr., September 14, 2005.

40 *"We don't think the rumored changes make much sense":* in Andrew Willis, "Bronfman Sells DuPont," *Maclean's,* April 17, 1995.

41 *"I told the board, 'Only one person gets to use this tax advantage'":* author interview with Edgar Bronfman Jr., September 14, 2005.

41 *"Even with this tax break":* in "Tax Loophole Aids DuPont and Seagram," *Weekly Corporate Growth Report,* June 19, 1995.

41 *"Perhaps it would have been better for Seagram":* in Graham D. Taylor, "From Shirt-sleeves to Shirtsleeves: The Bronfman Dynasty and the Seagram Empire," *Business History Conference,* 2006. Available at Business and Economic History On-Line.

42 *"He said, 'We see your purchase of Time Warner stock'":* author interview with Edgar Bronfman Jr., September 14, 2005.

43 *"Everyone naturally assumes that we sold DuPont to buy MCA":* author interview with Edgar Bronfman Jr., September 14, 2005.

43 Details on Seagram's purchase of MCA from Matsushita drawn from Edward Klein, "Edgar Bets the House," *Vanity Fair,* July 1995.

45 *"Why would you want to go to Universal":* in James B. Stewart, *Disney Wars* (New York: Simon & Schuster, 2005), p. 199.

45 *"There's a great saying":* author interview with Edgar Bronfman Jr., July 18, 2006.

45 *"I'm telling you right now I'm voting against this":* in Kolber, op cit, p. 199.

45 *"Everyone was uncomfortable from day one":* author interview with Edgar Bronfman Jr., July 18, 2006.

46 Ovitz's characterization of the Bronfmans drawn from a subsequent lawsuit against the Disney Corporation. See *In Re The Walt Disney Company Derivative Litigation, Opinion and Order,* August 9, 2005, pp. 11–12.

46 Diller sought to conceal his deal with MCA from Geffen: confidential source.

46 *"He's like a piñata":* in Connie Bruck, "Bronfman's Big Deals," *New Yorker,* May 11, 1998.

47 *"I didn't see any way we could be number one in film":* author interview with Edgar Bronfman Jr., September 14, 2005.

47 *"Al didn't always come across as if he believed it was Edgar's company"*: confidential source.

Chapter 3: The Rainmakers

Page
49 *"I realized that if you have good product you can do okay"*: author interview with Doug Morris, August 2, 2005. All subsequent quotes from this interview unless otherwise noted.

50 *"Doug is a terrific record guy"*: author interview with Ahmet Ertegun, July 18, 2006. All subsequent quotes from this interview unless otherwise noted.

51 *"Those were the cagiest cats on the planet"*: author interview with Jac Holzman, July 11, 2005. All subsequent quotes from this interview unless otherwise noted.

52 *"I remember the days of Steve Ross"*: author interview with Sheldon Vogel, June 7, 2005. All subsequent quotes from this interview unless otherwise noted.

53 *"Doug identified executive talent and nurtured it"*: author interview with Ron Shapiro, September 4, 2005. All subsequent quotes from this interview.

54 *"He was kind of the janitor"*: posted on Jimsteinman.com and simply entitled "rough transcription of Jim Steinman during a six-hour interview in 2003." No interviewer is credited.

54 *"Ahmet certainly had an austerity philosophy"*: author interview with Danny Goldberg, April 26, 2005. All subsequent quotes from this interview unless otherwise noted.

55 *"Mo turned us down"*: author interview with Seymour Stein, June 22, 2005.

56 *"Paul said, 'It's too bad Jimmy's already made his deal with Doug'"*: author interview with Ted Field, June 6, 2005. All subsequent quotes are from this interview.

57 *"When he smiled, you knew the knife was coming"*: in John Taylor, "The Warner Wars," *New York,* July 13, 1987.

58 *"I saw Ross once a month"*: author interview with Bob Krasnow, July 29, 2005. All subsequent quotes from this interview unless otherwise noted.

58 *"My feeling was always follow the artist"*: in Fred Goodman, "How a Legend Tapped the Rock Underground," *New York Times,* January 29, 1995.

58 *"We signed with Warner Bros. because of Mo"*: ibid.

60 *"Morgado came off as an innocent"*: author interview with Tom Silverman, July 21, 2005.

60 *"What I saw was the brilliance"*: confidential source.

60 *"He doesn't even say hello"*: author interview with Howie Klein, August 8, 2005.

61 *"There's a tendency within the music business to dis anyone who is a business person"*: author interview with Paul Vidich, August 1, 2005.

61 *"Morgado wanted to mold Doug into a force against the West Coast operation"*: confidential source.

63 *"Ted was very willing"*: author interview with Tom Whalley, July 20, 2006.

63 Marion "Suge" Knight's strong-arm tactics with Eazy-E are chronicled in Jerry

Heller and Gil Reavill's *Ruthless: A Memoir* (New York: Simon Spotlight Entertainment, 2006).

63   *"He was a really sweet guy back then":* author interview with Jimmy Iovine, March 9, 2006. All subsequent quotes from this interview unless otherwise noted.

65   *"I used to write rhymes before I knew there were raps":* in Alan Light, "Ice-T: The Rolling Stone Interview," *Rolling Stone,* August 20, 1992.

65   *"Mo and those guys were always supportive":* author interview with Jorge Hinojosa, July 23, 2005.

66   *"It was a typical Warner Bros. thing: 'Anybody can do anything' ":* author interview with Bob Merlis, July 15, 2005.

67   *"justification for murder"* and *"a sick mind running a sick company":* in Chris Morris, "Police, Time Warner Face Off Over 'Cop Killer,' " *Billboard,* July 25, 1992.

68   *"It's not a Warner Bros. fight, it's my fight":* in John Horn, "Ice-T Takes 'Cop Killer' Off His Album," *Chicago Sun-Times,* July 29, 1992.

69   *"So we put out the record, right?":* author interview with Josh Baran and Jaime Willett, undated.

70   *"He said, 'I'll teach you what it's like to play in the big leagues' ":* author interview with Craig Kallman, January 16, 2006.

71   *"Morgado wanted to stuff Atlantic down Mo's throat":* confidential source.

71   *"I think we provoked people":* confidential source.

73   *"I got an urgent message at one a.m.":* author interview with Rob Dickins, June 15, 2005. All subsequent quotes from this interview.

74   Details of conversation between Lewinter and Wistow: confidential sources.

75   *"Everyone was incredibly depressed":* confidential source.

76   Details of Jen Trynin signing: confidential sources.

77   *"You've got what? A twenty-seven percent market share?":* Danny Goldberg, op cit.

Chapter 4: A Rising Tide

Page

79   Details of meeting between record executives and Fuchs: author interview with Jimmy Iovine, March 9, 2006.

80   *"I couldn't figure out what they did":* confidential source.

80   *"when I got here, I discovered that this place was becoming organizationally dysfunctional":* in Mark Landler, "A Defender of Gangsta Rap is Dismissed at Warner Music," *New York Times,* June 22, 1995.

81   *"Have you seen* The Shawshank Redemption*?":* in James Bates, "Mr. Bronfman, Get Ready for Your Extreme Closeup: Can the New Head of MCA Teach the People Who Run Hollywood a Thing or Two About Entertainment?" *Los Angeles Times,* July 30, 2005.

81   *"How much money would it take?":* author interview with Doug Morris, August 2, 2005.

82 John Leo's criticism of Time Warner appeared in "The Leading Cultural Polluter," *US News & World Report,* March 27, 1995.

83 *"How long will Time Warner continue to put profit before principle?":* in Monica Fountain, "Tucker Battles Against Lyrics of Gangsta Rap," *Chicago Tribune,* November 10, 1996.

83 *"Some of us have known for many, many years":* in Richard Zoglin, "A Company
Under Fire: Targeted as the Chief Cultural Offender, Time Warner Struggles
to Define Itself," *Time,* June 12, 1995.

83 *"I'd like to ask the executives at Time Warner a question":* Dole made the remarks as
part of a speech delivered in Los Angeles on June 1, 1995.

84 *"I'm new on the job":* confidential source.

84 *"He wanted a deal with schmuck insurance":* confidential source.

85 *"Jimmy knows music":* in Patrick Goldstein, "Number One with a Bullet: Jimmy
Iovine," *New York Times Magazine,* April 16, 1995.

85 *"Hey, who's that guy we hate?"* and details of planned meeting: author interview
with Jimmy Iovine, March 9, 2006.

87 *"When we were still Time Warner shareholders":* author interview with Edgar Bronfman Jr., September 14, 2005.

87 *"I'm not saying the artist hasn't got a right to make these records":* in Patrick Goldstein,
"David Geffen: The Rolling Stone Interview," *Rolling Stone,* April 29, 1993.

88 *"You're not going to believe this":* author interview with Doug Morris, August 2,
2005.

88 Speculations on Fuchs's ouster taken from Geraldine Fabrikant and Deirdre
Carmody, "Time Warner Music Head Ousted in Shake-up," *New York Times,*
November 17, 1995; and Dana Kennedy, "Orchestral Maneuvers: Michael
Fuchs' Role as Chairman Rocks the Music Industry," *Entertainment Weekly,* May
19, 1995.

88 *"Semel and Daly want to know where you want your piano sent":* author interview
with Doug Morris, August 2, 2005.

89 *"Jimmy, if I had this job three weeks ago":* author interview with Jimmy Iovine,
March 9, 2006.

89 *"He felt Jimmy was asking for way too much":* author interview with Edgar Bronfman Jr., September 14, 2005.

89 *"There are lines we will not cross":* testimony of William Bennett before the Senate
Committee on Commerce on marketing violence to children, May 4, 1999.

91 *"They wanted a quantum shift":* author interview with Jay Boberg, November 13,
2006.

96 *"The music business is now going to be the most important business to us":* in Chuck
Philips, "Music Now Calls Tune at Seagram," *Los Angeles Times,* May 27, 1998.

Chapter 5: Lansky and the Hustlers' House of Higher Learning

Page

99   *"Lyor comes across almost like a fictional character"*: author interview with Bill Stephney, October 5, 2005. All subsequent quotes from this interview.

99   *"Lyor has a deaf ear to the world"*: author interview with Carmen Ashhurst, September 15, 2005. All subsequent quotes from this interview.

100   *"Lyor had an on-again, off-again relationship"*: author interview with Ziva Sirkis, August 11, 2005. All subsequent quotes from this interview.

100   *"When they failed, their first question was, what else can I scheme?"*: author interview with Lyor Cohen, July 25, 2005.

101   *"Lyor would become like a slave driver"*: author interview with Ovid Santoro, August 31, 2005. All subsequent quotes from this interview.

103   *"When I made thirty-six grand on Run-DMC"*: author interview with Lyor Cohen, July 25, 2005.

104   *"It was a way to get the things I wanted"*: in Russell Simmons and Nelson George, *Life and Def: Sex, Drugs, Money + God* (New York: Three Rivers/Random House, 2001), p. 17.

106   *"That's the blackest hip-hop record"*: in Stacy Gueraseva, *Def Jam, Inc: Russell Simmons, Rick Rubin, and the Extraordinary Story of the World's Most Influential Hip-Hop Label* (New York: One World/Ballantine Books, 2005), p. 33.

106   *"Lyor moves to New York and just shows up"*: author interview with Bill Adler, July 15, 2005. All subsequent quotes from this interview.

108   *"The secretary says there's a guy named Lyor outside"*: author interview with Charlie Stettler, August 31, 2005. All subsequent quotes from this interview.

108   Deal with Adidas for $1 million: according to the shoe company's website, the decision was made after the song was released and "Adidas eventually signed a $1-million deal with Run-DMC to continue promoting the shoes." See http://www.adidassuperstars.com.

108   *"Today hip-hop is used to advertise everything"*: author interview with Lisa Cortes, October 2, 2005. All subsequent quotes from this interview.

110   *"Lyor makes it so fucking hard"*: author interview with Sean Carasov, August 7, 2005. All subsequent quotes from this interview unless otherwise noted.

111   *"He's a music executive who didn't have to call the cops when a rapper raised his voice"*: author interview with Aaron Fuchs, September 6, 2005.

112   *"He was kind of gangster"*: in Rich Cohen, "How Lyor Cohen—the White, Jewish, Israeli-Raised President of Island Def Jam Records—Became One of the Most Important Men in Hip-Hop," *Rolling Stone,* June 21, 2001.

113   *"He let it be understood that he was connected to the Mossad"*: in Yossi Melman, "Disappearing Act," *Haaretz,* October 1, 2001. Melman's article is the primary source on Elisha Cohen's African career and subsequent Nigerian political intrigue.

116   *"Why don't we get covers?"*: author interview with Lyor Cohen, July 25, 2005.

117 *"Lyor was always very good about saying":* author interview with Julie Greenwald, November 10, 2005.

117 *"Even though Lyor's got a brusque demeanor":* author interview with Nelson George, January 31, 2005.

118 *"Island had all the incentive in the world":* in Simmons and George, op cit, p. 192.

119 *"Danny put a tremendous amount of insecurity in the company":* author interview with Lyor Cohen, March 8, 2005.

Chapter 6: Hurricane Shawn

Page

124 *"Everyone else in the industry told me I was insane":* author interview with Edgar Bronfman Jr., June 30, 2005.

124 *"Yes, it's well known":* in Calev Ben-David, "Charles in Charge," *Jerusalem Post,* June 29, 1999.

127 *"The heads of the record companies tended":* author interview with Hilary Rosen, May 21, 2006. All subsequent quotes from this interview unless otherwise noted.

128 *"Napster is not revolutionary":* author interview with Shawn Fanning, May 4, 2000.

128 Information on Napster's users from Joseph Menn, *All the Rave: The Rise and Fall of Shawn Fanning's Napster* (New York: Crown Business Books, 2003), pp. 125–26.

129 *"I already thought the record industry":* author interview with Roger Ames, June 29, 2005. All subsequent quotes from this interview unless otherwise noted.

129 *"Our urgent requests for a meeting were not taken seriously":* in Menn, op cit, p. 124.

130 *"Steven Spielberg will make his next movie":* in Fred Goodman, "Walter Yetnikoff: The Rolling Stone Interview," *Rolling Stone,* December 18, 1988.

130 *"I don't think you could find a recording artist":* in Jeffrey Kaye, "Music Revolt," *News Hour with Jim Lehrer,* July 4, 2002.

131 *"We were still trying to figure out which chorus to use":* author interview with Lars Ulrich, May 12, 2000. All subsequent quotes from this interview unless otherwise noted.

134 *"He's one of the few people around":* in Andrew Pollack, "Warner Music Gets New Chief," *New York Times,* August 17, 1999.

135 *"The PolyGram purchase was good":* author interview with Edgar Bronfman Jr., July 18, 2006.

136 *"The leaders of the net economy":* in Richard Siklos and Catherine Yang, "Welcome to the 21st Century," *BusinessWeek,* January 24, 2000.

136 *"The timing of this agreement could not be better":* joint press release of EMI and Time Warner announcing merger of their record operations, January 24, 2000.

137   *"AOL and Time Warner are the first to understand"*: in Jean-Marie Messier, *J6M.COM* (Paris: Hachette Littératures, 2000), English translation taken from Jo Johnson and Martine Orange *The Man Who Tried to Buy the World: Jean-Marie Messier and Vivendi Universal,* (London: Portfolio, 2003), p. 38. Johnson and Orange's book, an insightful portrait of Messier and his mania, contains the best and most complete history of the ill-conceived Vivendi-Universal merger.

138   *"He was absolutely calm, clear"*: in Johnson and Orange, op cit, p. 3.

139   *"Today is my father's birthday"*: in Barry Came, Brenda Branswell, and Patricia Chisholm, "Seagram-Vivendi Deal," *Maclean's,* July 1, 2000.

Chapter 7: Turf Wars

Page

140   *"I had a real anxiety that I would be known"*: author interview with Lyor Cohen, March 30, 2005.

142   *"Doug loved having a counter to Jimmy"*: author interview with Lyor Cohen, May 30, 2005.

145   *"Our strategy is we need to get more hits"*: quoted in Tamara Coniff, "Morris' UMG Plan: Sell More Records," *Hollywood Reporter,* October 2, 2001.

145   *"Here was an opportunity"*: in Menn, op cit, p. 250.

146   *"Things went backward from there"*: ibid., p. 251.

146   *"I decided I was willing to lose"*: in Shawn Tully, "Big Man Against Big Music: Think the Record Companies Will Bury Napster? John Hummer Is Betting You're Wrong, and He's Hired David Boies to Prove It," *Fortune,* August 14, 2000.

146   *"Napster, by its conduct"*: opinion in *A&M Records et al. v. Napster,* case 00–16401, United States Court of Appeals for the Ninth Circuit, filed February 12, 2001.

147   *"If you can get music from file-sharing"*: in Mark Hachman, "Linspire Chief to Launch DRM-Less Music Service," ExtremeTech.com, February 2, 2005.

148   *"The stage is set"*: testimony of Gerry Kearby before the US Senate Committee on the Judiciary hearing "Online Entertainment: Coming Soon to a Digital Device Near You," April 3, 2001.

148   *"Where are the internet businesses"*: testimony of Hank Barry before the US Senate Committee on the Judiciary hearing "Online Entertainment: Coming Soon to a Digital Device Near You," April 3, 2001.

148   *"We're starting to worry"*: testimony of Mike Farrace before the US Senate Committee on the Judiciary hearing "Online Entertainment: Coming Soon to a Digital Device Near You," April 3, 2001.

149   *"I thought what Bertelsmann did"*: author interview with David Pakman, June 5, 2006. All subsequent quotes from this interview.

150   *"The big record companies can't move with speed"*: author interview with Laurie Jakobson, May 19, 2006.

152   *"I really love things that change the whole game":* in Constance Loizos, "Why Tim Draper Feels Like Captain America," *Venture Capital Journal,* February 2006.

152   *"Students would come in":* author interview with Rene Baum, May 29, 2009.

153   *"The RIAA really wants to send a frightening message":* in Josh Brodie, "RIAA Sues Over File-Sharing Site, But Settles the Suit," *Daily Princetonian,* May 23, 2003.

153   *"When you sue one kid":* comments at WMG IPO road show, W Hotel, New York, NY, May 3, 2005.

153   *"I was a big advocate in 2000":* interview with Peter Paterno conducted and posted at Artistshousemusic.org, January 2006.

154   *"Your legal concepts of property":* in John Perry Barlow, "A Declaration of the Independence of Cyberspace," Davos, Switzerland, February 8, 1996.

154   *"Our goal is not to be vindictive":* in John Borland, "RIAA Sues 261 File Swappers," C-Net News, September 8, 2003.

154   Figure of 28,000 from the Electronic Frontier Foundation's report "RIAA v. the People," September 2008. Posted at eff.org/riaa-v-people.

155   *"You have to assume":* in Borland, op cit.

155   *"Virtually no one can claim":* in Mitch Bainwald and Cary Sherman, "Explaining the Crackdown on Student Downloading," *Inside Higher Education,* March 15, 2007.

155   Only 5 percent of downloads were paid for: those findings were included in *Digital Music Report 2009* published by the International Federation of the Phonographic Industry, London. The RIAA is a member.

155   *"There might not be any bigger scumbags":* in Kos's "DNC Hires RIAA Shill," *Daily Kos,* April 12, 2007.

155   *"There are those who believe":* in Edgar Bronfman Jr., "Property Is Property, Regardless of the Web," *Los Angeles Times,* June 11, 2000.

156   *"fairly certain":* Bronfman made the admission about his children's downloading while being interviewed by Adam Pasnik of Reuters, December 1, 2006. For blogger responses, see "WMG Boss' Kids 'Stole Music,'" p2pnetnews.com, December 4, 2006; and Eliot Van Buskirk, "Warner Music CEO Admits His Kids Stole Music; Didn't Get Sued," Wired Listening Post, December 4, 2006.

157   *At one point she walked:* Kat Giantis, "Top Ten Celebrity Meltdowns," Movie News, MSN.com, undated.

159   *"Jay-Z couldn't get his records on the radio":* testimony given by Irving "Irv Gotti" Lorenzo in the matter of *TVT Records et al. v. The Island Def Jam Music Group and Lyor Cohen,* March 12, 2002, p. 483.

159   *"It was a unique time":* in Ethan Brown, *Queens Reigns Supreme: Fat Cat, 50 Cent and the Rise of the Hip-Hop Hustler* (New York: Anchor Books, 2005), p. 139.

159   *"Irv Gotti was the best thing":* ibid, p. 147.

160   *"Every time you say no":* testimony of Lyor Cohen in the matter of *TVT Records et al. v. The Island Def Jam Music Group and Lyor Cohen,* March 14, 2002, p. 1059.

161   *"I'm putting up all the money in that proposition":* author interview with Steve Gottlieb, October 7, 2005. All subsequent quotes from this interview unless otherwise noted.

163   *"I messed up":* testimony of Lyor Cohen during the penalty phase of *TVT Records et al. v. The Island Def Jam Music Group and Lyor Cohen,* April 30, 2003, p. 309.

164   *"I had a five-year obligation":* author interview with Lyor Cohen, March 30, 2005.

Chapter 8: Le Divorce

Page

167   *"I was furious":* in Johnson and Orange, op cit, p. 106.

167   *"When I see a great book":* ibid., p. 110.

167   *"I think anybody who worked":* in *Special Report with Maria Bartiroma,* CNBC, October 21, 2002.

168   *"Up until the USA Networks transaction":* in Johnson and Orange, op cit, p. 117.

168   *"I've got the unpleasant feeling":* in John Carreyrou and Martin Peers, "Damage Control: How Messier Kept Cash Crisis at Vivendi Hidden for Months," *Wall Street Journal,* October 31, 2002.

169   *"He just did his homework":* in Brian Milner, "Broken Spirits," *Toronto Globe and Mail Magazine,* August 30, 2002.

169   *"Vivendi is in better-than-good health":* in Carreyrou and Peers, op cit.

171   *"His attitude was":* in Johnson and Orange, op cit, p. 232.

172   *"I flew to Paris":* author interview with Michael Klein, August 7, 2007.

172   *"There's an anti-American tinge":* in Johnson and Orange, op cit, pp. 239–40.

173   *"His reputation as a financial steward":* in Sorkin and Fabrikant, op cit.

173   *"My biggest mistake?":* Edgar Bronfman Jr. to Stephen Adler, *BusinessWeek*'s Captains of Industry Series at the 92nd Street Y, May 4, 2006.

Chapter 9: Redemption Song

Page

174   *"ludicrously vain pretender":* in Michael Wolff, *Autumn of the Moguls* (New York: HarperCollins, 2003), p. 63.

176   *"So I picked up the phone and called Dick Parsons":* author interview with Edgar Bronfman Jr., March 22, 2005.

177   *"You could buy the EMI Group right now for about that":* the speaker was analyst Michael Nathanson of Sanford C. Bernstein. In Laura M. Holson, "BMG to Buy Rest of Zomba, Home of Pop Stars," *New York Times,* June 12, 2002.

180   *"They figured the business was going to get better":* author interview with Edgar Bronfman Jr., March 22, 2005.

180   *"exactly the wrong outcome":* in Annie Lawson, "Bronfman Warns Vivendi Off NBC Bid," *Guardian,* August 29, 2003.

181   *"GE's the apple in their eye":* in Richard Verrier and Meg James, "NBC Gaining in Bid for Universal," *Los Angeles Times,* September 1, 2003.

181 *"not easy to feel sorry for a billionaire"*: in David D. Kirkpatrick and Andrew Ross Sorkin, "Comeback Glories Elude Seagram Heir," *New York Times,* September 3, 2003.

181 *"For a guy who certainly doesn't need to work for a living"*: ibid.

181 *"The most important part of it"*: ibid.

183 *"If you looked at the price"*: author interview with Scott Sperling, September 7, 2005.

184 *"Saban walked because he wanted to be chairman"*: confidential source.

Chapter 10: Of Animals and Treason

Page

186 *"I can't believe the company"*: confidential source.

186 *"This is a financial play"*: author interview with Bob Krasnow, July 29, 2005.

187 *"They're just in it to make money"*: confidential source.

187 *"unfairly knocked"* and *"The deal with Edgar"*: in Sorkin and Fabrikant, op cit.

187 *"I did not like reading it"*: author interview with Edgar Bronfman Jr., March 22, 2005.

188 *"We said, 'Here's what we're going to do'"*: author interview with Edgar Bronfman Jr., October 3, 2006.

189 *"I wouldn't be able"*: in Seth Mnookin, "Universal's CEO Once Called iPod Users Thieves. Now He's Giving Songs Away," *Wired,* November 27, 2007.

190 *"I said, 'Fuck, yeah'"*: author interview with Lyor Cohen, February 3, 2006.

190 *"Lyor's very good at artist relations"*: author interview with Scott Sperling, September 7, 2005.

191 *"After TVT I told my wife I was damaged goods"*: author interview with Lyor Cohen, March 30, 2005.

191 *"It was the look, the voice"*: author interview with Edgar Bronfman Jr., December 9, 2005.

193 *"The joke was going around"*: confidential source.

193 *"Could Tom Whalley have done the job instead of Lyor?"*: confidential source.

194 *"We lived for a long time"*: author interview with Brian Cohen, August 12, 2005.

195 *"She was insecure"*: confidential source.

195 *"He was talking about doing the job"*: confidential source.

196 *"I meet this big, tall Israeli"*: author interview with Julie Greenwald, October 11, 2005.

198 *"Lyor is the great thing Edgar did"*: author interview with Ahmet Ertegun, July 18, 2006.

198 *"The way he put the deal together was very smart"*: author interview with Jac Holzman, July 11, 2005.

200 *"Artist managers are happy with record companies almost never"*: author interview with Edgar Bronfman Jr., June 30, 2005.

200 Dennis Laventhal detested Cohen: confidential sources.

200 *"an 'artistic think tank' ":* in David D. Kirkpatrick, "Time Warner and Madonna Are at Odds on Her Label," *New York Times,* November 17, 2003.

202 *"I find myself in the ludicrous position":* in Chris Nelson, "Madonna Goes to War, This Time in Court," *New York Times,* April 29, 2004.

202 *"engaging in acts of self-dealing":* in Lionel Cironneau, "Madonna's Record Label Sues Warner Music," Associated Press, March 25, 2004.

202 *"It's a very strange way to make your most important artist happy":* in Phyllis Furman, "Madonna is Gunning for Edgar Bronfman Jr.," *New York Daily News,* March 26, 2004.

203 *"Warner Music Group is simply seeking to affirm":* ibid.

203 *"Look. You've been incredibly important":* author interview with Edgar Bronfman Jr., December 9, 2005.

Chapter 11: The "Try Anything" Company

Page

205 *"There are no hockey sticks":* author interview with Edgar Bronfman Jr., March 22, 2005.

205 *"In the old business, we were selling through ten thousand to twelve thousand retailers":* remarks made at Goldman Sachs Communacopia Conference, September 22, 2005.

206 *"There was a mission to switch":* in Matt Hartley, "How the iPod Changed Everything," *Toronto Globe and Mail,* May 19, 2009.

206 *"The beauty of the iPod":* ibid.

207 *"Roger and I did the Apple deal":* author interview with Paul Vidich, August 1, 2005.

208 *"I'm a huge believer":* author interview with Alex Zubillaga, January 30, 2006.

210 *"I view us as an indepedent producer of content":* author interview with Lyor Cohen, February 3, 2006.

211 *"I always believed the TVT case was bogus":* author interview with Edgar Bronfman Jr., June 30, 2005.

212 *"The disaggregation of the album":* author interview with Edgar Bronfman Jr., December 9, 2005.

213 *"The beauty of the internet is":* author interview with Alex Zubillaga, July 30, 2008.

214 Ringtone figures quoted in Edna G. Gunderson, "Master Tones Master Industry," *USA Today,* November 28, 2006.

215 *"There'll always be piracy":* author interview with Edgar Bronfman Jr., June 30, 2005.

215 *"Venture capital migrates away":* testimony of Gary Shapiro before the Senate Judiciary Committee hearing "Protecting Copyright and Innovation in a Post-Grokster World," September 28, 2005.

216   *"I think it's going to be difficult"*: author interview with Edgar Bronfman Jr., September 6, 2007.

217   *"I think Sony BMG is more a problem"*: author interview with Edgar Bronfman Jr., December 9, 2005.

217   *"He told me he wanted to set up a system for entrepreneurs to plug into"*: author interview with Todd Moscowitz, December 8, 2005.

218   *"Sometimes I go to the strip clubs"*: Julia Beverly's interview with Joie Manda, published in TheCrusade.net, October 17, 2005.

219   *"They had agreed"*: confidential source.

221   *"It becomes more and more attractive"*: confidential source.

221   *"The guys who are running this"*: in Jeff Leeds, "Wipe Egg Off Face. Try Again. Voilà!" *New York Times,* April 17, 2005.

222   *"These guys are superprogressive"*: in Paul Sloan, "Warner Music the Remix," *Business 2.0,* May 1, 2006.

222   *"the guy that's really sort of lighting the path"*: in Leeds, op cit.

Chapter 12: Ruling the Wasteland

Page

225   *"There's so much more in us buying them"*: author interview with Edgar Bronfman Jr., October 3, 2006.

225   *"In everyone's mind they were buying us"*: author interview with Will Tanous, July 23, 2006.

226   *"There'll be a merger between Warner"*: author interview with Tom Silverman, July 21, 2005.

226   *"More, more, more"*: Edgar Bronfman Jr. to Stephen Adler, *BusinessWeek*'s Captains of Industry Series at the 92nd Street Y, May 4, 2006.

227   *"We made wireless deals everywhere"*: author interview with Alex Zubillaga, July 30, 2008.

228   *"Any business that fails to innovate for twenty-five years"*: author interview with Edgar Bronfman Jr., October 3, 2006.

228   *"To be frank, we often get very frustrated"*: keynote speech to the 3GSM World Congress, Barcelona, February 14, 2007.

229   *"Ladies and gentlemen"*: keynote speech at GSMA Mobile Asia Congress, Macau, November 13, 2007.

231   *"Considering the RIAA will sue your grandma"*: in Mark Cuban, "The Coming Dramatic Decline of YouTube," posted at Blog Maverick: The Mark Cuban Weblog, September 17, 2006.

232   *"a lot of junk and stuff that's stolen"*: the speaker was Joel Waldfogel, a professor of public policy at the Wharton School of Business.

232   *"We believe these new businesses are copyright infringers"*: in Drew Cullen, "Warner Music Embraces YouTube," *Register,* September 18, 2006.

233   *"We've invested billions":* author interview with Edgar Bronfman Jr., September 6, 2007.

233   *"No one has mentioned payment":* in Peter Jenner, "YouTube, Google and the Majors—A Classic Example of How Not to Do It," *Record,* December 2006.

233   *"This changes everything":* in "Coming Attraction: YouTube's Business Model" posted at Knowledge@Wharton (http://knowledge.wharton.upenn.edu), October 4, 2006.

234   *"They were getting a pretty big audience":* confidential source.

236   *"The overall music business":* in Yinka Adegoke, "Music Companies Seek New Money in Old Partners," Reuters, August 7, 2007.

237   *"That was sort of a consolation prize":* confidential source.

238   *"I think the premium concert business":* author interview with Edgar Bronfman Jr., September 6, 2007.

238   *"The rich people they are targeting":* in Richard Johnson, "Hamptons Music Muzzled," *New York Post,* March 28, 2008.

238   *"Just because you buy a business":* in "Warner's Bulldog Chews Up Profits," *IQ,* undated.

239   *"It went before the independent directors":* author interview with Edgar Bronfman Jr., July 27, 2008.

240   *"something like a minimalist opera set for 'Cavalleria Rusticana'":* in Julie Iovine, "Bronfmans Tame a Town House," *New York Times,* September 23, 1999.

240   *"A shareholder could suggest that":* author interview with Nell Minow.

241   Complaint contained in *State of Minnesota v. National Arbitration Forum,* filed July 14, 2009.

241   Coverage of NAF in *BusinessWeek:* in Robert Berner and Brian Grow, "Banks vs. Consumers (Guess Who Wins)," *BusinessWeek,* June 6, 2008.

243   *"Clearly, that's not anywhere near":* in Dominic White, "EMI Not Worth Warner Offer Price," *Telegraph,* April 12, 2007.

244   *"The pressure was to say, 'Three hundred'":* confidential source.

244   *"If management was in control":* confidential source.

245   *"We won't deliver an album":* in Julia Finch, Owen Gibson, and Alex Needham, "Radiohead Quit, Robbie Williams on Strike—and Now 1,000 Jobs Cut," *Guardian,* January 12, 2008.

246   *"EMI is in a state of flux":* in James Robinson, "Radiohead Sound Off with Bum Notes for EMI," *Observer,* December 2, 2007.

246   *"EMI Music has not done very well":* in Dana Cimilluca and Aaron O. Patrick, "Guy Hands Resigns over EMI Deal," *Wall Street Journal,* March 18, 2009.

247   *"I just don't think this dance will end":* confidential source.

248   *"Everybody says YouTube has promoted your work":* in Pete Waterman, "100 Million Plays . . . and I Got £11," *Sun,* March 14, 2009.

248   *"It's absurd":* Amanda Palmer, posted on amandapalmer.net, December 24, 2008.

249   *"My video got 30,000 views":* comments of Oceanus57 in response to Mathew B.

Zeidman, "Warner Music Pulls the Plug on YouTube," Hollywoodtoday.net, December 28, 2008.

249   Figures on streaming income versus album sales taken from Glenn Peoples, "Today's Playlist Sites Are No Boon for Labels," *Coolfer,* December 26, 2008.

249   *"We do not intend to make":* WMG second quarter earnings call, May 7, 2009.

249   *"It's such an obvious idea":* in Dawn C. Chmielewski and Michelle Quinn, "MySpace Music Venture to Take on iTunes," *Los Angeles Times,* April 3, 2008.

Chapter 13: The Circle Game

Page

253   *"I had no money":* author interview with John Janick, undated.

253   *"John thrived on not having any money":* in Robert Levine, "An Alternative Approach to Marketing Rock Bands," *New York Times,* May 5, 2008.

254   *"If we had five executives":* confidential source.

255   *"We said, 'We think Hayley is something special' ":* author interview with Craig Kallman.

256   *"I'm not convinced it's in my best interests":* author interview with Edgar Bronfman Jr., April 14, 2005.

257   *"Most of the revenues and profits":* confidential source.

258   *"We kept expanding what we were asking for":* confidential source.

258   *"The record companies were circling the drain":* author interview with Ken Abdo, November 10, 2008.

258   2008 record figures taken from "Measuring Music Consumption," presentation of Nielsen SoundScan for NARM '09.

258   *"They were saying to the new artists":* Artists House Music interview with Kendall Minter at Artistshousemusic.org, April 30, 2009.

259   Details of Simon suit taken from Stephanie Clifford, "Instead of Retiring, Carly Simon Is Suing Her Label, *New York Times,* October 11, 2009.

260   Prince sales figures from Eliot Van Buskirk, "Prince Points the Way to a Brighter Future for Music," *Wired,* July 9, 2007.

260   *"It's direct marketing":* in Jumana Farouky, "Why Prince's Free CD Ploy Worked," *Time,* July 19, 2007.

260   *"The business is going to have to wake up":* in Brian Garrity, "Eagles Soar: Azoff Teaches Old Rockers New Tricks," *New York Post,* February 17, 2008.

262   *"providing the seed money":* Bronfman used this description in a Q&A for Wall Street analysts and investors sponsored by Goldman Sachs at the Grand Hyatt Hotel in New York, September 18, 2007.

263   *"It's been a little by design and a little by chance":* confidential source.

265   *"It's hard to tour these days":* in Andrew Orlowski, "The Music Wars from 30,000 Feet: Meet Chris Castle," *Register,* November 27, 2008.

265   *"A lot of people don't understand":* in Fred Goodman, "Rock's New Economy: Making Money When CDs Don't Sell," *Rolling Stone,* May 29, 2008.

265 *"The bass player is probably not going to do it":* in Daily Snapshot, *Digital Music News,* July 22, 2009.

268 *"We'll agree":* Paterno made the remarks as part of a mock panel on 360 negotiations webcast by Artistshousemusic.org in October 2008.

268 *"This is the music business now":* confidential source.

269 *"You have to be innovative* and *traditional":* author interview with Livia Tortella, July 27, 2009.

271 *"We're not sure we could have gotten credit then":* remarks at WMG leadership conference, May 18, 2009.

272 *"ten or twenty years":* author interview with Lyor Cohen, 2009.

Epilogue

Page

274 *"Unless the industry finds a way":* in Adam Sweeting and Juliette Garside, "Guy Hands: EMI Must Dump Artists to Survive," *Telegraph,* January 19, 2008.

275 *"the guerrilla savvy of kids":* in Dana Jennings's "Pandora's Boombox," a review of *Ripped: How the Wired Generation Revolutionized Music* by Greg Kot, *New York Times Book Review,* August 13, 2009.

275 *"sending in the internet storm troopers":* in Noz, "That's All Folks," Blunt Rapps, August 26, 2009.

276 *"The publishers, such as the recording industry":* in Russell Roberts, "An Interview with Lawrence Lessig on Copyrights," *Library of Economics and Liberty,* April 7, 2003.

277 *"The desire to attack the 'cartel' is fine":* in Patrick Ross, "The Market Challenges for Individual Artists," Copyright Alliance Blog, August 18, 2009.

279 *"What I'm really worried about":* in Orlowski, op cit.

280 *"Fame is fortune":* in John Perry Barlow, "The Next Economy of Ideas," *Wired,* August 2000.

282 *"People can use this model":* in Jeffrey Pepper Rodgers, "Jill Sobule Profile," *Acoustic Guitar,* December 2009.

284 *"I've met a lot of today's heroes of Silicon Valley":* Paul McGuinness, speech delivered at the MIDEM convention, Cannes, France, January 29, 2008.

284 *"a unique and exciting opportunity":* in Andrew Adam Newman, "Use Their Work Free? Artists Say No to Google," *New York Times,* June 14, 2009.

285 *"We have made a stand":* from "The Featured Artists Coalition Position on File Sharing," www.featuredartistsalliance.com, September 21, 2009.

Acknowledgments

This book could not have been written without the observations and input of the many people both inside and outside the Warner Music Group who took the time to speak with me. With the exception of the few who wished to remain in the background, those quoted are credited in the Notes section; my thanks to all.

Prior to seeking his cooperation for this book, I'd had no contact with Edgar Bronfman Jr. and so had no idea what to expect. What I did know was that he had just declined to be interviewed for a Canadian documentary on him. Yet when I suggested that the multibillion-dollar investment he and his partners had just made in Warner Music and the damage his own reputation had taken in the implosion of Vivendi Universal were likely to create a company highly motivated to address the enormous challenges facing the whole industry, he agreed to share his time and thoughts with me. In the course of an ongoing three-year conversation, I found him to be gracious, thoughtful, and a man of his word. I hope those qualities, as well as the focus and dedication I saw him bring to his work, are evident in the reporting.

Lyor Cohen opened his home and his office to me. He advertises himself as a commander who takes no prisoners, and assumed he would be subjected to the same treatment. I admire and thank him. At Atlantic Records, Craig Kallman went out of his way to be helpful, as did Julie Greenwald, Livia Tortella, and Sheila Richman.

I owe a special debt to Will Tanous. As head of corporate communications at Warner Music, he endured what could have been and certainly felt like a thousand phone calls and emails from me. Though he puts in ridiculous hours, Will's real calling card is an ability to keep focused on the outside picture—a rare and invaluable trait in a company spokesman that produces credibility. My admiration for him as a professional and my affection for him as a person are soul-deep. If you happen to be the CEO of a large and prosperous company, I encourage you to either steal him or introduce him to your daughter.

Thanks also to Walter Montgomery at Robinson Lerer & Montgomery for getting the ball rolling.

Copy editor Patty Romanowski Bashe's extensive knowledge of music and attention to detail were an unexpected and welcome boon, and I thank her for improving this book. I'm also grateful for the enthusiasm of everyone at Simon & Schuster, starting with David Rosenthal, who has been a welcoming and supportive publisher. Thanks also to Michelle Rorke, Jonathan Evans, Elisa Rivlin, Victoria Meyer, Tracey Guest, Alexis Welby, Julia Prosser, Aileen Boyle, Nina Pajak, and Kelly Welsh.

Thanks to Jeff Bumiller and Warne Goodman for their research assistance and to Bill Adler for access to his archives. I'm grateful for the support, information, and advice that came from Paula Batson, Anita Busch, Ed Christman, Bill Flanagan, Sam Freedman, Bill Holland, Laurie Jakobson, Michael Lynn, Geoff Mayfield, Bob Merlis, Jeffrey Ressner, Tony Scherman, Michael Sukin, Sam Sutherland, Roy Trakin, and Adam White.

For their friendship and support: Annie Ammann, Arlene and Barrie Bergman, Crescenzo and Alicia Capece, Paul Feinman,

Bill Fuchs, Eddie and Nancy Karp, Barbara Orentzel, Al and Marge Rosenthal, and Jim and Ann Whelan.

During the years I worked on this book, my family shrank in numbers but not in love. Without Janet, Joshua, and Warne, there's nothing.

And, of course, thanks always to Chuck Verrill. To paraphrase Jimmy Iovine, "I was always a Verrill guy—and I hope to be until I die."

Index